CHILE, CORN & CROISSANTS

Delicious Recipes from New Mexico Inns

by JOAN STROMQUIST

Tierra Publications

Tierra Publications
2801 Rodeo Road
Suite B-612
Santa Fe, New Mexico 87505
(505) 983-6300

Other books by Joan Stromquist:

Santa Fe Lite & Spicy Recipe
Santa Fe Hot & Spicy Recipe
Santa Fe Recipe
Taos Recipe
Southern California Beach Recipe

Additional copies may be obtained by contacting Tierra Publications. For your convenience, an order form is included in the back of this book.

Book Design by Carl Stromquist

Cover & Drawings by Beth Evans

Foreword & Inn write-ups by Sheila Tryk

Library of Congress Catalog Card Number: 94-60474

ISBN: 0-9622807-6-3

Printed in the United States of America

Foreword

The New Mexico Bed and Breakfast Association is a group of inns dedicated tc attaining and maintaining the highest standards of comfort, cleanliness, safety and service.

The few words describing each bed and breakfast establishment can't begin to tell the stories about these charming homes. Whether the inn consists of just one tiny, perfect casita or is a 12-suite complex in a rambling old adobe hacienda, each place has its own special enchantment, its own personality. If you are interested in visiting, write the inn of your choice for a brochure and rates.

Most rooms have private baths. Some have television sets, VCRs and even stereos. Many have fireplaces, or even small refrigerators. A great many are furnished with antiques, handmade furniture and works of art. Private entrances and great views are bonuses that come with some rooms, and there may be pools, saunas or Jacuzzis on the premises.

Most hosts and hostesses provide welcoming snacks for arriving guests.....anything from a plate of homemade chocolates to fresh cookies to hot muffins.....and cold or hot drinks. They'll help you with your sightseeing plans, guide you to local restaurants and take diet restrictions into consideration if you notify them in time. Breakfasts range from healthy buffets to sumptuous brunches, so ask ahead of time what to expect.

Some inns don't accept small children as guests, many are no-smoking establishments, and many don't allow pets.....but a few do, so inquire before you arrive.

As you'll see from the recipes in this book, every inn is different, every meal an adventure in good taste.

So, follow the highways and back roads of New Mexico to the mountains and rivers, the cities and villages, the deserts and forests and canyons, where you'll meet new friends, taste new delights and enjoy the warmth and hospitality of the innkeepers. Let us share with you the magic that is New Mexico.

Directory of Inns

1. Adobe Abode
202 Chapelle Street
Santa Fe, New Mexico 87501
(505) 983-3133

2. Alexander's Inn
529 East Palace Avenue
Santa Fe, New Mexico 87501
(505) 986-1431

3. American Artists Gallery House
Post Office Box 584
Taos, New Mexico 87571
(505) 758-4446 • (800) 532-2041

4. The Carter House
101 North Cooper Street
Silver City, New Mexico 88061
(505) 388-5485

5. Casa de las Chimeneas
405 Cordoba Road
Box 5303
Taos, New Mexico 87571
(505) 758-4777

6. Casa de Martinez
Post Office Box 96
Los Ojos, New Mexico 87551
(505) 588-7858

7. Casa de Patrón
Post Office Box 27
Lincoln, New Mexico 88338
(505) 653-4676

8. Casa del Granjero
414 C de Baca Lane N.W.
Albuquerque, New Mexico 87114
(505) 897-4144

9. Casa del Rio
Post Office Box 92
Española, New Mexico 87532
(505) 753-6049

10. Casa Europa
157 Upper Ranchitos Road
Taos, New Mexico 87571
(505) 758-9798

11. Casita Chamisa
850 Chamisal Road N.W.
Albuquerque, New Mexico 87107
(505) 897-4644

12. The Dancing Bear
Post Office Box 128
Jemez Springs, New Mexico 87025
(505) 829-3336

13. Eaton House
403 Eaton Avenue • P.O. Box 536
Socorro, New Mexico 87801
(505) 835-1067

14. El Paradero
220 West Manhattan
Santa Fe, New Mexico 87501
(505) 988-1177

15. El Rincón
114 Kit Carson Road
Taos, New Mexico 87571
(505) 758-4874

16. Four Kachinas Inn
512 Webber Street
Santa Fe, New Mexico 87501
(505) 982-2550 • (800) 397-2564

17. The Galisteo Inn
HC 75 Box 4
Galisteo, New Mexico 87540
(505) 466-4000

18. Grant Corner Inn
122 Grant Avenue
Santa Fe, New Mexico 87501
(505) 983-6678

19. Hacienda del Sol
109 Mabel Dodge Lane
Post Office Box 177
Taos, New Mexico 87571
(505) 758-0287

20. Hacienda de Placitas
491 Highway 165
Placitas, New Mexico 87043
(505) 867-3775

21. Hacienda Vargas
Post Office Box 307
Algodones, New Mexico 87001
(505) 867-9115

22. Inn of the Animal Tracks
707 Paseo de Peralta
Santa Fe, New Mexico 87501
(505) 988-1546

23. La Posada de Chimayó
Post Office Box 463
Chimayó, New Mexico 87522
(505) 351-4605

24. La Posada de Taos
309 Juanita Lane • P.O. Box 1118
Taos, New Mexico 87571
(505) 758-8164

25. Little Tree
Post Office Box 1100-255
Taos, New Mexico 87571
(505) 776-8467

26. Open Sky
Route 2, Box 918 • Turquoise Trail
Santa Fe, New Mexico 87505
(505) 471-3475

27. Orange Street Inn
3496 Orange Street
Los Alamos, New Mexico 87544
(505) 662-2651

28. Preston House
106 Faithway Street
Santa Fe, New Mexico 87501
(505) 982-3465

29. The Red Violet Inn
344 North 2nd Street
Raton, New Mexico 87740
(505) 445-9778 • (800) 624-9778

30. Salsa del Salto
Post Office Box 1468
El Prado, New Mexico 87529
(505) 776-2422

31. Sierra Mesa Lodge
Fort Stanton Road
Post Office Box 463
Alto, New Mexico 88312
(505) 336-4515

32. Territorial Inn
215 Washington Avenue
Santa Fe, New Mexico 87501
(505) 989-7737

33. Vogt Ranch House
Post Office Box 716
Ramah, New Mexico 87321
(505) 783-4362

34. Water Street Inn
427 West Water Street
Santa Fe, New Mexico 87501
(505) 984-1193

35. W.E. Mauger Estate
701 Roma Avenue N.W.
Albuquerque, New Mexico 87102
(505) 242-8755

Map of New Mexico Inns

Each numbered chile pepper represents the location of a New Mexico inn. The address and phone number of each inn can be found on the facing page, under the corresponding number.

Author's Notes

I wish to thank the participating members of the New Mexico Bed & Breakfast Association for supplying these wonderful recipes. Needless to say, without their generous cooperation, this cookbook would not be possible. They are a marvelous group of people.....friendly, intelligent, creative.....and completely dedicated to their profession.

Special thanks also go to Sheila Tryk, Beth Evans, Robyn Hunt, Kara Leigh and Sonya Moore. Each one made a special and valuable contribution to the production of this book.

For those of you who do not have access to the chile peppers and other Southwest ingredients called for in some of these recipes, page 8 lists mail order sources.

Altitude Cooking Adjustments

These recipes are designed to work at each inn's altitude, which ranges from approximately 4000 feet to 8000 feet above sea level. Most of the recipes should work fine at any altitude, although it is always wise to use a watchful eye and good judgment in the cooking times. (Remember, it takes longer to cook things at higher altitudes.)

If any problems do occur, they most likely will be with the dishes containing baking soda or baking powder (quick breads, coffee cakes, muffins, pancakes, etc.). Usually, a few minor adjustments will do the trick. My advice is to first try the recipe as it is written. Then, if necessary, follow these suggestions for cooking at lower altitudes:

1) Increase the baking powder and baking soda ¼ teaspoon for every teaspoon called for. This adjustment should be sufficient, but if not, go on to the next steps.

2) By very small amounts, uniformly decrease the flour and eggs, and increase the butter.

3) Decrease the oven temperature by not more than 25 degrees.

Table of Contents

Southwest Food Mail Order Sources

The Chile Shop
109 E. Water Street
Santa Fe, New Mexico 87501
(505) 983-6080

Coyote Cafe General Store
132 W. Water Street
Santa Fe, New Mexico 87501
(505) 982-2454

Josie's Best New Mexican Foods
Post Office Box 5525
Santa Fe, New Mexico 87502
(505) 473-3437

The Santa Fe School of Cooking
116 W. San Francisco Street
Santa Fe, New Mexico 87501
(505) 983-4511

Bueno Foods
2001 Fourth Street S.W.
Albuquerque, New Mexico 87102
(505) 243-2722

For information on the New Mexico Bed & Breakfast Association please write to:

New Mexico Bed & Breakfast Association
Post Office Box 2925
Santa Fe, New Mexico 87504-2925

Inn Recipe Table of Contents

Casa de las Chimeneas

Casa de Martinez

Casa de Patrón

Casa del Granjero

Casa del Rio

Casa Europa

Grant Corner Inn

Hacienda del Sol

Hacienda de Placitas

Hacienda Vargas

Inn of the Animal Tracks

La Posada de Chimayó

Food Category Table of Contents

Appetizers

Soups

Salads & Salad Dressings

Sauces, Dips & Condiments

Breakfast Dishes

Brunch, Eggs & Cheese Dishes

Main Entrées

Baked Goods

Side Dishes

Potpourri

Desserts

CHILE, CORN & CROISSANTS

Delicious Recipes from New Mexico Inns

by JOAN STROMQUIST

This book is dedicated to the memory of Jim Finnell, the talented artist who designed the covers of the ***Recipe*** series of cookbooks. He will be missed.

Adobe Abode

202 Chapelle Street
Santa Fe, New Mexico 87501
(505) 983-3133
Pat Harbour, Innkeeper

Just four blocks from the Plaza, this historic adobe-style inn combines the charm of a 1907 Santa Fe home with European traditions and modern conveniences. Southwestern furniture, designer bed linens, private phones and off-street parking make this the perfect hideaway even at the height of the summer season. Add to this a breakfast to die for, with homemade muffins and delectable entrées, and it's no wonder guests don't want to leave.

Recipes

Easy Garlic & Feta Cheese Appetizer

"This is a great appetizer to put together when unexpected guests show up. If you don't have feta cheese on hand you can substitute cream cheese."

- 1 **large clove garlic, minced**
- 1 **teaspoon whole green** *(or red)* **peppercorns, ground**
- 1 **tablespoon fresh** *(or 1 teaspoon dried)* **thyme leaves, chopped**
- 3 **tablespoons olive oil**
- 1½ **pounds feta cheese, drained and broken into small chunks**
- **toast rounds** *(or crackers or pita chips)*

- In a medium bowl place the garlic, peppercorns, thyme and olive oil. Mix the ingredients together. Add the feta cheese and mix it in well. Serve the mixture with the toast rounds.

serves 8 to 12

Jalapeño, Artichoke & Crab Dip

"If you are in the mood for something major, major mondo-delicious, and you aren't in the mood to worry about calories or cholesterol, then this is the perfect recipe. There will never be a bite left because it is so delicious people can't stop eating it."

- 1 **tablespoon vegetable oil**
- 1 **green bell pepper, seeded and finely chopped**
- 3 **jalapeño chile peppers** *(canned),* **seeded and finely chopped**
- 2 **14-ounce cans artichoke hearts, drained and finely chopped**
- ½ **cup scallions, thinly sliced**
- ½ **cup pimientos** *(or roasted red peppers),* **finely chopped**
- 2 **cups mayonnaise**
- 1 **cup Parmesan cheese, freshly grated**
- 1½ **tablespoons lemon juice, freshly squeezed**
- 4 **teaspoons Worcestershire sauce**
- 1 **teaspoon celery salt**
- 1 **pound fresh crab meat, cleaned and picked apart**
- ⅓ **cup sliced almonds, toasted**

- Preheat the oven to 375°.
- In a small sauté pan place the oil and heat it on medium high until it is hot. Add the bell peppers and jalapeño chile peppers, and sauté them for 5 minutes, or until they are tender.
- In a medium large bowl place the sautéed peppers, artichoke hearts, scallions, pimientos, mayonnaise, Parmesan cheese, lemon juice, Worcestershire sauce and celery salt. Mix the ingredients together well.
- Add the crab and gently mix it in.
- In a buttered medium baking dish place the mixture. Sprinkle the almonds on top. Bake the dip for 20 to 30 minutes, or until the top is golden and bubbly.

makes 10 servings

Ranch Potatoes with Sausage

"This is a wonderful dish to serve to your family when it's snowy and cold outside. It's spicy, tasty and very filling."

3 tablespoons butter
1 tablespoon olive oil
4 large baking potatoes, cleaned, halved lengthwise and sliced into ¼" thick pieces
1½ cups yellow onions, diced medium
3 hot Italian sausages, chopped, cooked, crumbled and drained
¼ teaspoon fresh rosemary, finely chopped
2 cloves garlic, mashed
½ teaspoon paprika
salt and pepper *(to taste)*
¼ cup fresh parsley, finely chopped
1 teaspoon red chile flakes

- In a large, heavy skillet place the butter and olive oil, and heat them on medium high until they sizzle. Reduce the heat to low.
- Add the potatoes and onions, and cook them for 30 minutes, or until the potatoes are lightly browned on all sides.
- Add the cooked sausage, rosemary, garlic, paprika, salt and pepper. Cook and stir the ingredients for 5 minutes.
- Sprinkle on the parsley and red chile flakes.

serves 4 to 6

"If you are thinking of opening a Bed & Breakfast, then don't read the books that are discouraging and say it is too hard. Realize that it is quite possible to be successful in this business, especially if you are organized and don't get rattled when things go wrong."

Pat Harbour

Black Bean Salad

"I cannot describe how good this salad is, and I believe the secret is the fresh lemon juice. Whenever I serve it, there is never so much as one bean left, which is too bad, because it tastes even better the next day!"

- **1 15-ounce can black beans, rinsed and drained thoroughly**
- **1 10-ounce package frozen corn, broken apart**
- **1½ cups tomatoes, seeded and chopped**
- **¾ cup scallions, thinly sliced**
- **⅛ cup fresh cilantro leaves, minced**
- **½ cup olive oil**
- **½ cup lemon juice, freshly squeezed**
- **1 teaspoon salt**

- In a large bowl place the beans, corn, tomatoes, scallions and cilantro. Mix the ingredients together.
- In a small bowl place the olive oil, lemon juice and salt. Whisk the ingredients together.
- Pour the dressing over the salad and mix it in well.
- Cover the bowl with plastic wrap and refrigerate it overnight.
- Serve the salad at room temperature.

serves 4

"One of the big attractions of staying at a Bed & Breakfast in Santa Fe is that they are so homey and warm. As the innkeeper, I know just about everything to do with Santa Fe, and can impart this information to my guests. I'm especially good at knowing all the shopping secrets!"

Pat Harbour

Fiesta Baked Tomatoes

"Because of its bright red color, this makes a wonderful accompaniment to a main entrée that has a strong white, green or yellow color. It is especially nice with quiche."

- 6 **large tomatoes**
- **salt** *(as needed)*
- 5 **slices bacon, diced, cooked and drained** *(reserve the grease)*
- 2 **cups corn**
- 1 **medium yellow onion, diced small**
- ½ **red bell pepper, seeded and diced small**
- ½ **green bell pepper, seeded and diced small**
- 1 **teaspoon sugar**
- **pepper** *(to taste)*
- 1 **tablespoon flour**
- ½ **cup heavy cream**
- ½ **cup Parmesan cheese, freshly grated**
- 2 **tablespoons butter, cut into small pieces**

- Preheat the oven to 375°.
- Cut out the stem of each tomato and scoop out the center. Sprinkle the insides with the salt. Turn the tomatoes upside down to drain.
- In a medium large skillet place the reserved bacon grease and heat it on medium so that it is hot. Add the corn, onions and bell peppers. Sauté the ingredients so that they are lightly browned.
- Add the diced bacon, sugar, pepper and some more of the salt *(to taste)*, and stir them in.
- In a small bowl place the flour and cream, and stir them together so that they are smooth.
- Add the mixture to the skillet with the corn mixture, and stir it in. While stirring constantly, cook the mixture for 5 minutes, or until it is thickened.
- In a shallow lightly greased baking dish place the hollowed drained tomatoes so that they are upright. Fill them with the cooked mixture.
- Sprinkle the tops with the Parmesan cheese and dot them with the butter.
- Place several tablespoons of water in the bottom of the dish.
- Bake the tomatoes for 15 to 20 minutes, or until the skins begin to wrinkle. Serve them immediately.

serves 6

Santa Fe Cheese Casserole

"This is delicious served for breakfast with a homemade bread that is thickly sliced, because it's good for dunking. Add jalapeño strips if you want it spicier, and serve salsa on the side."

- 1 **pound Monterey Jack cheese, grated**
- 1 **pound cheddar cheese, grated**
- 2 **4-ounce cans green chile peppers, drained and chopped**
- 4 **egg yolks**
- 2/3 **cup evaporated milk**
- 1 **tablespoon flour**
- 1/2 **teaspoon salt**
- 1/8 **teaspoon pepper**
- 4 **egg whites, stiffly beaten** *(but not dry)*
- 2 **medium tomatoes, sliced**
- 1 **tablespoon fresh cilantro sprigs**

- Preheat the oven to 325°.
- In a medium large bowl place the two cheeses and green chile peppers *(reserve 1 tablespoon)*, and mix them together.
- In another medium bowl place the egg yolks, evaporated milk, flour, salt and pepper. Beat the ingredients together.
- Add the egg whites and fold them in.
- Add this mixture to the cheese mixture, and fold it in.
- Place the mixture in a buttered 3-quart casserole dish.
- Bake it for 30 minutes.
- Arrange the tomatoes on top.
- Bake the casserole for 30 minutes more.
- Garnish the casserole with the reserved green chile peppers and the cilantro sprigs.

serves 10 to 12

"New Bed & Breakfasts open every year in New Mexico, but there don't seem to be enough to fill the need. We are always booked. I get 20 calls every weekend for rooms I don't have."

Pat Harbour

Apricot Almond Muffins

"The combination of apricots and almonds gives these muffins a delicious flavor and a nice, crunchy texture."

1½ cups flour
¼ cup almonds, ground
2 teaspoons baking powder
1 teaspoon salt
½ teaspoon sugar
2 large eggs
4 tablespoons butter, melted
¾ cup milk
1 cup dried apricots, finely chopped
1 teaspoon lemon juice, freshly squeezed
⅓ cup almonds, sliced

- Preheat the oven to 400°.
- In a large bowl sift together the flour, ground almonds, baking powder, salt and sugar. Make a well in the center. Add the eggs, butter and milk, and mix them in lightly.
- Add the apricots and lemon juice, and mix them in.
- Fill 12 individual greased muffin tins with the batter so that they are ⅔ full.
- Sprinkle the sliced almonds on top.
- Bake the muffins for 25 to 30 minutes, or until they are golden brown.

makes 12 muffins

"My mother was such a bad cook that she often would serve a half-cooked turkey for Thanksgiving dinner. Luckily my sisters and I did not follow in her footsteps, and we all grew up to be pretty good chefs."

Pat Harbour

Caramelized French Toast

"Once I was staying at the Plantation Inn in Maui, Hawaii, and ordered this French Toast. It had a wonderful soufflé texture in the center, and I really wanted to know how to make it. The chef, who was a hotshot cook on the island, not only refused to give me the recipe, but also would not let me set foot in his kitchen! So I ordered the same thing for three days in a row, trying to analyze it. Finally, with the help of a friendly waitress, I came up with this very good reproduction."

- ¾ **stick unsalted butter**
- 1 **cup brown sugar** *(loosely packed)*
- ½ **cup corn syrup**
- 5 **eggs**
- ¾ **cup milk**
- 1 **teaspoon vanilla extract**
- ½ **teaspoon ground cinnamon**
- 1 **tablespoon sugar**
- 6 **thick slices French bread, cut on an angle**

- Preheat the oven to 375°.
- Place the butter in a small glass bowl and melt it in the microwave.
- Pour the melted butter on the bottom of a baking pan that is large enough to hold the 6 slices of bread, one layer deep. Swirl it around so that the bottom is evenly coated.
- Crumble the brown sugar evenly over the melted butter.
- Dribble the corn syrup in streams on top of the brown sugar.
- In a medium bowl place the eggs, milk, vanilla, cinnamon and sugar. Whisk the ingredients together well.
- Dip each piece of bread in the mixture so that it is well soaked.
- Place the bread in the baking pan on top of the other ingredients.
- Bake the bread for 20 to 25 minutes, or until it is lightly browned and the sauce underneath is bubbling.
- Flip each slice of bread over in the pan so the other side is coated with the sauce.
- Serve the French Toast on an attractive platter.

serves 6

Honeydew Compote

"Once I ate a similar dish that contained a flavored liqueur. Since I wanted to serve it for breakfast, I eliminated the alcohol and substituted fresh lime juice. It's a very simple recipe that tastes delicious."

- 1 **lime, zested** *(outer green part grated off)* **and juiced**
- ½ **cup sugar**
- 1 **tablespoon fresh ginger root, peeled and grated**
- ⅓ **cup water**
- 1 **honeydew melon, halved, seeds removed, and cut into small melon balls**
- 1 **tablespoon fresh mint leaves**
- 6 **strawberries** *(stems on)*

- In a small, heavy saucepan place the lime zest, lime juice, sugar, ginger and water. Bring the mixture to a boil and stir it so that the sugar is dissolved. Boil the mixture for 5 minutes.
- Strain the mixture through a fine sieve into a medium bowl and let it cool. Add the melon balls and mix them in. Add the mint leaves and stir them in.
- Cover the bowl with plastic wrap and chill it in the refrigerator overnight.
- Into each of 6 attractive compote bowls place the melon balls with some juice. Place a strawberry on top of each serving.

serves 6

"I used to be the head of advertising for a large company and traveled all over the world with my work. Eventually I got sick to death of chain hotels, so I began seeking out small Bed & Breakfast inns. They were so charming that I decided to open one when I retired. I still haven't retired, but it has been the best decision I've ever made."

Pat Harbour

Apple Skillet Cake

"This is an old recipe that my grandmother used to make. I enjoy eating it as much now as an adult as I did as a child!"

3 large eggs
¾ cup flour
2 tablespoons sugar
¾ cup milk
1 teaspoon vanilla extract
1 teaspoon ground cinnamon
2 cups tart green apples, peeled, cored and thinly sliced
½ stick unsalted butter
maple syrup *(as needed),* **heated**

- Preheat the oven to 375°.
- In a large bowl place the eggs, flour and sugar. Whisk them together so that they are smooth.
- Add the milk, vanilla and cinnamon, and whisk them in.
- Add the apples and stir them in.
- In a 10" cast-iron skillet place the butter and melt it over medium heat. Pour the batter in the skillet and spread the apples out evenly.
- Place the skillet in the oven. Bake the cake for 30 minutes, or until it is puffed and begins to pull away from the sides of the skillet.
- Cut the cake into wedges and serve it with the maple syrup.

serves 6 to 8

"When I was first married I was given a Julia Child cookbook as a wedding gift, and essentially learned to cook from it. I had no idea that most women knew nothing of fancy French cooking and only used the **Joy of Cooking** or **Betty Crocker's Cookbook**. To this day my recipes reflect that Julia Child influence."

Pat Harbour

The Best Apple Pie in the World
(Made in a Paper Bag)

"Years ago I was a Woman's Editor for a newspaper in Tennessee. We did a wedding issue that featured a young couple about to be married. This is the bride's recipe, which had been a family secret for generations. She told me that after her boyfriend tasted this pie, he got down on his knees and begged her to marry him. Without a doubt, it is the best apple pie I have ever eaten. Be sure not to open the oven door before the pie is done..... otherwise the bag might catch fire. While you are cooking it, the bag smells like it is burning, but it is not."

2 tablespoons lemon juice, freshly squeezed
½ cup sugar
2 tablespoons flour
1 teaspoon ground cinnamon
4 large green apples, peeled, cored and sliced
½ cup sugar
½ cup flour
½ stick butter, cut into small pieces
1 9-inch unbaked pie shell

- Preheat the oven to 425°.
- In a large bowl place the lemon juice, the first ½ cup of sugar, the 2 tablespoons of flour and the cinnamon. Mix the ingredients together.
- Add the apples and gently toss them in.
- In a medium bowl place the second ½ cup of sugar and the ½ cup of flour, and mix them together.
- Add the butter and cut it in with a pastry blender so that the mixture is crumbly.
- Place the apple mixture in the pie shell. Sprinkle the crumbled butter mixture on top.
- Place the pie in a large paper bag. Fold the opening over twice and secure each end with a paper clip.
- Place the bag in the center of the oven and bake the pie for 1 hour *(do not open the oven during this time).*
- Remove the pie from the oven, cut open the paper bag and let the pie cool on a rack.

serves 8

Fabulous Cheesecake

"Once I was in a wine-tasting club and all the members compiled their cheesecake recipes to come up with this unique version. We would make it to serve with sweet white wines. It is the best!"

2 8-ounce packages cream cheese, softened
1 pound creamed cottage cheese
1½ cups sugar
4 eggs, lightly beaten
3 tablespoons cornstarch
3 tablespoons flour
1½ tablespoons lemon juice, freshly squeezed
1 teaspoon vanilla extract
½ cup butter, melted
1 pint sour cream

- Preheat the oven to 325°.
- In a large bowl place the cream cheese and cottage cheese. With an electric mixer beat them on high speed so that they are well combined and creamy.
- Gradually add and beat in the sugar.
- Add the eggs one at a time, and beat them in.
- With the mixer running on high speed, add the cornstarch, flour, lemon juice and vanilla. Beat them together.
- Add the melted butter and sour cream, and beat them in so that the batter is smooth.
- Place the mixture in a greased 9" springform pan.
- Bake the cheesecake for 1 hour and 10 minutes, or until it is firm around the edges.
- Turn off the heat and let the cake sit in the oven for 2 hours.
- Remove the cake from the oven and let it cool completely.
- Refrigerate the cheesecake for 2 hours, or until it is well chilled.
- Loosen the sides with a spatula. Remove the side of the springform pan and leave the bottom of the pan in place.

serves 10 to 12

"People who stay in Bed & Breakfasts are very open and interesting individuals. They derive such joy from discovering the secrets of Santa Fe that it is contagious, and I find myself seeing things through their eyes. They help to remind me why I moved here in the first place."

Pat Harbour

Alexander's Inn

529 East Palace Avenue
Santa Fe, New Mexico 87501
(505) 986-1431
Carolyn Lee, Innkeeper

Late Victorian ambience combines with an appreciation of healthful living at Alexander's Inn. This cozy old home, built in 1903 and filled with antiques, shows an aspect of Santa Fe that many visitors never get to see. The renovated house and two cottages are set in blossoming gardens in a residential area on the historic east side.....a short stroll from the Plaza and the city's many great restaurants.

Recipes

Baboli Delight

"I got this recipe while on a women's raft trip down the Chama River in New Mexico. We brought the mix already prepared in a Tupperware container, along with the spinach, walnuts and other ingredients. We spread everything on top of the bread and heated it over the campfire. It was delicious and took no time at all to make."

- 1 **cup Gruyere cheese, grated**
- 1 **cup Fontina cheese, grated**
- 1 **cup Parmesan cheese, freshly grated**
- 1 **cup pitted black olives, sliced**
- 2 **packages frozen spinach, thawed**
- 1 **can water chestnuts, drained and chopped**
- 1 **cup walnuts, chopped**
- 1 **tablespoon fresh dill** *(or 1 teaspoon dried)*
- 2 **large rounds Baboli bread**

- Preheat the oven to 400°.
- In a large bowl place all of the ingredients *(except for the bread)* and mix them together so they are well combined.
- Spread the mixture evenly on top of the bread.
- Bake the bread for 10 to 15 minutes, or until the topping is hot and bubbly. Cut the bread into wedges.

serves 12

Caesar Salad

"My boyfriend Ted likes to make this recipe, which he got from his mother. I've eaten hundreds of Caesar salads in different restaurants, and this one is in the top 10 percent."

- 5 **anchovies**
- 4 **cloves garlic, coarsely chopped**
- 1 **cup Parmesan cheese, freshly grated**
- 2 **eggs**
- 2 **tablespoons dry vermouth**
- 1 **cup olive oil**
- 2 **heads romaine lettuce, washed, dried and torn**
- 1 **cup croutons**

- In a blender place the anchovies, garlic, cheese, eggs, vermouth and olive oil. Blend the ingredients so they are creamy.
- In a large salad bowl place the lettuce. Add the dressing and toss it in well.
- Serve the salad with the croutons sprinkled on top.

serves 8

Sesame Noodles

"I serve this both as a main course and an appetizer. There is no secret to making these noodles.....just follow the recipe and you will be happy!"

1 tablespoon tahini
2 tablespoons peanut butter
2 teaspoons hot mustard
2 teaspoons honey
½ orange, freshly juiced
3 tablespoons rice vinegar
2 tablespoons tamari
1 tablespoon chili oil
⅓ cup sesame oil
¼ cup vegetable oil
1 pound sesame noodles, cooked al dente and drained
¼ cup scallions, thinly sliced
¼ cup sesame seeds, toasted
1 cucumber, peeled, seeded and finely chopped

- In a large bowl place the tahini, peanut butter, mustard, honey, orange juice, vinegar, tamari, chili oil, sesame oil and vegetable oil. Whisk the ingredients together so they are well blended.
- Add the sesame noodles and toss them in well.
- Sprinkle the scallions, sesame seeds and cucumbers on top of each serving.

serves 4

Chile Relleno Casserole

"This recipe comes from a native New Mexican friend of mine. It's quick and easy to put together, and everyone loves it."

10 eggs, lightly beaten
3 cups large curd cottage cheese
2 4-ounce cans green chile peppers, diced
2 cups Monterey Jack cheese, grated
½ cup flour
½ teaspoon baking powder
1 large avocado, peeled, pitted and thinly sliced

- Preheat the oven to 350°.
- In a large bowl place all of the ingredients *(except for the avocados)* and mix them together. Place the mixture in a greased 8" x 12" baking pan.
- Bake the casserole for 30 to 40 minutes, or until it is set.
- Place the avocados on top of each serving.

serves 8

Savory Pizza with Sundried Tomato Pesto

"I once ate an incredible pizza at the Taos Ski Valley and then tried to re-create it when I came home. This recipe is the result, and it is excellent. My boyfriend enjoys making the pesto because he loves to use the food processor."

Savory Pizza

2 12" pizza rounds
¼ cup olive oil
1 cup Sundried Tomato Pesto *(recipe follows)*
2 cups mozzarella cheese, grated
1 can artichoke hearts, drained and chopped
¾ cup walnuts, chopped
1 cup pitted black olives, sliced

- Preheat the oven to 550°.
- Place the pizza rounds on a flat baking sheet *(or stone)*.
- Spread the olive oil over each pizza round.
- Spread on the Sundried Tomato Pesto.
- Sprinkle on the cheese, artichoke hearts, walnuts and olives.
- Bake the pizzas for 10 minutes, or until the crust is browned and the cheese is hot and bubbly.

serves 4 to 6

Sundried Tomato Pesto

8 sundried tomatoes, reconstituted in boiling water for 5 minutes and drained
½ cup walnuts, chopped
¾ cup Parmesan cheese, freshly grated
2 cloves garlic
1 tablespoon dried basil
⅓ cup extra virgin olive oil

- Place all of the ingredients in a food processor and purée them so that the mixture is smooth.

makes approximately 1½ cups

David's Salmon Pasta Dish

"David, who is a very sophisticated, cosmopolitan European friend of mine, once invited me to dinner and cooked this wonderful dish. I begged him to give me the recipe for publication in this cookbook, and he did. The black squid pasta is more for the color than the taste."

½ **cup olive oil**
¼ **cup fresh dill, chopped**
1 **pound salmon fillet, cut into ¾" cubes**
1 **large yellow onion, finely chopped**
1 **stalk celery, finely chopped**
1 **carrot, finely chopped**
2 **cloves garlic, minced**
½ **cup white wine**
1 **cup fish broth**
2 **tablespoons tomato purée** *(from a tube, if possible)*
1 **cup heavy cream**
½ **whole nutmeg, freshly grated**
salt and pepper *(to taste)*
1 **pound black squid pasta, cooked al dente and drained**

- In a medium large bowl place the olive oil and dill, and mix them together. Add the salmon and marinate it for 1 hour at room temperature.
- In a medium large skillet place 1 tablespoon of the olive oil from the salmon marinade and heat it on medium high until it is hot. Add the onions, celery, carrots and garlic. Sauté the ingredients for 5 minutes, or until the onions are translucent. Place the vegetables in a small bowl and set them aside.
- To the same skillet add another tablespoon of the olive oil from the marinade and heat it on medium high until it is hot. Add the salmon and sauté it for 2 minutes, or until it is seared on the outside and raw on the inside. Place the salmon in another small bowl and set it aside.
- Return the skillet to the stove and heat it on medium high. Add the white wine, fish broth and tomato purée, and deglaze the pan.
- Add the cooked vegetables, salmon, cream, nutmeg, salt and pepper. Stir the ingredients together for 2 to 3 minutes, or until everything is hot.
- Spoon the mixture over the pasta and serve it immediately.

serves 4

Rosalia's Pasta

"Rosalia is an Italian woman from Santa Fe who worked to develop recipes that combined flavors from both New Mexico and Italy. The avocados are delicious in this dish, and provide a rich, creamy texture."

- **2 cloves garlic, crushed**
- **2 medium tomatoes, diced medium**
- **3 medium avocados, peeled, pitted and diced medium**
- **¼ cup olive oil**
- **¾ cup walnuts, coarsely chopped**
- **1 pound spaghetti, cooked al dente and drained**
- **½ cup Parmesan cheese, freshly grated**

- In a large bowl place the garlic, tomatoes, avocados and olive oil. Mash the ingredients together with a large fork so that the mixture is chunky. Add the walnuts and mix them in.
- Add the mixture to the spaghetti and toss it in well.
- Sprinkle the Parmesan cheese on top.

serves 4

Chicken with Artichoke Hearts

"I invented this recipe while living in Paris, when I had no cares about eating sour cream or other rich foods. It's quick and easy to make, and only dirties one skillet. To me, not making a big mess in the kitchen is quite important, since I usually am the one who has to clean it up!"

- **2 tablespoons olive oil** *(or as needed)*
- **2 tablespoons butter** *(or as needed)*
- **2 tablespoons yellow onions, minced**
- **4 cloves garlic, minced**
- **1 cup mushrooms, thinly sliced**
- **4 whole chicken breasts**
- **1 cup white wine**
- **1 16-ounce can artichoke hearts, drained**
- **1 cup heavy cream**

- In a large skillet place the olive oil and butter, and heat them on medium until the butter is melted and they are hot. Add the onions and garlic, and sauté them for 2 minutes, or until they are tender. Remove the onions and garlic with a slotted spoon, and set them aside.
- To the same skillet add the mushrooms and sauté them for 5 minutes. Place the mushrooms in the bowl with the onions and garlic.
- To the same skillet add the chicken breasts and sauté them so they are golden brown on both sides.
- Return the onions and mushrooms to the skillet. Add the wine and stir it in.
- Cover the skillet and cook the chicken for 15 minutes on low heat, or until it is done. Add the artichoke hearts and cream, and stir them in so that they are heated.

serves 4

Chicken Breasts à la Suisse

"This is a very good 'company dish' to serve at a nice dinner party. It looks elegant and gourmet, but really is so simple to make! I like to sew the chicken breasts up with a needle and thread instead of using a toothpick, because it works better. But then I have to warn my guests before they eat it, which probably detracts from the overall effect."

4 whole chicken breasts, boned, skinned and pounded 1/4" thin
4 thin slices cooked ham
4 thin slices Swiss cheese
1/4 cup butter
3/4 cup dry white wine
1/4 teaspoon ground nutmeg
salt and pepper *(to taste)*
2 tablespoons yellow onions, minced
1/4 cup dry white wine
1 cup sour cream
2 egg yolks, lightly beaten

- Preheat the oven to 150°.
- In the center of each chicken breast place a slice of both the ham and the cheese. Fold and roll the chicken breast up. Secure it with a toothpick.
- In a large skillet place the butter and heat it on medium high so that it is melted and hot. Add the rolled chicken breasts and sauté them so that they are golden brown on all sides.
- Reduce the heat to low and add the 3/4 cup of wine, the nutmeg, salt and pepper. Cover the pan and simmer the chicken for 15 minutes, or until it is done.
- Remove the chicken and place it in a baking pan. Cover it with foil and place it in the oven to keep it warm.
- To the same skillet add the onions and cook them for 3 minutes on medium heat.
- Add the 1/4 cup of wine and stir it in.
- Add the sour cream and egg yolks, and mix them in well. Stir the sauce for 2 to 3 minutes, or until it is thickened *(do not let it boil).*
- Serve the sauce over the chicken.

serves 4

Breast of Chicken Veronique

"This is a dish that I learned to make while I was living in Paris. It's quite simple to make, but appears to be very fancy and elegant. It's one of those perfect things to make for company."

½ cup butter
4 whole chicken breasts, halved, boned and skinned
¼ cup butter
24 medium size mushroom caps, quartered
4 tablespoons flour
2 cups half & half
½ cup dry white wine
1¼ cups ham, diced
salt and pepper *(to taste)*
2 cups fresh seedless grapes

- Preheat the oven to 350°.
- In a large heavy skillet place the ½ cup of butter and heat it on medium so that it is melted and hot. Add the chicken and sauté it for 2 to 3 minutes on each side, or until it is browned. Place the chicken in a casserole dish with a lid and set it aside.
- In the same skillet place the ¼ cup of butter and heat it on medium high so that it is melted and hot. Add the mushrooms and sauté them for 3 minutes. Remove them with a slotted spoon so the excess juices return to the skillet. Place the mushrooms evenly over the chicken.
- Reduce the heat to medium low. Add the flour to the butter and juices in the skillet, and stir it in for 1 minute.
- Add the half & half and wine, and stir them for 5 minutes, or until the mixture thickens.
- Add the ham and stir it in for 2 minutes. Add the salt and pepper, and stir them in.
- Pour the sauce over the chicken and mushrooms.
- Cover the dish and bake it for 30 to 40 minutes, or until the chicken is tender and everything is hot and bubbly.
- Remove the cover and place the grapes evenly on the top of the chicken. Bake the chicken for 10 minutes more.

serves 8

Our Daily Granola

"We serve this granola at the inn, and I have given out the recipe hundreds of times to our guests. You can play around with the ingredients and make it very fat-free by using much less oil and nuts. Or, you can really go to town, like I did with this version."

1 **large box** *(42 ounces)* **old-fashioned rolled oats**
½ **cup wheat bran**
½ **cup wheat germ**
½ **cup oat bran**
1 **cup walnuts, chopped**
1 **cup almonds, slivered**
1 **cup sunflower seeds**
1½ **cups canola oil**
¾ **cup honey**
¾ **cup maple syrup**
½ **cup molasses**
4 **tablespoons vanilla extract**
1 **tablespoon salt**
1½ **cups coconut**
1 **cup dried fruit** *(your favorite)*

- Preheat the oven to 350°.
- In a very large bowl place the oats, wheat bran, wheat germ, oat bran, walnuts, almonds and sunflower seeds. Mix everything together well.
- In a medium large bowl place the canola oil, honey, syrup, molasses, vanilla and salt. Mix everything together well.
- Pour the liquid mixture into the dry mixture, and stir it in so that everything is well coated.
- Place the mixture in a roasting pan and bake it for 20 minutes *(stir it occasionally)*, or until everything is lightly toasted.
- Add the coconut and dried fruits, and stir them in.

makes approximately 3 quarts

"I believe that I was born and raised to run a Bed & Breakfast. As the eldest of five children, I learned at a young age to cook for a lot of people, and became quite good at it. There was a short period when I worked on Wall Street and tried my hand at advertising, but finally I accepted the fact that this is my destiny."

Carolyn Lee

The Best Apple Muffins

"These muffins are so delicious that previous guests, who have since moved to Santa Fe, still come by my place to purchase them."

- **3 cups apples, peeled, cored and finely chopped**
- **3½ cups all-purpose flour**
- **1 cup white sugar**
- **1 cup brown sugar**
- **1 tablespoon baking soda**
- **1 teaspoon salt**
- **4 eggs, lightly beaten**
- **2 cups walnuts, chopped medium**
- **1 teaspoon ground cinnamon**
- **1 cup canola oil**
- **1 teaspoon vanilla extract**

- Preheat the oven to 350°.
- In a large bowl place the apples, flour, white sugar, brown sugar, baking soda and salt. Mix the ingredients together.
- Add the eggs, walnuts, cinnamon, oil and vanilla. Mix the ingredients together.
- Fill 24 individual greased muffin tins with the batter so that they are ⅔ full. Bake the muffins for 30 minutes, or until a wooden toothpick inserted in the center comes out dry.

makes 24 muffins

Lemon Poppy Seed Bread

"I make this bread on a regular basis for our guests, and am always getting requests for the recipe. We serve it with yogurt and fresh fruit."

- **2 sticks butter, softened**
- **2 cups sugar**
- **8 eggs**
- **4 cups all-purpose flour**
- **1 tablespoon baking powder**
- **1 teaspoon salt**
- **1½ cups milk**
- **½ cup poppy seeds**
- **4 lemons, zested** *(outer yellow part grated off)* **and juiced**

- Preheat the oven to 325°.
- In a large mixing bowl place the butter and sugar. Cream them together with an electric beater. Add the eggs and mix them in well.
- Sift in the flour, baking powder and salt, and mix them in well. Add the milk and mix it in. Add the poppy seeds, lemon zest and lemon juice, and fold them in.
- Place the batter in 2 greased and floured loaf pans. Bake the bread for 1 hour, or until the center springs up when lightly pushed down with a finger.

makes 2 loaves

Pineapple Bran Muffins

"My ex-manager, Mary Jo, concocted this recipe and we always served it while she was working here. The pineapple makes the muffins moist, and the walnuts give them a nice crunchy texture."

1 pint vanilla yogurt
1 teaspoon baking soda
2 eggs, lightly beaten
1½ cups brown sugar
2½ cups all-purpose flour
1 teaspoon salt
½ cup canola oil
3 cups Nabisco 100% bran cereal, mixed with 1 cup boiling water
1 8-ounce can crushed pineapple
1 cup raisins
1 cup walnuts, chopped

- Preheat the oven to 375°.
- In a medium bowl place the yogurt and baking soda, and mix them together.
- In a large bowl place the eggs, brown sugar, flour, salt and oil. Mix the ingredients together.
- Add the cereal and yogurt, and mix them in well.
- Add the pineapple, raisins and walnuts, and mix them in.
- Fill 30 individual greased muffin tins with the batter so that they are ⅔ full.
- Bake the muffins for 20 minutes, or until a toothpick inserted in the center comes out clean.

makes 30 muffins

"Running a Bed & Breakfast is very labor intensive. However, it also is very rewarding because the guests are wonderful, and they give me much positive feedback for all my hard work."

Carolyn Lee

Marvelous Carrot Cake with Fantastic Frosting

"During my teenage years I had a girlfriend who made this cake for everyone's birthday. Everyone loved it, and we all loved her for making it."

Marvelous Carrot Cake

4 eggs
1 cup vegetable oil
2 cups sugar
2½ cups all-purpose flour
2 teaspoons ground cinnamon
2 teaspoons ground cloves
1½ teaspoons baking soda
1 teaspoon salt
2 cups carrots, grated
2 cups walnuts, chopped medium
Fantastic Frosting *(recipe follows)*

- Preheat the oven to 350°.
- In a medium bowl place the eggs, oil and sugar. Mix the ingredients together so that they are well combined.
- In a large bowl place the flour, cinnamon, cloves, baking soda and salt. Mix the ingredients together.
- Add the egg mixture to the flour mixture, and beat them together so that a sticky dough is formed. Add the carrots and walnuts, and fold them in.
- Place the mixture in a 9" x 12" greased and floured baking pan.
- Bake the cake for 45 minutes, or until center of the cake springs up when lightly pushed down with a finger.
- Let the cake cool. Spread the Fantastic Frosting on top.

serves 8 to 10

Fantastic Frosting

1 pound powdered sugar
1 stick butter, softened and cut into quarters
1 8-ounce package cream cheese, softened and cut into quarters
1 teaspoon vanilla extract
½ cup walnuts, chopped

- In a medium bowl place the sugar, butter, cream cheese and vanilla. Beat the ingredients together so that they are smooth and creamy.
- Add the walnuts and mix them in.

frosts 1 cake

American Artists Gallery House

Post Office Box 584
Taos, New Mexico 87571
(505) 758-44466 • (800) 532-2041
Elliot & Judie Framan, Innkeepers

Even the breakfast menu is a work of art at this delightful Taos inn, where paintings, pottery and weavings decorate the charming Southwest-style rooms. A menu that features elegant hot dishes is sure to lure guests from under their down comforters or from in front of their kiva fireplaces to face a day of skiing, hiking or whitewater rafting.

Recipes

Herbed Liver Paté

"If you like paté, you will really love this recipe. Because it is quite rich, you should treasure each bite."

1 stick butter
1 cup yellow onions, finely chopped
1 pound chicken livers, trimmed and cut into thirds
1 small bay leaf
½ teaspoon dried thyme
½ teaspoon dried oregano
1 teaspoon salt *(or to taste)*
½ teaspoon pepper *(or to taste)*
½ stick butter, softened

- In a large skillet place the 1 stick of butter and heat it on medium until it is melted and hot. Add the onions and sauté them for 5 minutes, or until they are lightly browned. Remove them with a slotted spoon and set them aside.
- Add the chicken livers, bay leaf, thyme, oregano, salt and pepper. Sauté the ingredients for 15 minutes, or until the livers are brown on the outside and slightly pink in the middle. Discard the bay leaf.
- In a blender place the reserved onions. Add the livers a few at a time and blend them so that the mixture is smooth.
- Push the mixture through a fine sieve into a bowl. Add the ½ stick of butter and blend it in. Add more salt and pepper if necessary.
- Place the paté in a small loaf pan and chill it in the refrigerator.

makes 1 small loaf

Piñon Rice

"This is a very basic white rice recipe that is enhanced by the flavor of the piñon nuts and parsley. Our guests don't like the spicy red Spanish rice for breakfast.....they prefer something more mild, like this dish."

¼ cup unsalted margarine
2 cups uncooked white rice
3 cups chicken broth
½ cup piñon nuts *(pine nuts),* **lightly roasted**
¾ cup fresh parsley, chopped

- In a large saucepan place the margarine and heat it on medium until it is melted and hot. Add the rice and stir it constantly for 6 to 8 minutes, or until it is lightly browned.
- Add the broth and bring the mixture to a boil. Cover the pan and reduce the heat to low. Simmer the rice for 30 minutes, or until it is done. Add the piñon nuts and parsley, and toss them in.

serves 8

Jalapeño Corn Cakes

"These are delicious, slightly spicy corn cakes that you can serve with any meal. They are especially good with some sour cream and hot tomato salsa on the side."

1½ cups flour
½ cup cornmeal
1 teaspoon baking powder
6 egg yolks
6 ounces cream cheese
1½ cups milk
½ cup unsalted butter, melted
1 cup fresh corn kernels, roasted
¼ cup jalapeño chile peppers *(or to taste),* **finely chopped**
¼ cup red bell peppers, seeded and finely chopped
⅛ teaspoon Tabasco sauce *(or to taste)*
1 teaspoon salt
6 egg whites
1 pinch of salt
1 teaspoon butter
1 teaspoon corn oil
Papaya & Avocado Salsa *(recipe on next page)*

- In a medium bowl sift together the flour, cornmeal and baking powder.
- In a large bowl place the egg yolks and cream cheese. Mix them together with an electric beater. Add the flour mixture and mix it in. Slowly add the milk and mix it in.
- Add the ½ cup of butter, the corn, jalapeño chile peppers, red bell peppers, Tabasco and the 1 teaspoon of salt. Mix the ingredients together.
- In another large bowl place the egg whites and the pinch of salt, and beat them so that the egg whites are stiff but not dry. Add ⅓ of the egg whites to the batter, and fold them in.
- Gently fold the batter into the remaining egg whites.
- In a large nonstick frying pan place the 1 teaspoon of butter and the corn oil, and heat them on medium high until the butter is melted and hot. Drop the batter into the pan by rounded tablespoons. Cook the patties until bubbles form and burst on top. Turn the cakes over and cook them for 30 seconds more.
- Serve the corn cakes with the Papaya & Avocado Salsa on the side.

makes approximately 5 dozen cakes

"I learned how to cook as a little girl from my sweet mother, who was very patient in teaching me. As I got older, I took over the cooking for the whole family. It's something that I both enjoy and do well."

Judie Framan

Papaya & Avocado Salsa

"I have a good friend in California who is a very creative cook. When she heard I was moving to New Mexico, she developed this recipe for me as a going away gift. The flavor of the papaya and avocado together is exquisite."

- 1 **papaya, peeled, seeded and coarsely chopped**
- 1 **small red onion, finely chopped**
- 6 **scallions** *(green part only),* **finely chopped**
- ½ **cup fresh cilantro leaves, chopped**
- 1 **orange, zested** *(outer orange part grated off)* **and juiced**
- 2 **limes, zested and juiced**
- 1 **teaspoon brown sugar**
- ⅛ **teaspoon Tabasco sauce**
- ½ **cup cider vinegar**
- **salt and pepper** *(to taste)*
- 2 **medium avocados, peeled, pitted and diced medium**

- In a large bowl place all of the ingredients *(except for the avocados)* and mix them together. Cover the salsa and chill it in the refrigerator for at least 1 hour.
- Just before serving, add the avocados and gently toss them in.

makes approximately 2 cups

Chile Verde con Carne

"I was given this recipe by Sarah Martinez, a native of Taos, whose family dates back to the early sixteenth century. She told me the recipe has changed very little over all those years. It's really great over breakfast burritos."

- 1 **5-pound pork roast**
- 10 **cups water**
- ⅓ **cup vegetable oil**
- ⅓ **cup flour**
- 1 **medium yellow onion, finely chopped**
- 1 **clove garlic, minced**
- 10 **green chile peppers, roasted, peeled and chopped**
- 1 **teaspoon salt** *(or to taste)*

- In a large heavy stockpot place the pork roast and water. Simmer the pork for 2 hours, or until it is done.
- Remove the meat from the broth. Let it cool, and then shred it. Place the meat in the refrigerator until it is to be used.
- Refrigerate the broth so that the fat rises and congeals on top. Skim off the fat and discard it.
- In a medium sauté pan place the vegetable oil and heat it on medium high until it is hot. Add the flour and stir it continuously so that a smooth roux is formed. Add the onions, garlic and green chile peppers. Stir and cook them for 5 minutes, or until the roux is golden brown.
- Heat the refrigerated broth until it is hot. Add the roux, pork and salt to the broth, and stir them in well. Simmer the stew for 30 minutes.

serves 8

New Mexico Coleslaw

"Originally this coleslaw was designed to go in a grilled swordfish sandwich with a sourdough roll, but I like to serve it as a side dish for brunch. It's very colorful, with the green, red and white vegetables."

- ¼ **cup lime juice, freshly squeezed**
- ¼ **cup vegetable oil**
- ½ **cup fresh cilantro, minced**
- **salt and pepper** *(to taste)*
- 4 **cups green cabbage, shredded**
- 1 **cup red cabbage, shredded**
- 1 **avocado, peeled, pitted and thinly sliced**
- 2 **cups jicama, peeled and thinly sliced**

- In a small bowl place the lime juice, oil, cilantro, salt and pepper. Mix the ingredients together well.
- In a large bowl place the green and red cabbage. Add the dressing and toss it in.
- Garnish each serving with the avocados and jicama.

serves 8

Indian Corn Bake

"This is a very moist and delicious soufflé-like casserole that we serve for breakfast. It's nourishing, filling and quick to make. Serve it with your favorite salsa on the side."

- ¾ **cup cornmeal**
- 2 **cups creamed corn**
- 2 **eggs, lightly beaten**
- 2 **4-ounce cans green chile peppers, chopped**
- 2 **cups cheddar cheese, grated**
- ½ **teaspoon garlic powder**

- Preheat the oven to 350°.
- In a medium bowl place all of the ingredients and mix them together.
- Place the mixture in a greased and floured baking pan.
- Bake the casserole for 35 minutes, or until it is set.

serves 8

Broiled Grapefruit

"Normally I don't like grapefruit, but I love it in this recipe. This is the perfect thing to serve before a rich main cheesy dish, because the acid seems to cut the fat. Make sure you don't use the ruby red grapefruit....they are too sweet."

1 large orange, peeled, seeds removed, and cut into small pieces

4 tablespoons frozen orange juice concentrate

4 tablespoons port wine

¼ teaspoon ground cinnamon *(or as needed)*

4 large yellow grapefruit, halved, seeded and sections separated from rind and membranes

- Preheat the broiler.
- In a medium bowl place the orange pieces, juice concentrate and wine. Stir the ingredients together.
- On top of each grapefruit half place some of the fruit mixture. Top each half with a sprinkling of cinnamon.
- Broil the grapefruit for 1 minute.

serves 8

"We are very environmentally and health aware at our inn. Our food is as fat-free and nutritious as possible, and we recycle everything that we can."

Judie Framan

Cucumber Soup

"Some time ago I acquired this recipe from a health spa. It's cool, light and refreshing...... just the perfect thing for a hot summer day."

2 pounds cucumbers, peeled, seeded and chopped
2½ cups chicken broth
½ cup half & half
½ teaspoon lemon juice, freshly squeezed
pepper *(to taste)*
4 fresh dill sprigs

- In a large stockpot place the cucumbers *(reserve ½ cup)* and chicken broth. While stirring occasionally, bring them to a boil.
- Reduce the heat to low and simmer the cucumbers for 20 minutes. Remove the pot from the heat and let it cool.
- Place the mixture in a food processor and purée it so that it is smooth.
- In a medium bowl place the puréed mixture and chill it in the refrigerator for 1 hour, or until it is cold.
- In a small bowl place the half & half, lemon juice, pepper and reserved cucumbers. Mix the ingredients together.
- Add the chilled purée and stir it in so that everything is well blended.
- Garnish each serving with a sprig of dill.

serves 4

"Our Bed & Breakfast is also an art gallery, which makes us rather unique. I really enjoy working with the local artists, who sometimes come to give demonstrations or to have breakfast with our guests."

Elliot Framan

Sundried Tomato Olive Strata

"Stratas are great things to serve for breakfast because they can be prepared the day before and then popped in the oven the next morning while you are enjoying hot coffee and reading the paper."

8 **slices firm white bread** *(or as needed)*
2 **cups Monterey Jack cheese, grated**
¼ **cup sundried tomatoes** *(packed in oil),* **drained and chopped**
1 **2¼-ounce can pitted olives, drained and chopped**
5 **large eggs**
2½ **cups milk**
½ **teaspoon pepper**

- In a buttered 8" x 11" baking dish place 4 of the bread slices so that they cover the bottom.
- Sprinkle ½ of the cheese on top.
- Sprinkle on the tomatoes and olives.
- Place the rest of the bread slices on top.
- Sprinkle on the rest of the cheese.
- In a medium bowl place the eggs and milk, and beat them together.
- Pour the mixture on top of the bread.
- Sprinkle on the pepper.
- Cover the dish with plastic wrap and refrigerate it overnight.
- Preheat the oven to 350°.
- Bake the strata *(uncovered)* for 50 minutes, or until the edges are lightly browned and the center is firm.
- Let the strata cool for 10 minutes. Cut it into squares.

serves 8

"Many famous writers and artists have been captivated by the charms of Taos. Some of the most notable are Georgia O'Keeffe, Aldous Huxley, Thomas Wolfe, D.H. Lawrence and Willa Cather."

Judie Framan

Spicy Chicken Strips

"This is my alternative to a traditional buffalo chicken wings recipe. It's much better because you don't have to deal with the bones, and it's made with white meat instead of dark. Also, the spices give the chicken an excellent flavor."

1 medium yellow onion, coarsely chopped
1 whole head garlic, peeled
5 tablespoons peanut oil
¼ cup red wine vinegar
3 tablespoons fennel seeds
2 tablespoons ground cumin
2 tablespoons ground paprika
20 whole peppercorns
1 1-inch piece fresh ginger root, peeled and chopped
2 tablespoons cardamom seeds
8 whole cloves
2 teaspoons ground cilantro
2 teaspoons salt
1 teaspoon ground cinnamon
¼ teaspoon cayenne pepper
3 pounds chicken breast, boned, skinned and cut into ½" wide strips

- In a food processor place all of the ingredients *(except for the chicken)*. Blend them together so that a smooth paste is formed.
- In a large bowl place the chicken. Add the paste and stir the ingredients together so that the chicken is thoroughly coated.
- Cover the bowl and chill the chicken for 4 to 6 hours.
- Preheat the broiler.
- In a shallow baking pan place the chicken.
- Broil it for 4 minutes, or until it is cooked and browned.

serves 6

"Taos is a most unique and special place. Many people come here because of its natural beauty, but I love it because of the people. They are just wonderful, and embrace newcomers as if they were members of their own family."

Judie Framan

Chicken & Blueberry Pasta Salad

"If you can find fresh blueberries, this is the best pasta salad in the world. I've made it with leftover chicken in about ten minutes, and my guests thought I slaved in the kitchen all day. You can substitute balsamic vinegar for the blueberry vinegar."

3 cups boneless chicken breast, cooked and shredded
3 cups fusilli *(or shell pasta),* **cooked al dente and drained**
1 9-ounce package frozen French cut green beans, thawed and drained
1 cup fresh blueberries
¾ cup celery, thinly sliced
¼ cup scallions, thinly sliced
2 tablespoons fresh oregano, finely chopped
¾ cup plain low-fat yogurt
¼ cup mayonnaise
3 tablespoons blueberry vinegar
½ teaspoon coarsely ground pepper
6 lettuce leaves, rinsed and patted dry

- In a large bowl place the chicken, pasta, green beans, blueberries, celery and scallions. Combine the ingredients together.
- In a small bowl place the oregano, yogurt, mayonnaise, vinegar and pepper. Mix the ingredients together well.
- Add the dressing to the salad and gently mix it in.
- Cover the bowl with plastic wrap and refrigerate it for 3 hours.
- On each of 6 individual salad plates place a lettuce leaf. Place the chicken salad on top.

serves 6

"To me, good food should be nutritious, filling and delicious. I work hard to come up with recipes that satisfy all of these requirements."

Judie Framan

Eggs Denise

"A friend of mine gave me this recipe when she found out I was moving to New Mexico and opening a Bed & Breakfast. It's simple, but very, very good."

12 **eggs**
8 **ounces cream cheese**
½ **cup milk**
8 **ounces lox** *(or smoked trout),* **chopped**
6 **scallions, thinly sliced**
½ **teaspoon ground nutmeg**
pepper *(to taste)*
1 **round loaf rye bread, hollowed out**

- Preheat the oven to 350°.
- In a medium bowl place the eggs and cream cheese. Beat them together with an electric mixer so that they are well blended. Add the milk and blend it in well.
- Add the lox, scallions, nutmeg and pepper. Stir the ingredients together so that they are well blended.
- In a greased large skillet place the mixture and scramble it on medium high heat until the eggs are firm.
- Place the egg mixture in the loaf of bread.
- Bake it for 15 minutes, or until the bread is crispy and the center is set.

serves 8

Egg Chile Relleno

"I love this recipe because not only is it extremely popular with our guests, it also is healthy. The flavor and texture are not at all diminished by using low-fat mozzarella and cottage cheese."

10 **eggs, beaten**
½ **cup flour**
½ **teaspoon baking powder**
1 **24-ounce carton low-fat cottage cheese**
2 **4-ounce cans green chile peppers, diced**
1 **cup low-fat mozzarella cheese, grated**
1 **avocado, peeled, pitted and thinly sliced**

- Preheat the oven to 350°.
- In a large bowl place the eggs, flour, baking powder, cottage cheese, green chile peppers and mozzarella cheese. Mix the ingredients together so that they are well combined.
- In a greased medium baking pan place the mixture. Bake the rellenos for 25 to 30 minutes, or until they are golden brown on top.
- Garnish each serving with some of the avocado.

serves 8

American Artists' Cioppino

"When I was in college I majored in marine biology, and this is something I used to make during that time. If available, Dungeness crab is the best."

1/4 cup olive oil
1 medium yellow onion, finely chopped
1 clove garlic, minced
2 15-ounce cans tomato sauce
1 8-ounce can tomatoes
1 1/2 tablespoons fresh basil, finely chopped
1 teaspoon Tabasco sauce
1 teaspoon salt
1/2 teaspoon pepper
1 1/2 cups red wine
2 large crabs, scrubbed
12 prawns
12 cherrystone clams, scrubbed
1/2 cup fresh parsley, chopped
8 thick slices French bread, buttered and toasted

- In a large stockpot place the oil and heat it on medium high until it is hot. Add the onions and sauté them for 5 minutes, or until they are translucent.
- Add the garlic, tomato sauce, tomatoes, basil, Tabasco, salt and pepper. Stir the ingredients together.
- Add the wine and stir it in. Cover the pan and simmer the ingredients on low heat for 1 hour.
- Add the crabs, cover the pot and cook them for 5 minutes.
- Add the prawns and clams. Sprinkle on the parsley. Cover the pot and cook the ingredients for 10 minutes more.
- Serve the cioppino with the toasted French bread on the side.

serves 8

"Don't try to start a Bed & Breakfast unless you really know yourself well. You must be a people-person, be service oriented, and be willing to work very hard for 365 days a year."

Elliot Framan

Pasta Primavera

"Make this recipe only when you have very, very fresh vegetables. It is a wonderful, light pasta dish with a heavenly flavor."

3 tablespoons butter
3 tablespoons extra virgin olive oil
1 medium yellow onion, minced
2 cloves garlic, minced
⅓ cup fresh parsley, minced
⅓ cup carrots, thinly sliced
2 cups cauliflower, broken into florets
10 cherry tomatoes
10 asparagus spears, blanched and cut into 1" pieces
1 cup mushrooms, sliced
⅓ cup petite peas
½ cup chicken broth
⅓ cup heavy cream
3 tablespoons Parmesan cheese, freshly grated
6 fresh basil leaves, coarsely chopped
pepper *(to taste)*
1 pound fettucine, cooked al dente and drained

- In a large skillet place the butter and olive oil, and heat them on medium until the butter is melted and hot. Add the onions and sauté them for 5 minutes, or until they are translucent.
- Add the garlic and parsley, and sauté them for 1 minute.
- Add the carrots and cauliflower, and sauté them for 5 minutes.
- Add the tomatoes, asparagus, mushrooms and peas. Stir the ingredients together.
- Add the chicken broth and stir it in. Reduce the heat to low and simmer the mixture for 5 minutes.
- Add the cream and blend it in well.
- Add the cheese, basil and pepper. Gently stir the ingredients together.
- Pour the mixture over the pasta and toss it well.

serves 4

Stuffed French Toast

"I call this a 'world-famous recipe' because our return guests from all over the globe always request it. If you eat this for breakfast before a big day on the ski slopes, you won't need to have lunch."

16 thick slices French bread
4 ounces cream cheese, softened
4 tablespoons pecans, finely chopped
8 eggs, slightly beaten
½ tablespoon vanilla extract
½ teaspoon ground nutmeg
½ teaspoon orange zest *(outer orange part grated off)*
½ cup milk
1 stick margarine

- Match the slices of bread into pairs. On one slice of bread, heavily spread on some of the cream cheese. On the other slice, lightly spread a small amount of the cream cheese.
- On each of the heavily spread slices of bread sprinkle on some of the pecans. Top it with the second slice of bread so that a sandwich is made. Set the sandwiches aside.
- In a medium bowl place the eggs, vanilla, nutmeg, orange zest and milk. Mix the ingredients together so that they are well blended.
- In a large frying pan place the margarine and heat it on medium until it is melted and hot. One at a time, dip each sandwich into the batter. Fry it for 2 minutes on each side, or until it is golden brown.

serves 8

"Owning a Bed & Breakfast is very similar to having a public relations business, which was my former occupation. It is very intense, and is based on developing personal relationships with your clients. Over the years I have made life-long friends through both businesses."

Elliot Framan

The Carter House

101 North Cooper Street
Silver City, New Mexico 88061
(505) 388-5485
Lucy Dilworth, Innkeeper • Brenna Brown, Chef

The echoes of Silver City's early copper-mining days still can be heard in the Carter House, a Queen Ann-Colonial revival home conveniently situated in the historical district. The handsome old oak-trimmed house with its wrap-around front porch is at the edge of a mountainous area renowned for its hiking, rock hounding, art galleries, prehistoric Indian ruins, ghost towns, hot springs, the Gila Wilderness.....and wild west history.

Recipes

Tomatillo & Raspberry Mint Salsa

"Usually I make my salsa with tomatillos or tomatoes, but one day I decided to add some fresh raspberries from my garden. They blended in to produce a most surprising and delicious flavor."

1 tablespoon butter
1 pound tomatillos, skinned and quartered
1 red bell pepper, seeded and finely chopped
1 serrano chile pepper, thinly sliced
2 cloves garlic, minced
2 tablespoons water
1 pint fresh raspberries
3 tablespoons fresh mint, chopped

- In a medium sauté pan place the butter and heat it on medium until it is melted and hot. Add the tomatillos, bell peppers, serrano chile peppers and garlic. Sauté them until the tomatillos turn bright green.
- Add the water, cover the pan and cook the salsa for 2 minutes.
- Add the raspberries and mint, and gently stir them in.
- Place the salsa in a medium bowl and refrigerate it for at least 2 hours.

makes approximately 2 cups

"I really love running a Bed & Breakfast inn. Perhaps the best part about it is that I am now my own boss. Although there is a lot of hard work, there is also a wonderful variety."

Lucy Dilworth

Green Sauce Dip

"This is a beautiful, emerald-colored dip that I serve with a fresh vegetable platter. Make sure that you really purée it well so that there are no strings left from the spinach. If you have time for the preparation, fresh spinach tastes much better than frozen."

1 cup water
1 pound tomatillos, blanched, skins removed, and quartered
1 green bell pepper, seeded and chopped medium
2 serrano chile peppers, chopped
2 cloves garlic, chopped
1 package frozen spinach, thawed
1 ripe avocado, peeled, pitted and coarsely chopped
½ cup sour cream
2 tablespoons lemon juice, freshly squeezed
1 tablespoon fresh tarragon, chopped
salt *(to taste)*

- In a large saucepan place the water and heat it on medium high until it comes to a boil. Add the tomatillos, bell peppers, serrano chile peppers and garlic. Cover the pan and simmer the vegetables for 5 minutes.
- Add the spinach and simmer the ingredients for 1 minute.
- In a food processor place the cooked vegetables and blend them together well. Place the mixture in a medium bowl and set it aside.
- In the food processor place the avocado, sour cream, lemon juice and tarragon. Blend the ingredients together so that a smooth paste is formed.
- Add the spinach mixture and blend it in so that the sauce is smooth.
- Add the salt and pulse it in.

makes approximately 3 cups

"Silver City is an old mining town with a lot of wonderful Victorian architecture. I like living here because the people are friendly, the climate is temperate and the scenery is spectacular."

Lucy Dilworth

Baked Pumpkin Soup

"Many years ago I read a recipe for a baked butternut squash soup. At the time I wanted to make it there was no squash in the kitchen, but I did have pumpkin, which I decided to use instead. The flavor came out to be incredibly rich and the color was a deep orange. In addition to the fresh parsley sprinkled on top, it's nice to add some freshly ground nutmeg."

1½	**pounds pumpkin, seeds removed**	2	**tablespoons flour**
5	**cloves garlic, peeled and wrapped in foil**	1	**quart chicken broth**
1	**medium yellow onion, halved**	1	**cup heavy cream**
2	**carrots, cut into 2" long pieces**	1	**tablespoon fresh thyme**
2	**stalks celery, cut into 2" long pieces**	2	**tablespoons fresh parsley, minced**
¼	**cup butter**		

- Preheat the oven to 350°.
- On a large baking sheet place the pumpkin, garlic, onion, carrots and celery. Wrap the pan tightly in foil so that all of the vegetables except the pumpkin are covered. Bake the vegetables for 1½ hours. Remove the foil and let the vegetables cool.
- Peel off the skin from the pumpkin and discard it.
- Place the cooked vegetables in a food processor and blend them so that they are smooth.
- In a large saucepan place the butter and heat it on medium until it is melted and hot. Add the flour and stir it in so that a smooth roux is formed. While stirring constantly, slowly add the chicken broth. Simmer and stir the mixture for 5 minutes.
- Add the vegetable mixture and stir it in. Add the cream and thyme, and stir them in well.
- Remove the soup from the heat and let it sit for 5 minutes.
- Sprinkle the parsley on top.

serves 6

"I used to be a strict vegetarian, but then gradually started including fish, chicken and a small amount of meat in my diet. I have learned that when you are a professional chef who cooks for hundreds of different people, it is not wise to be inflexible in your tastes!"

Brenna Brown

Cold Cucumber Soup

"I thank my grandmother for the creation of this recipe. She has been a tremendous influence in my cooking. To make the soup lighter, eliminate the sour and heavy creams, and substitute more broth."

3 large cucumbers, peeled, seeded and thinly sliced
1 cup scallions, chopped
½ cup green bell peppers, seeded and chopped
1 cup chicken broth
4 tablespoons butter
2 tablespoons flour
1 cup chicken broth
1 teaspoon dried dill
¼ teaspoon dried chervil
¼ teaspoon ground cayenne pepper
1 cup sour cream
¼ cup heavy cream

- In a large saucepan place the cucumbers, scallions, bell peppers and the first cup of chicken broth. Cook and stir the ingredients over low heat for 15 minutes.
- Place the mixture in a food processor and blend it so that it is smooth.
- In the same saucepan place the butter and heat it on medium until it is melted and hot. Add the flour and stir it in so that the mixture is smooth.
- Add the second cup of chicken broth, the dill, chervil and cayenne pepper. Stir the ingredients together well.
- Add the blended cucumber mixture to the saucepan and stir it in well.
- Add the sour cream and heavy cream, and stir them in.
- Remove the soup from the heat, transfer it to a bowl and refrigerate it for at least 4 hours.

serves 6 to 8

"My job as a youngster was to prepare the family meals with the helpful instruction from my two grandmothers. As a result, I became a competent cook at a very young age."

Brenna Brown

Tofu-Stuffed Grape Leaves

"I've always loved to cook with grape leaves, and found that I could easily substitute tofu for the traditional ground lamb. This dish is a big hit with our guests who either are vegetarians or who are cutting down their meat intake. If people aren't told there is tofu in this recipe, they can't tell."

½ **pound tofu, drained and mashed**
1 **cup basmati rice, cooked**
2 **tablespoons wild rice, cooked**
½ **cup red bell peppers, chopped medium**
½ **cup yellow onions, finely chopped**
garlic salt *(to taste)*
20 **grape leaves**
1 **cup white wine**
½ **cup lemon juice, freshly squeezed**

- Preheat the oven to 375°.
- In a large bowl place the tofu, basmati rice, wild rice, bell peppers, onions and garlic salt. Mix the ingredients together well.
- In the center of each grape leaf place 1 tablespoon of the filling. Fold in the sides, top and bottom of each leaf toward the center so that a small roll is formed.
- In a small baking pan place the rolls with the seam sides down.
- In a small bowl place the white wine and lemon juice, and mix them together. Pour the liquid over the tofu rolls.
- Cover the pan tightly with aluminum foil. Bake the stuffed grape leaves for 1 hour.

serves 10

"The presentation of food is very important to me. I want the colors, textures and proportions of the food all to be perfect on the plate, so that everything tastes as good as it looks."

Brenna Brown

Green Chile Chicken Gumbo with Griddle Cakes

"I'm a Southern girl and chicken gumbo has always been a part of my life. So when I moved to New Mexico I decided to add some green chile to my family gumbo recipe, and it proved to be delightful. The Griddle Cakes, being very light, are a perfect accompaniment to the gumbo."

Green Chile Chicken Gumbo

¼ cup canola oil
2 cups okra, sliced ¼" thick
1 pound red bell peppers, seeded and chopped
2 cups green chile peppers, roasted, peeled and chopped
2 cups potatoes, coarsely chopped
2 cups carrots, coarsely chopped
1½ cups yellow onions, sliced
1½ cups celery, sliced
2 cups fresh tomatoes, crushed
6 cloves fresh garlic, peeled and crushed
2 pounds boneless chicken, cooked, skin removed, and shredded
2 tablespoons gumbo filé
3 tablespoons shrimp powder
2 quarts chicken broth
½ cup fresh parsley, chopped
2 tablespoons paprika
salt *(to taste)*
Griddle Cakes *(recipe on next page)*

- In a large Dutch oven place the oil and heat it on medium until it is hot. Add the okra, bell peppers, green chile peppers, potatoes, carrots, onions, celery, tomatoes and garlic. Sauté the ingredients for 5 minutes.
- Cover the pot and cook the ingredients on low heat for 15 minutes.
- Add the chicken, gumbo filé and shrimp powder. Stir the ingredients together well.
- Add the chicken broth and stir it in. Simmer the ingredients for 45 minutes.
- Add the parsley, paprika and salt. Simmer the gumbo for 15 minutes, or until the vegetables are tender.
- Serve the gumbo with the Griddle Cakes on the side.

serves 8

Griddle Cakes

1 cup yellow cornmeal
1 cup whole wheat flour
2 teaspoons sugar
½ teaspoon salt
1 teaspoon baking powder
½ cup hot water
2 eggs, lightly beaten
2 cups buttermilk
2 tablespoons butter, melted
2 tablespoons sesame seeds

- In a large bowl sift together the cornmeal, flour, sugar, salt and baking powder. Pour the hot water over the dry ingredients and let them sit for 5 minutes.
- Add the eggs and buttermilk, and mix them in well. Pour the butter over the batter and let it sit for 2 minutes.
- Add the sesame seeds and stir them in well.
- On a greased and hot griddle, pour out the cakes with a ½ cup measuring cup. Cook the cakes until bubbles around the edges pop. Turn the cakes over and cook them until they are lightly browned.

serves 8

"I purchased this building in 1989 and completely renovated it to its present state. The unusual thing about my Bed & Breakfast is that I am also licensed by Hostelling International to run a hostel on the ground floor of the house. Many of my guests are from countries around the world, which always keeps the conversations interesting!"

Lucy Dilworth

Tri-Color Pasta Salad with Arugula Pesto

"This is a common Italian recipe that is a nice change from the more popular basil pesto. I love the bitter flavor of the arugula and the way it dances with the tri-color pasta."

Tri-Color Pasta Salad

1 pound tri-color pasta, cooked al dente and drained
3 medium tomatoes, cut into thin wedges
1 cup pitted black olives, cut into halves
1 red bell pepper, seeded and coarsely chopped
½ cup fresh chives, minced
½ cup slivered almonds, roasted
Arugula Pesto *(recipe follows)*

- In a large bowl place the pasta.
- Add the tomatoes, olives, bell peppers, chives and almonds.
- Gently toss the ingredients together.
- Add the Arugula Pesto and toss it in.

serves 4

Arugula Pesto

½ cup olive oil
½ cup piñon nuts *(pine nuts)*
3 cloves garlic, chopped
½ pound fresh arugula, chopped
¼ cup Romano cheese, freshly grated
salt *(to taste)*

- In a food processor place the olive oil, piñon nuts and garlic. Blend the ingredients together.
- Add the arugula in small amounts, and blend it in well between each addition so that the mixture is smooth.
- Add the cheese and blend it in.

makes approximately 1½ cups

Vegetable Medley with Cashew Gravy

"For many years I was a vegetarian, and the Cashew Gravy is a recipe that I developed during that time. It enhances the flavor of the vegetables and really makes them come alive. Be sure to pour the gravy on top of the vegetables.....don't mix it in."

Vegetable Medley

2 cups water
1 cup carrots, sliced into ¼" thick rounds
½ pound snow peas, strings removed
1 red bell pepper, seeded and sliced into thin strips
½ cup zucchini, sliced into ½" thick rounds
5 scallions, white part only, left whole
½ teaspoon fresh thyme, chopped
Cashew Gravy *(recipe follows)*

- In a large saucepan place a steamer and the water. Heat the water on medium high heat until it boils. Reduce the heat to low. Add the carrots, cover the pan and steam them for 3 minutes.
- Add the remaining vegetables and cover the pan. Steam the vegetables for 5 minutes, or until they are tender.
- Place the vegetables on a serving plate and sprinkle them with the thyme. Pour the Cashew Gravy on top.

serves 6

Cashew Gravy

1 stick butter
2 cups cashews, crushed
2 tablespoons flour
½ cup yellow onions, finely chopped
½ cup red bell peppers, seeded and finely chopped
1 cup vegetable broth
salt *(to taste)*

- In a medium skillet place the butter and heat it on medium until it is melted and hot. Add the cashews and flour. Stir the mixture constantly until the flour is browned *(be sure not to burn the nuts)*.
- Add the onions and red bell peppers, and stir them in well.
- Add the vegetable broth and salt, and stir them in so that the ingredients are well mixed.
- Cover the skillet and let the gravy simmer for 10 minutes.

makes approximately 1 quart

Lemon Ginger Raspberry Chicken

"One year I had a bonanza raspberry harvest, and so decided to try adding them to my lemon chicken recipe. The result was outstanding! Everyone loved it and wanted to know how I came up with the idea."

6 8-ounce boneless chicken breasts, skins removed, and cut into thin strips
½ cup lemon juice, freshly squeezed
2 teaspoons lemon zest *(outer yellow part grated off)*
1 teaspoon fresh garlic, minced
1 teaspoon ground paprika
¼ teaspoon ground ginger
¾ cup flour
¼ cup cornmeal
½ teaspoon ground ginger
½ teaspoon white pepper
1 teaspoon salt
2 eggs, lightly beaten
¼ teaspoon cayenne pepper
1 teaspoon sugar
2 cups canola oil
1 small can lemonade concentrate, thawed
¼ cup yellow onions, finely minced
2 tablespoons fresh ginger root, peeled and grated
1 quart fresh raspberries

- In a large bowl place the chicken strips, lemon juice, lemon zest, garlic, paprika and the ¼ teaspoon of ground ginger. Cover the bowl and marinate the chicken for at least 1 hour *(or overnight)*.
- Preheat the oven to 375°.
- Remove the chicken strips from the marinade and drain them on paper towels.
- In a medium bowl place the flour, cornmeal, the ½ teaspoon of ground ginger, the white pepper and salt. Mix the ingredients together.
- In another medium bowl place the eggs, cayenne pepper and sugar. Mix the ingredients together.
- One at a time, dip the chicken strips into the egg mixture and then into the flour mixture so that each piece is evenly coated.
- In a large heavy skillet place the oil and heat it on medium high until it is hot. Add the chicken strips and brown them on both sides. Place the chicken in a shallow baking pan.
- In a small bowl place the lemonade, onions and fresh ginger. Mix the ingredients together and pour them over the chicken.
- Cover the pan tightly with foil.
- Bake the chicken for 45 minutes.
- Remove the chicken from the oven. Remove the foil, add the raspberries and mix them in.
- Cover the pan again with the foil and let the chicken sit for 20 minutes.

serves 8

Double Chocolate Brownie with Chocolate Ganache Topping

"This is so rich and decadent that I suggest that people not eat more than one small piece. If you'll notice, the brownies contain cocoa powder with very little flour, which makes them incredibly sweet and chocolately."

Double Chocolate Brownie

2 sticks butter, softened to room temperature
1 cup unsweetened cocoa *(Dutch, if possible)*
1½ cups sugar
1 teaspoon heavy cream
3 tablespoons flour
4 eggs, lightly beaten
1 teaspoon vanilla extract
Chocolate Ganache Topping *(recipe follows)*
1 pint fresh raspberries
1 cup pecans, chopped

- Preheat the oven to 375°.
- In a medium bowl place the butter, cocoa, sugar and cream. Blend the ingredients together with an electric mixer so that they are smooth and creamy.
- Add the flour, eggs and vanilla. Stir the ingredients together so that the flour is just moistened *(do not overmix)*.
- Into a greased 13" x 9" baking pan pour the batter and bake it for 20 minutes.
- Let the brownies cool for 1 hour.
- Spread the Chocolate Ganache on top.
- Cut the brownies into 24 squares.
- Sprinkle on the raspberries and pecans.

makes 24 brownies

Chocolate Ganache Topping

16 ounces semisweet baking chocolate squares
1 egg yolk, lightly beaten
1½ cups heavy cream

- In a double boiler place the chocolate and heat it on medium low heat until it is melted.
- Add the egg yolk and heavy cream, and stir them in well.

makes approximately 2 cups

Casa de las Chimeneas

405 Cordoba Road • Box 5303
Taos, New Mexico 87571
(505) 758-4777
Ron Rencher & Susan Vernon, Innkeepers

The House of the Chimneys is the place to go for romantic rooms, brilliantly flowered gardens and sumptuous breakfasts. The two-room Library Suite in the 50-year-old adobe hacienda provides a year's worth of good reading and board games, and all rooms feature kiva fireplaces, antique furniture and talavera-tiled bathrooms. If you're not skiing the famed Taos slopes, walk just a few blocks to the town center with its many art galleries, restaurants and shops.

Recipes

Fruit Frappé

"This drink has the consistency of a milk shake although it has no dairy. It's a delicious treat to serve at breakfast or as a cold drink on a hot summer day."

2 cups small ice cubes
1 cup papaya nectar
¾ cup pineapple juice
½ ripe banana
⅓ cup frozen blackberries
1 tablespoon canned cream of coconut

- In a blender place all of the ingredients and purée them on high speed so that the mixture is smooth.

serves 4

Casa Chimeneas Ham Salad

"This ham salad is a regular feature of our hors d'oeuvre spread, thanks to our assistant innkeeper, Jacalyn Libby, who shared her grandmother's recipe with us. Serve it as a spread on crackers or as a sandwich filling."

4 eggs, hard boiled and peeled
12 ounces cooked ham, coarsely chopped
2 large dill pickles, coarsely chopped
½ small yellow onion, coarsely chopped
2 tablespoons mayonnaise

- In a food processor place all of the ingredients *(except for the mayonnaise)* and blend them together.
- Place the mixture in a small bowl. Add the mayonnaise and stir it in well.
- Cover the bowl and refrigerate the salad for 2 hours.

makes approximately 2 cups

Casa Chimeneas Guacamole

"There are thousands of guacamole recipes in the world, but this is one of the best I have ever eaten. It was a collaborative effort by our staff. The secret is the mayonnaise, which makes it creamier."

2 ripe avocados, peeled, pitted and mashed
1 medium tomato, skinned and chopped
1 teaspoon lemon juice, freshly squeezed
3/4 teaspoon garlic powder
3/4 teaspoon red chile powder
1½ teaspoons mayonnaise
3/4 teaspoon salt

- In a medium bowl place all of the ingredients and mix them together well.

makes approximately 1 cup

"I've been running this Bed & Breakfast for over six years, and there is no way I could do that if I didn't enjoy it. This business is something you either like or don't like. There is no gray area!"

Susan Vernon

Homemade Salsa

"This is a basic fresh salsa that you can serve with chips, or as a garnish with other dishes. It will last for several days in the refrigerator."

2½ cups tomatoes, chopped
½ cup white onions, finely chopped
½ teaspoon jalapeño chile peppers, minced
1 clove garlic, minced
1 teaspoon chile pequin *(or to taste)*
½ teaspoon salt *(or to taste)*

- In a medium bowl place all of the ingredients and mix them together. Chill the salsa in the refrigerator overnight.

makes approximately 3 cups

Breakfast Burritos

"Breakfast burritos are very popular in New Mexico and this is the version we serve at our inn. They are quick and easy to make, and taste wonderful."

1 tablespoon butter
½ cup cooked ham, diced small
1 clove garlic, minced
¼ medium red onion, diced medium
½ green bell pepper, seeded and diced medium
8 eggs, beaten
4 flour tortillas, warmed
2 cups Casa Chimeneas Green Chile Stew *(recipe on page 78),* **heated**
½ cup Monterey Jack cheese, grated
4 tablespoons sour cream

- In a large sauté pan place the butter and heat it on medium high until it is melted and hot. Add the ham, garlic, onions and bell peppers. Sauté the ingredients for 5 minutes, or until the onions are translucent.
- Add the eggs and scramble them so they are just done.
- On each of 4 individual serving plates place a tortilla. Spread the egg mixture across the center. Roll the tortilla up and tuck the ends under.
- Pour the Casa Chimeneas Green Chile Stew on top. Sprinkle on the grated cheese. Place a dollop of sour cream on top.

serves 4

Oven Hash Browns

"These potatoes are brown and crispy on the outside and moist and tender on the inside. You can make them in large batches to feed lots of people, or in small amounts for your family. They go with everything."

6 small red potatoes, cut into ¼" cubes, soaked in salt water and drained
3 tablespoons vegetable oil
½ teaspoon pepper
½ teaspoon garlic powder
¼ teaspoon Mrs. Dash

- Preheat the oven to 400°.
- In a medium bowl place all of the ingredients and toss them together so that the potatoes are well coated with the oil.
- Spread the potatoes on a cookie sheet.
- Bake the potatoes for 25 minutes, or until they are browned.

serves 4

"When my husband Ron and I travel, we always stay at the very most expensive Bed & Breakfasts available. We notice all the details that they offer and then try to incorporate them into our own inn."

Susan Vernon

Huevos Rancheros

"We based this recipe on the traditional way Huevos Rancheros are made in Taos. It is a layered dish, where the different ingredients are stacked. People just love it!"

2 tablespoons butter
4 corn tortillas
1½ cups cooked pinto beans
4 eggs, poached
¾ cup cheddar cheese, grated
1 cup Casa Chimeneas Green Chile Stew
(recipe on next page)
4 strips bacon, cooked crisp, drained and crumbled
½ cup sour cream

- In a medium skillet place the butter and heat it on medium until it is melted and hot. Place 1 tortilla at a time in the skillet and heat it for 30 seconds, or until it is just limp. Drain them on paper towels.
- On each of 4 individual serving plates place a tortilla.
- In this order, layer on the beans, poached egg, cheese, Casa Chimeneas Green Chile Stew and crumbled bacon.
- Top each serving with a dollop of sour cream.

serves 4

"We have one of the most amazing gardens in Taos, with more than 2300 tulips, daffodils and crocus blooming in April and masses of daisies, poppies and peonies (to name only a few) bursting with color in the summer. As the days shorten, Korean mums bloom until the first frost."

Susan Vernon

Casa Chimeneas Green Chile Stew

"One of our employees, Paul Higdon, developed this recipe, which is a variation of the popular New Mexico green chile stew. We use mild chiles so that the heat is not too strong. Green chile stew can be used with burritos, enchiladas, or huevos rancheros, or just in a bowl by itself. In the latter case, I would serve it with bread or tortillas, which will absorb the spiciness in case your mouth starts to heat up."

1 **pound ground pork, browned** *(fat drained off and reserved)*
3 **cloves garlic, crushed**
6 **tablespoons flour**
2 **teaspoons ground cumin**
2 **pounds fresh green chile peppers, roasted peeled and chopped**
salt *(to taste)*
4 **cups water** *(or as necessary)*

- In a large stockpot place the reserved fat from the browned pork. Heat it on low until it is melted and warm. Add the garlic and sauté it for 2 minutes.
- Add the flour and stir it in well.
- Add the pork, cumin, green chile peppers and salt. Stir the ingredients together well.
- Add the water so that the ingredients are covered.
- Simmer the stew *(uncovered)* for 30 minutes.

serves 4

"When our guests notice and comment on all of the attention to detail and extra special touches that we provide, I am very gratified. Their compliments make all of the hard work seem worth it!"

Susan Vernon

Taos Pueblo Bread Pudding

"This recipe is based on a traditional Taos Pueblo 'sopa' developed by Isabelle Herion for our inn. The cheddar cheese is just delicious with the apples and raisins. We serve it warm for breakfast, in place of a fruit course."

- **4 cups water**
- **1 cup brown sugar**
- **5 tablespoons butter**
- **1 teaspoon vanilla extract**
- **1 teaspoon ground allspice**
- **1 teaspoon ground nutmeg**
- **1 teaspoon ground cinnamon**
- **½ loaf white bread**
- **2 large baking apples, peeled, cored and thinly sliced**
- **4 cups medium cheddar cheese, grated**
- **1 cup raisins**

- Preheat the oven to 350°.
- In a medium saucepan place the water, brown sugar, butter, vanilla, allspice, nutmeg and cinnamon. Heat the ingredients on medium so that the sugar dissolves and a syrup is formed. Keep it warm.
- Toast the bread on a cookie sheet in the oven. Break the bread into small pieces.
- Place the bread in a greased 13" x 9" x 2" baking pan. Place the apples on top. Sprinkle on the cheese. Pour the warm syrup on top. Sprinkle on the raisins. Cover the pan tightly with foil.
- Bake the pudding for 20 minutes, or until the liquid steams and bubbles.

serves 8

"I learned how to cook as a child by watching cooking shows on television. My girlfriends and I would make elaborate cakes and dirty up every dish in the kitchen, all the while pretending we were performing for the camera."

Susan Vernon

Fancy French Toast with Banana Maple Butter

"You can use any kind of a sweet, fruit bread for this recipe. We like to use an orange datenut bread that a local Taos bakery makes. This is so good that people literally lick their plates clean."

Fancy French Toast

4 eggs, beaten
1 cup milk
½ teaspoon vanilla extract
½ teaspoon ground cinnamon
¼ teaspoon ground nutmeg
¼ teaspoon pepper
12 slices cinnamon raisin bread
¼ cup butter
Banana Maple Butter *(recipe follows),* **heated**

- In a large bowl place the eggs, milk, vanilla, cinnamon, nutmeg and pepper. Mix the ingredients together well.
- Place each bread slice in the egg mixture and soak it well on both sides.
- In a large skillet place the butter and heat it on medium until it is melted and hot. Fry the bread for 3 minutes on each side, or until it is browned.
- Serve the Fancy French Toast with the Banana Maple Butter on the side.

serves 6

Banana Maple Butter

1 stick butter
1½ cups maple syrup
1 teaspoon ground cinnamon
2 bananas, peeled and sliced into ¼" thick rounds

- In a medium skillet place the butter and heat it on medium until it is melted and hot. Add the syrup and cinnamon, and stir them together.
- Reduce the heat to low. Add the bananas and cook them for 5 minutes, or until the syrup is warm and bubbly *(do not overcook the bananas).*

makes approximately 2 cups

Paul's Apple Bread

"One of our first assistant innkeepers was Paul Higdon. He had many talents, including culinary skills, which contributed to our developing business. This recipe is a gift from him. We love it because it uses up the apples from our apple tree, and our guests love it because it tastes so good."

4 eggs
1 cup vegetable oil
2½ cups apples, peeled, cored and diced
3 cups flour
2 cups sugar
2 teaspoons baking powder
1½ teaspoons baking soda
2 teaspoons ground cinnamon
½ teaspoon ground nutmeg
¼ cup raisins
¼ cup walnuts, chopped
¼ cup apples, peeled, cored and finely diced

- Preheat the oven to 350°.
- In a food processor place the eggs, oil and the 2½ cups of apples.
- Blend the ingredients together so that the apples are finely chopped.
- In a large bowl place the flour, sugar, baking powder, baking soda, cinnamon and nutmeg. Stir the ingredients together so that they are well combined.
- Add the apple mixture to the flour mixture, and stir them together well.
- Add the raisins and walnuts, and stir them in.
- Pour the batter into a greased medium loaf pan.
- Bake the bread for 25 minutes.
- Sprinkle the ¼ cup of apples on top.
- Bake the bread for 25 minutes more, or until a wooden toothpick inserted in the center comes out clean.

makes 1 loaf

"Our Bed & Breakfast has caught the attention of various magazines, including **Ski**, **Bon Appetit** and **Gourmet**. We also are a 3-star Mobil-rated inn."

Susan Vernon

Ice Box Gingerbread Muffins

"We serve these muffins on a regular basis to our guests. The recipe is courtesy of Grace Marshall, who always served them with Thanksgiving dinner. The batter can be stored in the refrigerator for up to a month, so you can make just a few muffins at a time. If you make the batter fresh and bake the muffins immediately, the cooking time will be shorter."

- 2 **sticks butter, softened**
- 1 **cup sugar**
- 4 **eggs, lightly beaten**
- 1 **cup molasses**
- 4 **cups flour**
- 2 **teaspoons ground ginger**
- ¼ **teaspoon ground cinnamon**
- ¼ **teaspoon ground allspice**
- 1 **cup sour milk** *(add 2 teaspoons lemon juice to make the milk sour)*
- 2 **teaspoons baking soda**
- ½ **cup raisins**
- ½ **cup walnuts, chopped**

- Preheat the oven to 400°.
- In a large bowl place the butter, sugar, eggs and molasses. Blend the ingredients together with an electric mixer so that they are creamy. Set the mixture aside.
- In a medium bowl sift together the flour, ginger, cinnamon and allspice.
- In another small bowl place the sour milk and baking soda, and mix them together.
- While stirring constantly, alternately add the flour mixture and the milk mixture to the butter mixture, so that a batter is formed.
- Add the raisins and nuts, and stir them in well.
- Fill individual greased muffin tins with the batter so that they are ⅔ full. Bake the muffins for 15 to 18 minutes, or until a wooden toothpick inserted in the center comes out clean.
- Cover the remaining batter tightly and store it in the refrigerator for up to 4 weeks.

makes approximately 36 muffins

Frozen Rum Pie

"My mother gave me this recipe and it is just outstanding! If you are having a dinner party you can make it up a week in advance and store it in the freezer. You don't even need a garnish because the grated chocolate on top looks so pretty."

6 egg yolks
1 cup sugar
1/8 teaspoon salt
1/2 cup cold water
1 envelope gelatin
1 pint heavy cream, whipped
3 tablespoons rum
1 9-inch prepared graham cracker crust
2 ounces bitter chocolate, grated

- In a large bowl place the egg yolks and beat them with an electric mixer so that a thick liquid is formed. Add the sugar and salt, and beat them in well.
- In a small saucepan place the water and gelatin. While stirring constantly, heat the water on medium until it comes to a boil and the gelatin is dissolved. Remove the pan from the heat and let it cool to room temperature.
- Add the gelatin to the egg mixture, and stir it in well.
- Place the mixture in the refrigerator for 30 minutes, or until it thickens *(stir it occasionally)*.
- Add the whipped cream and the rum to the egg mixture, and mix them in well.
- Pour the batter into the pie crust.
- Sprinkle on the chocolate.
- Freeze the pie until it is solid.
- Let the pie thaw for 10 minutes before cutting it.

serves 8 to 10

"I grew up with a mother who loved to entertain, and I think that is one reason why I enjoy this work so much. It's a very social business, with a lot of personal interaction with the guests."

Susan Vernon

Casa de Martinez

Post Office Box 96
Los Ojos, New Mexico 87551
(505) 588-7858
Clorinda Martinez de Sanchez, Innkeeper

In the village of Los Brazos in the historic Tierra Amarilla country, you will find Casa de Martinez. The old adobe home was built in 1861 and is owned and managed by a great-granddaughter of the builders. The peaked tin roofs above thick adobe walls seen in this area are typical in the far north of the state. This wild, sparsely populated area, with its once-isolated tiny villages, forests, rocky peaks and rushing waterfalls, lures those who want to hunt, fish, cross-country ski or ride the narrow-gauge railway into the mountains. Or just relax and enjoy the historic ambience and sparkling clear skies.

Recipes

Eggs Olé Soufflé

"For a heavenly, easy to make soufflé, this is the perfect recipe. It is always a hit with my guests, and everyone wants to know how to make it. Serve it with my Papas Fritas recipe and some red or green chile."

9 eggs, well beaten
1 cup milk
1 cup cheddar cheese, grated
1 cup bacon, cooked, drained and crumbled
½ cup yellow onions, chopped medium
2 cups fresh mushrooms, sliced
¼ teaspoon ground nutmeg

- Preheat the oven to 325°.
- In a large bowl place all of the ingredients *(except for the nutmeg)* and blend them together well.
- Place the mixture in a greased medium casserole dish. Sprinkle on the nutmeg.
- Cover the dish tightly with foil and bake the soufflé for 1 hour, or until it is firm.

serves 8

Clorinda's Special Breakfast Toast

"The secret to this recipe is that you fry the toast at a very low heat for 45 minutes, while constantly turning it. Do this while you are frying bacon, making an omelette, and squeezing fresh orange juice for the meal. The result is superb! Many of my guests are repeat customers and they all request that I serve my special toast. It's delicious with warm maple syrup and plain yogurt or cream cheese."

3 eggs, beaten well
1 tablespoon orange juice, freshly squeezed
1 teaspoon ground cinnamon
4 slices whole wheat bread, lightly toasted
1½ cups granola
1 stick light butter

- In a medium bowl place the eggs, orange juice and cinnamon. Mix them together well.
- Dip each piece of toast into the egg batter so that both sides are coated. Dredge it in the granola so that each side is well coated.
- In an electric skillet place the butter and heat it on the lowest heat possible until it is melted. Place the toast in the skillet. While turning the bread slices every few minutes, fry them for 45 minutes, or until they are golden brown.

serves 2

Papas Fritas con Queso

"My mother used to make this dish with her white, homemade cheese from cow's milk. That is too complicated for me to make, so I use fresh Parmesan instead. These potatoes are excellent with carne adovada and calabacitas."

½ cup olive oil
10 medium-size red potatoes, peeled and sliced into ¼" thick rounds
salt and pepper *(to taste)*
¼ cup Parmesan cheese, freshly grated

- In a large nonstick skillet place the olive oil and heat it on medium low until it is hot. Add the potatoes and sprinkle them with the salt and pepper.
- Cover the skillet tightly with a lid. Cook the potatoes for 15 minutes, or until they are browned *(turn them occasionally)*.
- Sprinkle the potatoes with the cheese. Cook them for 5 minutes, or until they are tender.

serves 8

Calabacitas Verdes

"I grew up eating calabacitas, or 'baby squash', which is a typical New Mexican dish. This recipe is a little richer than a more traditional version because of the sour cream, but I like it because it adds a delicious taste."

2 cups water
4 cups zucchini, sliced into ¼" thick rounds
1 large yellow onion, sliced into ¼" thick pieces
¼ teaspoon salt
½ pint sour cream
½ cup green chile peppers, roasted, peeled and diced
1 cup cheddar cheese, grated

- Preheat the oven to 350°.
- In a large pot place the water and heat it on medium high so that it comes to a boil. Add the zucchini, onions and salt. Cover the pot, reduce the heat to low and simmer the vegetables for 5 minutes.
- Remove the pot from the heat and drain off the water.
- Add the sour cream and green chile peppers, and gently stir them in.
- Place the mixture in a greased baking dish and sprinkle the cheese on top.
- Bake the casserole for 15 minutes, or until the cheese is melted and bubbly.

serves 6 to 8

New Mexican Creamed Chicken Casserole

"Here is a simple, tasty side dish to serve with a main entrée of roast beef, leg of lamb or pork chops. The tortilla chips are what give it such a great flavor."

1 can cream of chicken soup
1 can evaporated milk
2 tablespoons jalapeño chile peppers, finely chopped
½ cup yellow onions, chopped medium
3 cups corn tortilla chips, crushed
2 cups cheddar cheese, grated

- Preheat the oven to 350°.
- In a large bowl place all of the ingredients *(except for the cheese)* and mix them together well.
- Place the mixture in a greased baking dish. Sprinkle the cheese on top.
- Cover the dish tightly with foil. Bake the casserole for 20 minutes, or until the cheese is melted and everything is hot.

serves 8

Casa Baked Pork Chops & Vegetables

"This is an old family recipe that my grandmother and mother used to make, and I loved to eat it as a little girl. It's simple to prepare and has a wonderful flavor."

3 tablespoons olive oil
4 thick pork chops
1 tablespoon yellow onions, finely chopped
2 tablespoons green bell peppers, seeded and finely chopped
2 cups canned crushed tomatoes
salt and pepper *(to taste)*
½ cup uncooked rice

- Preheat the oven to 350°.
- In a medium skillet place the oil and heat it on medium high until it is hot. Add the pork chops and cook them for 5 minutes, or until they are browned on both sides. Place the pork chops in a greased medium baking dish and set them aside.
- To the remaining oil in the same skillet place the onions and green bell peppers. Sauté them on medium low heat for 5 minutes, or until the onions are translucent.
- Add the tomatoes, salt and pepper. While stirring occasionally, simmer the ingredients for 30 minutes, or until a thick sauce is formed.
- Add the rice and stir it in.
- Pour the mixture over the pork chops. Cover the pan tightly with foil. Bake the pork chops for 40 minutes, or until the meat and rice are done.

serves 4

Miquelita's Tortillas

"I had never been able to make good tortillas until I got this recipe from Miquelita, who is the grandmother of Ursula, a girl who used to work with me. In my opinion, these are the perfect tortillas!"

4 cups white flour
¼ cup whole wheat flour
1 tablespoon baking powder
1 teaspoon salt
¼ cup vegetable oil
¼ cup milk
1½ cups warm water

- In a large bowl place the white flour, whole wheat flour, baking powder and salt. Mix the ingredients together well.
- Add the oil, milk and water. Mix the ingredients together so that they are well blended and a dough is formed.
- On a floured surface, knead the dough for 2 minutes.
- With oiled hands, form twelve 2" balls by rolling some of the dough in your palms.
- Roll out each ball so that it forms a ⅛" thick circle.
- On a heated grill place the tortillas. Cook them for 2 minutes on each side, or until they are done.

makes 1 dozen tortillas

"My grandmother Tita spent much time teaching me how to cook when I was a little girl. Of Spanish descent, she was truly wonderful in the kitchen. I remember a big pot of stew always simmering on her stove, and fresh bread baking in the oven. Unlike myself, who might make a mad dash to the local convenience store if unexpected guests show up, she was always prepared."

Clorinda Martinez de Sanchez

Apple Delight

"I used to eat this as a child growing up, and it is absolutely delicious. To me, the best food in the world is simple to prepare and simple in the flavors. You don't really need the vanilla ice cream, but I must admit that it elevates the dessert to a higher level."

6 medium baking apples, peeled, cored and thinly sliced
1/3 cup water
1/2 cup white sugar
1 teaspoon ground nutmeg
1 teaspoon ground cinnamon
1/4 cup butter, softened
1 cup brown sugar
1 cup flour
1 quart vanilla ice cream *(your favorite)*

- Preheat the oven to 350°.
- In a greased medium baking dish place the apples and water.
- In a small bowl place the white sugar, nutmeg and cinnamon. Mix the ingredients together well and then sprinkle them over the apples.
- In another small bowl place the butter, brown sugar and flour. Cut the ingredients with a pastry blender so that fine crumbs are formed.
- Sprinkle the mixture on top of the apples.
- Bake the apples for 45 minutes, or until they are tender.
- Top each serving with a scoop of vanilla ice cream.

serves 8 to 10

"My Bed & Breakfast is my family home, which dates back for many generations. It has always been filled with loving family members and lots of wonderful cooking. Now my guests help to maintain that tradition of good feelings, good smells and good eating."

Clorinda Martinez de Sanchez

Casa de Patrón

Post Office Box 27
Lincoln, New Mexico 88338
(505) 653-4676
Jeremy & Cleis Jordan, Innkeepers

The famed Western writer John L. Sinclair, who lived here many years, always said Lincoln, in the Rio Bonito Valley, was the most idyllic place in the world. Once the scene of rampaging violence during the Lincoln County Wars, the now peaceful village seems to shimmer with ghostly figures.....Billy the Kid, Pat Garrett, Juan Patrón. Patrón's historic adobe home, with its welcoming courtyard and sheltering trees, big country breakfasts and antique furnishings, puts guests right in the mood for the town, a National Historic Landmark.

Recipes

Quilters' Delight Fruit Salad

"One time I served this fruit salad to a group of ladies who were at my home for a quilting party. After they tasted it, they insisted not only that I change the name of the recipe to 'Quilters Delight Fruit Salad', but also that I serve it at all future quilting functions."

1 pint sour cream
2 tablespoons lemon juice, freshly squeezed
¾ cup sugar
⅛ teaspoon salt
1 banana, peeled and sliced
1 8-ounce can crushed pineapple, drained
¼ cup maraschino cherries, sliced
¼ cup piñon nuts *(pine nuts)*
2 kiwis, peeled and sliced
6 lettuce leaves

- In a medium bowl place the sour cream, lemon juice, sugar and salt. Blend the ingredients together well.
- Add the banana, pineapple, cherries and piñon nuts. Stir the ingredients together so that they are well combined. Set the bowl aside.
- In the bottom of 6 individual greased cupcake tins place a slice of kiwi. Place the fruit mixture on top. Place the muffin tins in the freezer for 2 hours.
- Invert each individual salad onto a leaf of lettuce. Let them partially thaw before serving.

serves 6

Chilled Tropical Soup

"I used to make this as a smoothie and then got the idea to thin it out for a soup. When my bananas get so ripe that they cannot be eaten fresh, I put them in the freezer until I'm ready to use them in this recipe. Their coldness really makes the soup good."

1 medium cantaloupe, peeled, seeded and coarsely chopped
1 ripe mango, peeled, seeded and coarsely chopped
1 very ripe banana, frozen, peeled and coarsely chopped
1 lemon, freshly juiced
1 cup vanilla yogurt
1 tablespoon fresh mint leaves, finely chopped
4 whole mint leaves

- In a food processor place the cantaloupe, mango and banana. Blend the ingredients together well.
- Add the lemon juice, yogurt and chopped mint leaves. Purée the mixture on high speed so that it is smooth.
- Garnish each serving with a whole mint leaf.

serves 4

Avocado Soup

"This is a nice variation for serving avocados, instead of the traditional guacamole. The avocado flavor really comes through, and the Tabasco and lemon juice give it a nice bite."

- 2 **large ripe avocados, peeled, pitted and minced**
- 3 **cups chicken broth**
- 1 **cup half & half**
- 1 **teaspoon Tabasco sauce**
- 1/3 **cup lemon juice** *(or to taste),* **freshly squeezed**
- 1 **teaspoon garlic powder**
- **salt** *(to taste)*

- In a food processor place all of the ingredients and blend them together so that the mixture is smooth. Refrigerate the soup for at least 24 hours before serving it.

serves 4 to 6

Squash & Chile Casserole

"Originally we came from the midwest and were not at all familiar with green chile peppers. My first exposure was this casserole, which was served at a village potluck dinner..... and I've been serving it ever since."

- 1/3 **cup fresh bread crumbs**
- 2 **tablespoons butter, melted**
- 1 **teaspoon red chile powder**
- 1 1/2 **cups zucchini, thinly sliced**
- 3/4 **cup yellow crookneck squash, thinly sliced**
- 1/2 **cup fresh corn kernels**
- 2 **eggs, well beaten**
- 1/4 **cup milk**
- 1/2 **teaspoon baking powder**
- 1/2 **teaspoon salt**
- 1 1/2 **tablespoons flour**
- 1 **cup Monterey Jack cheese, grated**
- 2 **cloves garlic, minced**
- 1/4 **cup fresh cilantro, chopped**
- 1/2 **cup green chile peppers, roasted, peeled and chopped**

- Preheat the oven to 350°.
- In a small bowl place the bread crumbs, butter and red chile powder. Stir them together well.
- In a greased baking pan spread out 1/2 of the bread crumb mixture. Place the squash on top. Sprinkle on the corn. Set the pan aside.
- In a medium bowl place the eggs, milk, baking powder, salt, flour, cheese, garlic, cilantro and green chile peppers. Mix the ingredients together well. Pour the mixture over the vegetables. Sprinkle the remaining bread crumbs on top.
- Bake the casserole for 30 minutes, or until it is done.

serves 6

Huevos Giraldo

"This dish is much more interesting than a regular breakfast of scrambled eggs with bacon on the side. If I had my way, I would mix the salsa right in with the eggs. But, in consideration of our guests, who have variable tastes for spiciness, we serve the salsa on the side. One excellent suggestion is to use the Chipotle Sauce recipe on page 95."

8 eggs
⅔ cup sharp cheddar cheese, grated
½ teaspoon garlic powder
2 teaspoons Mrs. Dash
2 tablespoons butter
½ cup yellow onions, minced
salt and pepper *(to taste)*
4 strips bacon, cooked, drained and chopped
1 cup salsa *(your favorite)*

- In a medium bowl place the eggs and beat them with a wire whisk so that they are frothy.
- Add the cheese, garlic powder and Mrs. Dash, and whisk them in well. Set the bowl aside.
- In a large skillet place the butter and heat it on medium until it is melted and hot. Add the onions and sauté them until they are slightly transparent.
- Reduce the heat to low. Add the egg mixture, salt and pepper, and stir them in.
- Cook and stir the mixture for 5 minutes, or until the eggs are almost done.
- Add the bacon and stir it in. Cook the eggs until they are just set.
- Serve the salsa on the side.

serves 4

"This may sound strange, but one time my husband and I were driving in southern New Mexico, and we decided to take a route that went through Lincoln. The moment we arrived in town I had an overpowering feeling that I had come 'home'.....I felt that I had been here before. Because of this experience, we eventually moved here and bought our home."

Cleis Jordan

Copper Pennies

"These are marinated, cooked carrots that are served cold. They have a delicious sweet and sour taste, which makes them somewhat unusual. If you put them on lettuce leaves, you can serve them as a salad. They also are good as an appetizer, or as a side dish to an entrée."

1 pound carrots, sliced into 1/8" thick rounds and cooked al dente
1 green chile pepper, roasted, peeled and chopped
1 small yellow onion, minced
1/2 cup brown sugar
1/4 cup balsamic vinegar
1/4 cup canola oil
1/2 can tomato soup

- In a medium bowl place the carrots, green chile peppers and onions. Set the bowl aside.
- In a small saucepan place the brown sugar, vinegar, oil and tomato soup. Cook the mixture over medium heat until it comes to a boil.
- Pour the hot mixture over the vegetables. Let the ingredients cool. Refrigerate them for 8 hours.

serves 8

"The Casa de Patrón used to be a rest stop for Billy the Kid. In fact, the opening line of the movie **Young Guns** is 'Now, I say we stop off at Juan Patrón's for one jolly big dram and one ginger beer with a dollop of whipped cream.' That's our house!"

Jeremy Jordan

Southwest Meat Loaf with Chipotle Sauce

"This was an experiment to see if I could find a formula for a really flavorful meat loaf. The chorizo sausage and chipotle chile peppers are the secret."

Southwest Meat Loaf

10 ounces chorizo sausage, cooked, crumbled and drained well
1½ pounds lean ground beef
1 small yellow onion, freshly chopped
½ cup Chipotle Sauce *(recipe follows)*
1 cup bread crumbs
1 egg, beaten until frothy
1 teaspoon salt
½ teaspoon pepper
Chipotle Sauce *(as needed)*
sour cream *(as needed)*

- Preheat the oven to 350°.
- In a large bowl place the chorizo, beef, onions, the ½ cup of Chipotle Sauce, the bread crumbs, egg, salt and pepper. Mix the ingredients together well with your hands.
- Place the meat mixture in a 9" x 5" x 3" loaf pan and shape it into a loaf.
- Bake it for 40 minutes, or until it is done.
- Let the meat loaf sit for 5 minutes and then slice it.
- Serve each slice on top of a bed of Chipotle Sauce. Place a dollop of sour cream on top.

serves 8

Chipotle Sauce

3 chipotle peppers in adobo sauce
½ lime, juiced
1 clove garlic, minced
1 egg
1 cup extra virgin olive oil

- In a blender place all of the ingredients *(except for the olive oil)* and purée them so that the mixture is smooth.
- With the blender constantly running, slowly dribble in the oil.
- Place the sauce in a bowl and cover it with foil. Chill it in the refrigerator until you are ready to serve it.

makes approximately 1½ cups

Patrón English Toffee

"This is an old family recipe that has been around forever. I think it's much better than store-bought toffee because it is fresher tasting, and you know exactly what's in it. Last Christmas season we sold over 900 pounds of our candies to guests and neighbors."

1½ cups pecans, chopped
1¼ cups sugar
2 sticks butter
2 tablespoons water
1 8-ounce package chocolate chips

- On a cookie sheet spread out the pecans.
- In a medium saucepan place the sugar, butter and water. Cook and stir the ingredients on medium high heat until the mixture is light brown in color and a candy thermometer reads 300°.
- Pour the mixture over the pecans. Immediately sprinkle the chocolate chips on top.
- Let the candy cool and then break it into bite-size pieces.

makes approximately 1 pound

"I love to talk to our guests and find out all about them....what they do for a living, where they come from, what makes them tick. This is one of the perks of owning a Bed & Breakfast."

Jeremy Jordan

Mango Upside Down Cake

"My mother used to make a pineapple upside cake that I really loved, and one day I took her recipe and substituted mangos. They give a delicious and interesting flavor, not to mention a beautiful color. The cake is very light, not dense, which I really like. Serve it with fresh whipped cream on top."

3 ripe mangos, peeled and sliced
¼ cup butter
1 cup brown sugar
½ cup butter, softened
⅔ cup white sugar
2 egg yolks, lightly beaten
½ teaspoon vanilla extract
1½ cups flour
3 teaspoons baking powder
½ teaspoon salt
⅔ cup water
2 egg whites

- Preheat the oven to 375°.
- In a 9" square baking pan arrange the sliced mangos and set the pan aside.
- In a small saucepan place the ¼ cup of butter and heat it on medium until it is melted and hot Add the brown sugar and stir it until it dissolves.
- Pour the mixture over the mangos.
- In a large bowl place the ½ cup of butter and the white sugar. Blend the ingredients together with an electric mixer so that they are creamy.
- Add the egg yolks and vanilla, and blend them in well.
- In a medium bowl sift together the flour, baking powder and salt.
- While mixing constantly, alternately add the flour mixture and the water to the butter mixture.
- In another small bowl place the egg whites and beat them with an electric mixer on high so that stiff peaks are formed. Gently fold the egg whites into the batter.
- Pour the mixture over the mangos and syrup.
- Bake the cake for 35 minutes, or until a wooden toothpick inserted in the center comes out clean.

serves 6 to 8

Casa del Granjero

414 C de Baca Lane N.W.
Albuquerque, New Mexico 87114
(505) 897-4144
Victoria Farmer, Innkeeper

The kiva fireplaces, handmade tiles and carved Mexican furniture of this old Territorial adobe home in Albuquerque's far North Valley bring memories of days that used to be. Hummingbirds entertain in the garden during the warm summer days and the massive Great Room fireplace takes the chill off cold evenings throughout the year. Extra touches include a hot tub under the stars, a garden room, lily pond, old willow furniture on the portal and a yard full of flowers.

Recipes

Butch's Guacamole

"My husband Butch is a wonderful cook of native New Mexican dishes. His family has lived here for many generations, and this is a recipe they have passed down over the years. By covering the top with sour cream, the guacamole will not turn brown, and can be made up to a day ahead."

- **4 ripe avocados, peeled, pitted and cut into ½" pieces**
- **1 tablespoon green chile peppers, roasted, peeled, seeded and chopped**
- **3 hot yellow chile peppers, seeded and coarsely chopped**
- **3 jalapeño chile peppers, seeded and coarsely chopped** *(reserve 1 whole pepper for the garnish)*
- **3 Roma tomatoes, seeded and coarsely chopped**
- **½ medium white onion, coarsely chopped**
- **½ tablespoon fresh cilantro, chopped**
- **½ tablespoon fresh garlic, minced**
- **1 tablespoon lemon juice, freshly squeezed**
- **½ teaspoon salt**
- **½ cup sour cream**
- **½ cup cheddar cheese, grated**
- **½ cup pitted black olives, chopped**

- In a medium bowl place the avocados, green chile peppers, yellow chile peppers, jalapeño chile peppers, tomatoes, onions, cilantro, garlic, lemon juice and salt. Mix the ingredients together well.
- Place the guacamole in a medium serving dish.
- Cover the entire surface with a layer of sour cream, so that there is no green showing.
- Sprinkle the grated cheese on top.
- Sprinkle on the olives.
- Place the reserved jalapeño chile pepper on top.
- Cover the bowl with plastic wrap and refrigerate it for at least 1 hour before serving.

makes approximately 4 cups

"If you are thinking of opening a Bed & Breakfast, make sure that you like the idea of opening your home to guests. Unless you live in a separate residence, there is not much privacy."

Victoria Farmer

Lemon Wine Cream Sauce

"This is a delicious sauce with fish or chicken. The key is to keep the heat very low and whisk the sauce for a long time."

½ **stick butter**
1 **tablespoon flour**
1 **cup heavy cream**
¼ **cup lemon juice, freshly squeezed**
¼ **cup dry white wine**
salt and pepper *(to taste)*

- In a medium saucepan place the butter and heat it on low until it is melted and hot. Add the flour and whisk it in for 5 minutes.
- Add the heavy cream and whisk it in.
- Add the lemon juice and wine, and whisk them in for 8 minutes, or until the sauce thickens.
- Add the salt and pepper, and stir them in.

makes approximately 2 cups

Creamy Fresh Mushroom Soup

"I used to own a restaurant and catering business in Oklahoma, and this is a recipe that I developed out of my kitchen. It is delicious, and you can make it as rich or as light as you want by using either heavy cream or low-fat milk."

1 **stick butter**
2 **tablespoons flour**
2 **cups milk**
2 **tablespoons butter**
½ **pound white button mushrooms, sliced**
⅛ **teaspoon mace**
¼ **cup cream sherry**
salt and white pepper *(to taste)*
2 **tablespoons fresh cilantro, chopped**

- In a large saucepan place the stick of butter and heat it on medium until it is melted and bubbly. Add the flour and stir it in for 3 minutes.
- While stirring constantly, slowly add the milk.
- Cook and stir the mixture for 5 minutes, or until it thickens.
- In a large skillet place the 2 tablespoons of butter and heat it on medium until it is melted. Add the mushrooms and sauté them for 5 minutes, or until they are tender.
- Add the sautéed mushrooms to the milk mixture.
- Cook the soup on low heat until it begins to simmer.
- Add the mace, sherry, salt and white pepper. Mix them in well.
- Garnish each serving with the cilantro.

serves 4 to 6

Casa del Granjero

Farmer's Potato Salad

"Since I was a little girl my mother has made this potato salad and I have always loved it. The piñon nuts were added in this version to give it a Southwest twist, but the real secret to the good taste is the bacon, and the sweetness from the sugar and relish."

- 5 **pounds white potatoes, cooked, peeled and diced into 1" pieces**
- 5 **eggs, hard-boiled, peeled and coarsely chopped**
- ½ **pound bacon, cooked, drained and chopped**
- 1 **cup celery, chopped medium**
- 1 **medium white onion, chopped medium**
- ½ **cup green bell peppers, seeded and chopped medium**
- ½ **cup red bell peppers, seeded and chopped medium**
- ½ **cup yellow bell peppers, seeded and chopped medium**
- 1 **cup fresh parsley, chopped**
- ½ **cup piñon nuts** *(pine nuts),* **roasted**
- 2 **teaspoons salt** *(to taste)*
- ½ **teaspoon pepper** *(to taste)*
- 2 **cups mayonnaise**
- ¼ **cup yellow mustard**
- ½ **cup sweet relish**
- ¼ **cup sugar**
- ¼ **cup white vinegar**

- In a large bowl, place the potatoes, eggs, bacon (reserve ¼ cup), celery, onions, bell peppers, parsley *(reserve ¼ cup),* piñon nuts, salt and pepper. Gently mix everything together.
- In a medium bowl place the mayonnaise, mustard, relish, sugar and vinegar. Whisk them together well.
- Add the dressing to the potato mixture and gently fold it in.
- Sprinkle the reserved bacon and parsley on top.
- Cover the bowl tightly with plastic wrap and refrigerate it for at least 1 hour before serving.

serves 10 to 12

"When we found this adobe nestled in the historic North Valley we knew we were 'home'. From the very beginning our friends and visitors encouraged us to open our home to Bed & Breakfast guests, saying that 'This is the kind of house everyone wants to see and explore'."

Victoria Farmer

Breakfast Swiss Soufflé

"Add chunks of ham or chicken to this dish and you will have an outstanding luncheon entrée. Everybody always wants to know the recipe!"

1 small loaf sourdough French bread, broken into small pieces
⅓ pound Swiss cheese, grated
¼ pound Monterey Jack cheese, grated
2 cups milk
10 eggs, lightly beaten
¼ cup dry white wine
2 scallions, minced
2 teaspoons yellow mustard
salt *(to taste)*
¼ teaspoon pepper, freshly ground
1 cup sour cream
½ cup Parmesan cheese, freshly grated
1 cup chunky salsa *(your favorite)*

- In a 9" x 13" x 2" buttered baking dish place the pieces of bread. Sprinkle the two cheeses on top.
- In a large bowl place the milk, eggs, wine, scallions, mustard, salt and pepper. Beat the ingredients together well. Pour the mixture over the bread.
- Cover the baking dish with foil and refrigerate it overnight.
- Remove the baking dish from the refrigerator and let it come to room temperature.
- Preheat the oven to 325°.
- Bake the soufflé for 1 hour, or until it is firmly set.
- Remove the soufflé from the oven and take off the foil cover.
- In a small bowl place the sour cream and Parmesan cheese, and mix them together. Spread the mixture on top of the soufflé.
- Return the soufflé to the oven and bake it for 10 minutes more, or until it is lightly browned.
- Remove the soufflé from the oven and let it sit for 10 minutes.
- Cut it into squares.
- Place a spoonful of salsa on top of each piece *(or on the side)*.

serves 12

Chile Relleno Casserole

"My mother used to make this recipe, which came out of an old WW II cookbook. She always used green bell peppers, but I decided to try New Mexico green chiles instead.....and they just worked beautifully. You may also add bacon, ham or chicken."

1 cup green chile peppers, roasted, peeled and chopped
2 eggs, lightly beaten
1¼ cups sharp cheddar cheese, grated
1¼ cups Monterey Jack cheese, grated
½ cup flour
1 teaspoon baking powder
1½ cups milk
½ cup sour cream *(or as needed)*
1 avocado, peeled, pitted and sliced
1 cup salsa *(your favorite)*

- Preheat the oven to 350°.
- In a large bowl place the green chile peppers, eggs, the two cheeses, flour, baking powder and milk. Mix the ingredients together well.
- Place the mixture in a 10" buttered pie pan.
- Bake the casserole for 50 minutes, or until it is firmly set.
- Remove the casserole from the oven. Let it sit for 5 minutes.
- Cut it into 6 pie-shape wedges.
- Garnish each serving with a dollop of sour cream and some slices of avocado. Serve the salsa on the side.

serves 6

"Cooking is very therapeutic to me. It not only offers the chance to share great recipes, but also provides a sense of artistic fulfillment."

Victoria Farmer

Stuffed Whole Loin of Pork

"This is a wonderful special occasion dish, because not only does it taste delicious, but the presentation is spectacular. The stuffing puffs up out of the pork and the whole thing looks like a golden crown. Bake any remaining stuffing in a small casserole dish and serve it on the side."

¼ cup Parmesan cheese, freshly grated
5 cups dried bread crumbs
1 cup fresh parsley, chopped
1 stick butter
1 large white onion, minced
1 cup celery, minced
1½ cups chicken broth
1 pound lean ground sausage, browned, drained and crumbled
2 eggs, lightly beaten
1 whole boneless loin of pork, deep pockets cut every 2"
2 tablespoons butter
1 cup apricot jam

- In a large bowl place the Parmesan cheese, bread crumbs, and parsley. Mix the ingredients together and set them aside.
- In a large skillet place the stick of butter and heat it on medium until it is melted and hot. Add the onions and celery, and cook them for 5 minutes, or until the onions are translucent. Reduce the heat to low.
- Add the chicken broth and sausage, and cook them for 10 minutes on low heat.
- Add the contents of the skillet to the bread crumb mixture, and mix them together well. Add the eggs and blend them in well.
- Cover the bowl and refrigerate the dressing for 1 hour, or until it is cool.
- Preheat the oven to 350°.
- Loosely stuff several tablespoons of the dressing into each pocket of the pork loin *(do not overstuff because the dressing will expand as it cooks).*
- On a rack in a large baking pan place the stuffed pork loin. Add 1" of water to the bottom of the pan. On the dull side of a large piece of aluminum foil rub on the 2 tablespoons of butter. With the buttered side next to the meat, make a tent of the foil and place it over the pork, being careful not to let the foil touch the meat.
- Roast the pork loin for 1½ hours, or until it is done.
- Remove the foil and discard it. Brush the pork loin with the apricot jam.
- Return the roast to the oven and cook it for 10 minutes more, or until the jam is bubbly.

serves 8 to 10

Custard French Toast

"The big secret to this recipe is that the bread must be dense, very thickly sliced, and must have soaked overnight. The bread puffs up like a soufflé. Everybody tells me it is the best French Toast in the world!"

12 very thick slices dense French bread
10 eggs, lightly beaten
3 cups milk
¾ cup sugar
½ cup apricot nectar
2 tablespoons vanilla extract
2 tablespoons butter
1 tablespoon canola oil

- In a large buttered baking dish lay out the slices of bread in 1 layer.
- In a large mixing bowl place the eggs, milk, sugar, apricot nectar and vanilla. Mix the ingredients together. Pour the mixture over the bread.
- Cover the dish with plastic wrap and refrigerate it overnight.
- In a large nonstick skillet place the butter and canola oil, and heat them on medium until the butter is melted and hot. Add the bread slices and cook them for 3 minutes on each side, or until they are lightly browned.

serves 6

"By owning a Bed & Breakfast, I do not have to seek out a social life.....my social life comes to me. The guests are interesting, entertaining and most considerate. They represent an ever widening circle of friends from all over the world."

Victoria Farmer

Lemon Piñon Rice

"My husband doesn't like rice because he ate so much of it when he was in Vietnam, but he does like this dish. I think that the lemon is what makes it taste so good."

- **1 stick butter**
- **½ cup piñon nuts** *(pine nuts)*
- **½ cup red bell peppers, seeded and chopped small**
- **¼ cup green bell peppers, seeded and chopped small**
- **¼ cup yellow bell peppers, seeded and chopped small**
- **1 tablespoon fresh garlic, minced**
- **4 scallions, minced**
- **1½ cups white rice, cooked**
- **½ cup lemon juice, freshly squeezed**
- **½ cup fresh parsley, minced**
- **1 lemon, cut into wedges**
- **6 fresh parsley sprigs**

- In a large skillet place the butter and heat it on medium until it is melted and hot. Add the piñon nuts and sauté them for 3 minutes, or until they are lightly browned.
- Add the bell peppers, garlic and scallions. Sauté the ingredients for 5 minutes, or until the vegetables are crisp and tender.
- Add the cooked rice and mix it in well.
- Add the lemon juice and minced parsley, and mix them in.
- Garnish each serving of rice with a lemon wedge and parsley sprig.

serves 6

Ambrosia

"I used to serve orange juice for breakfast, but found that a lot of my guests were bored with it. So I came up with this recipe and now I always put a big pitcher of it out on the table.....and there's never a drop left!"

- **1 cup pear nectar**
- **1 cup peach nectar**
- **1 cup apricot nectar**
- **1 cup pineapple juice**
- **1 ripe banana, peeled**
- **4 ½" thick slices pineapple**
- **4 sprigs mint leaf**

- In a blender place the 4 fruit juices and blend them together.
- Add the banana and blend it in.
- Into each of 4 individual drinking glasses pour the ambrosia.
- Garnish each serving with a slice of pineapple and a sprig of mint.

serves 4

Mom's Best Pound Cake

"I truly have never tasted another pound cake as good as this one. It's rich and moist, yet has no butter. It's a wonderful base that you can decorate in any way you please. I like to serve it with fruit, ice cream or a light rum glaze."

1 cup milk
1 cup vegetable oil
4 eggs, lightly beaten
1 tablespoon vanilla extract
3 cups flour
2 cups sugar
1 teaspoon baking powder
1 dash salt
1 ounce light rum
1 cup whole pecans, shelled

- Preheat the oven to 325°.
- In a medium bowl place the milk, oil, eggs and vanilla. Mix the ingredients together.
- In a large bowl sift together the flour, sugar, baking powder and salt.
- Add the liquid mixture to the flour mixture, and beat them with an electric mixer on medium speed for 5 minutes.
- Add the rum and blend it in on low speed for l minute.
- Add the pecans and mix them in.
- Place the batter in a greased and floured tube pan.
- Bake the cake for 1¼ hours, or until a wooden toothpick inserted in the center comes out clean, and the top springs back when you touch it with your finger.
- Let the cake cool in the pan for 10 minutes.
- Remove the cake from the pan and let it cool on a rack for 10 minutes more.

serves 8

Heavenly Rice Custard

"My rice-hating husband just loves this custard. Be sure to use the hot water bath when making it, because that is the key to its success."

- 2 **cups cooked long grain white rice**
- 10 **eggs, lightly beaten**
- 2 **cups sugar**
- 5 **cups milk**
- 3 **cinnamon sticks**
- **water** *(as needed)*

- Preheat the oven to 300°.
- In a buttered 10" x 12" x 3" baking dish place the cooked rice and spread it evenly over the bottom.
- In a large bowl place the eggs and sugar, and beat them together.
- In a large saucepan place the milk and cinnamon sticks. Heat the mixture to the scalding point and then remove it from the heat.
- Remove the cinnamon sticks.
- With an electric mixer constantly running on low speed, add the milk to the eggs in small amounts at a time.
- Strain the mixture through a fine sieve onto the rice.
- In a large baking pan filled with very hot water place the baking dish.
- Bake the custard for 2 hours, or until it is set but not firm.
- Remove the custard from the oven and place it on a rack to cool.
- Refrigerate the custard for 2 hours.

serves 12

"Although my mother was a great cook herself, she would not let me in the kitchen as a girl. Instead, she wanted me to study hard so that I could have a professional career, and not end up being 'just a housewife'. Eventually I became a clinical psychologist and traveled all over the world. But now, here I am cooking and cleaning for a living.....and loving every minute of it!"

Victoria Farmer

Victoria's Apple Cake

"This is one of those wonderful cakes that seems to stay moist forever. Add other fruits or nuts if you have them on hand."

- **3 cups flour**
- **1½ cups sugar**
- **3 teaspoons baking powder**
- **4 eggs**
- **1 cup vegetable oil**
- **2 teaspoons vanilla extract**
- **¼ cup lemon juice, freshly squeezed**
- **1 dash salt**
- **4 Granny Smith apples, peeled, cored and thinly sliced**
- **sugar** *(as needed)*
- **ground cinnamon** *(as needed)*

- Preheat the oven to 325°.
- In a large bowl place the flour, sugar, baking powder, eggs, oil, vanilla, lemon juice and salt. Mix the ingredients together well.
- Into a greased and floured 10" tube pan spoon ⅓ of the batter.
- Place ½ of the apple slices on top. Sprinkle them generously with the sugar and cinnamon.
- Place another ⅓ of the batter on top. Add the rest of the apples. Sprinkle on some more sugar and cinnamon.
- Place the final ⅓ of the batter on top.
- Bake the cake for 1¼ hours, or until a wooden toothpick inserted in the center comes out clean.
- Let the cake cool for 10 minutes.
- Remove the cake from the pan and let it cool on a rack for 10 minutes longer.

serves 8

"We have spent a great deal of time and effort to make our Bed & Breakfast both unique and comfortable for our guests, and yet to remain true to the land and the spirits that dwell here. It has truly been a labor of love."

Victoria Farmer

Casa del Rio

Post Office Box 92
Española, New Mexico 87532
(505) 753-6049
Eileen Sopanen-Vigil, Innkeeper

This jewel of an adobe guest cottage on a small Chama Valley horse ranch has all the charm of New Mexico's early days.....with modern conveniences. The guest house features a ceiling of vigas and latillas, a kiva fireplace, a Mexican-tile bathroom and hand-carved furniture. From the patio, visitors may view migrating cranes and the cliffs above the nearby Rio Chama. A sumptuous hot breakfast is served in the main house.

Recipes

Del Rio Quesadilla

"Traditionally a quesadilla consists of two tortillas with melted cheese in the middle. This recipe is an elaborate variation, which evolved as a way to use leftovers from the night before."

4 flour tortillas
1 cup refried beans
1 cup potatoes, diced and cooked
1 cup cooked beef *(or elk or antelope)*
2 eggs, scrambled
1 cup Chama Red Chile Sauce *(recipe on next page)*
1 cup cheddar cheese, grated
4 tablespoons sour cream
1 jalapeño chile pepper, thinly sliced

- Preheat the oven to 350°.
- On each of 4 oven-proof plates place a tortilla. Spread on the refried beans. In this order, layer on the potatoes, meat, eggs, Chama Red Chile Sauce and cheese.
- Bake the quesadillas for 6 to 8 minutes, or until the cheese is melted and everything is hot.
- Top each quesadilla with the sour cream and jalapeño peppers.

serves 4

Rio Refried Beans

"Beans are the basis of New Mexican cooking, and each family makes a big pot of them every week. You can eat them alone or with meat, as a filling for burritos, as a side dish with vegetables, in a salad, or as a base for many New Mexican dishes."

1 pound pinto beans, cleaned, rinsed and drained
1 tablespoon baking soda
1 clove garlic
water *(as needed)*
½ cup yellow onions, chopped medium
2 teaspoons salt
1 tablespoon vegetable oil

- In a large stockpot place the beans, baking soda and garlic. Cover the beans with water and let them sit overnight.
- Rinse both the beans and the pot. Return the beans and garlic to the pot.
- Add the onions and enough water to cover the beans. While stirring occasionally, heat the beans on medium high until they come to a boil. Reduce the heat to low and simmer the beans for 1½ hours. Add the salt and gently stir it in. Simmer the beans for 30 minutes, or until they are tender.
- Place the beans in a food processor and blend them so that they are smooth.
- In a large skillet place the oil and heat it on medium until it is hot. Place the beans in the skillet and fry them for 3 minutes. Reduce the heat to low. While stirring the beans occasionally, simmer them until they are of a medium-dry consistency.

serves 6

Chama Red Chile Sauce

"My husband's family gave me this recipe, which is a very plain, basic chile sauce. You can serve it with beans and tortillas, as an enchilada sauce, or with eggs. The red chile powder is made from dried New Mexico red chiles, and grinding it up makes chopping onions seem like a piece of cake. The fumes are awesome!"

1 tablespoon vegetable oil
2 cloves garlic, peeled and finely chopped
3 tablespoons ground red chile powder
2 cups water, boiling
1 teaspoon cornstarch, dissolved in 3 teaspoons cold water
½ teaspoon beef bouillon
¼ teaspoon sugar
salt *(to taste)*

- In a medium skillet place the oil and garlic, and heat them on medium until the garlic is lightly browned.
- Remove the skillet from the heat. Add the red chile powder and stir it in so that a smooth roux is formed.
- Return the skillet to the heat *(be sure not to let the chile burn)*. While stirring constantly, slowly add the boiling water. Continue to stir the sauce until it comes to a boil.
- Add the cornstarch, beef bouillon, sugar and salt. Stir the sauce until it starts to thicken.
- Remove the sauce from the heat.

makes approximately 2 cups

"I believe in cooking food that not only tastes delicious, but also is as healthy as possible. However, I do not advertise the health aspect of my dishes to my guests for fear of scaring them off. Over the years I have learned to be very clever in serving them food that they love, but that is also good for them."

Eileen Sopanen-Vigil

Chile Relleno Casserole

"My neighbor Rosina Martinez gave me this recipe, which is an old favorite of her family. When she first told me about it I was slightly dubious, but now it is one of my favorite dishes."

¾ **cup green chile peppers, roasted, peeled and diced**
½ **pound longhorn cheese, grated**
3 **scallions, thinly sliced**
½ **cup flour**
2 **cups milk**
2 **eggs**
salt *(to taste)*

- Preheat the oven to 350°.
- In a small bowl place the green chile peppers, cheese and scallions. Mix the ingredients together.
- Spread the mixture in the bottom of a greased 1½-quart casserole dish.
- In a medium bowl place the flour, milk, eggs and salt. Mix the ingredients together so that they are smooth. Pour the batter over the chile mixture.
- Bake the casserole for 30 minutes, or until it is lightly browned.

serves 4

"My husband is a native New Mexican cowboy, born and bred in Santa Fe. I met him when we were working on a film together, and he was my head wrangler. We fell in love, rode off into the sunset and are living happily ever after!"

Eileen Sopanen-Vigil

Spinach Baked Eggs

"Some people might know this dish as a version of Eggs Florentine. The seasoned cream cheese gives it a most delicious flavor. If you cannot find commercially flavored cheese, then add minced onions and garlic to your taste."

- **2 10-ounce packages spinach, thawed, chopped and excess moisture squeezed out**
- **3 tablespoons onions, finely chopped**
- **½ cup cooked ham, chopped**
- **⅓ cup onion & garlic cream cheese, softened**
- **4 large eggs**
- **¾ cup longhorn cheese, grated**

- Preheat the oven to 375°.
- In a medium bowl, place the spinach, onions, ham and cream cheese. Mix the ingredients together well.
- Spray 4 individual casserole dishes with Pam.
- Place the mixture in each dish. Make a depression in the center. Break an egg into the center.
- Sprinkle the cheese on top.
- Bake the eggs for 20 to 25 minutes, or until they are set.

serves 4

"I learned to cook as a young person by using classical French cookbooks. Over the years I have modified different recipes to retain their flavors but to eliminate the high fat content."

Eileen Sopanen-Vigil

Rio Zucchini Pancakes

"This is a great recipe to make when you are drowning in zucchini in the summer. The pancakes are moist and have a wonderful flavor. They are extra good with some applesauce on the side."

1 cup sour cream
3 tablespoons fresh chives, finely chopped
4 cups zucchini, grated
½ cup flour
1 teaspoon lemon juice, freshly squeezed
½ cup scallions, minced
½ cup mayonnaise
½ cup Parmesan cheese, freshly grated
4 eggs, lightly beaten
½ cup vegetable oil *(or as needed)*

- In a small bowl place the sour cream and chives, and mix them together. Set the bowl aside.
- In a large bowl place the zucchini and flour, and mix them together well.
- Add the lemon juice, scallions, mayonnaise, Parmesan cheese and eggs. Blend the ingredients together well.
- In a large skillet place some of the oil and heat it on medium until it is hot. Using a ⅓ measuring cup, pour the batter into the skillet. Fry the pancakes for 2 minutes on each side, or until they are browned.
- Serve the pancakes with the sour cream on the side.

serves 4

"Casa del Rio is a micro-mini Southwestern ranch with beautiful Arabian horses, fine wool sheep, authentic adobe construction and beautiful 'Georgia O'Keeffe' pink cliffs."

Eileen Sopanen-Vigil

Finnish Pancakes

"My guests absolutely adore these pancakes. They make a spectacular presentation because they get so fluffy and light with air. If you cook one in a six-inch cast-iron skillet, it often will rise to be six inches high."

- **3** **tablespoons butter**
- **3** **medium eggs, room temperature**
- ½ **cup plus 2 tablespoons milk**
- ½ **cup plus 2 tablespoons flour**
- ¼ **cup powdered sugar**
- ½ **teaspoon ground nutmeg**
- **Apricot Sausage Compote** *(recipe on next page)*
- **1** **cup plain yogurt**

- Preheat the oven to 425°.
- In each of two small oven-proof skillets place 1½ tablespoons of the butter. Place the skillets in the oven so that the butter melts and turns a little brown.
- In a blender place the eggs and mix them on low until they are well beaten.
- While blending on low speed, slowly add the milk.
- A little at a time, slowly add the flour. Blend the mixture for 2 minutes.
- Remove the skillets from the oven.
- Very slowly pour ½ of the batter into each skillet and return it to the oven.
- Bake the pancakes for 20 minutes, or until they are lightly browned.
- Gently remove the pancakes from the skillets. Sprinkle the powdered sugar and nutmeg on top.
- Serve the pancakes with the Apricot Sausage Compote and plain yogurt on the side.

serves 2

"Our guests enjoy a coffee or tea tray delivered to their room as a wake-up call in the morning, and then a full breakfast served later on in the dining room."

Eileen Sopanen-Vigil

Apricot Sausage Compote

"This sausage has a very interesting flavor because of the apricots. I love to eat it with pancakes or by itself with fresh yogurt."

½ pound uncooked sausage
1 15-ounce can apricot halves, drained
2 tablespoons brown sugar

- In a medium skillet place the sausage. While stirring constantly, cook the sausage on medium high heat until it is well done.
- Drain off the grease.
- Add the apricots and brown sugar, and stir them in.
- Cook the compote until it is well heated.

makes approximately 2½ cups

"To me, New Mexico is all about the people. They are kind, warm, generous and loving.....the most wonderful people in the world! I feel blessed to live here."

Eileen Sopanen-Vigil

Finnish Potato Barley Bread

"Americans are not used to barley bread and never think of making it. This is a pity, because barley bread is one of the most wonderful tasting things in the world. I love to eat this with hot soup."

2 tablespoons cornmeal
2¼ cups potatoes, cooked and mashed
1 large egg
¾ teaspoon salt
1½ cups barley flour
2 tablespoons barley flour

- Preheat the oven to 500°.
- Line 2 cookie sheets with brown paper. Sprinkle on the cornmeal and set the sheets aside.
- In a large bowl place the potatoes, egg and salt. Mix them together well.
- Add the 1½ cups of barley flour and stir it in well.
- On a flat surface sprinkle 1 tablespoon of the barley flour.
- Use the remaining flour to dust your hands.
- Divide the dough into 4 equal parts. Place each portion on the floured surface and pat it into a ¼" thick round loaf.
- Place the rounds on opposite ends of the cookie sheets.
- Bake them for 15 minutes, or until they are browned.

makes 4 loaves

"Casa del Rio is located halfway between Taos and Santa Fe, so it is very convenient for many wonderful day trips. To name a few: Bandelier National Monument, Ghost Ranch Living Museum, Chama train trips, the Abiquiu reservoir, and eight local Indian pueblos."

Eileen Sopanen-Vigil

Finnish Good Bread

"If you slice this very thin, it makes a super sandwich bread. In fact, I think it makes the best toasted cheese sandwiches in the world!"

2 tablespoons butter, softened
1 tablespoon sugar
2 teaspoons salt
1½ cups hot water
1 package dry yeast
½ cup water
1½ cups whole wheat flour
2½ cups rye flour
1½ cups bread flour
2 tablespoons cornmeal
2 tablespoons butter, melted

- In a large bowl place the first 2 tablespoons of butter, the sugar, salt and the 1½ cups of hot water. Mix the ingredients together so that they are well combined. Set the mixture aside and let it cool to room temperature.
- In a small bowl place the yeast and the ½ cup water, and stir them together so that the yeast is dissolved.
- Add the yeast to the liquid mixture and blend it in well. Add the liquid to the whole wheat flour and stir it in. Add the rye flour and 1 cup of the bread flour, and stir them in well.
- Place the dough on a floured surface and knead it for 10 minutes. Add the remaining ½ cup of bread flour *(as necessary)* so that the dough is smooth.
- In another large oiled bowl place the dough and turn it so that it is well coated with the oil. Cover the bowl tightly with plastic wrap. Set it aside in a warm place for 1½ hours, or until the dough is double in size.
- Punch the dough down and knead it 4 times. Divide the dough in half. Shape each half into a 1" thick round loaf.
- Place the loaves on a cookie sheet that has been covered with brown paper and sprinkled with the cornmeal. Cover the loaves with a damp cloth and set them aside for 1 hour, or until they are double in size.
- Preheat the oven to 400°.
- Place the loaves on the cookie sheet.
- Bake them for 25 minutes, or until the crusts are lightly browned.
- Brush the melted butter on top of the loaves. Let them cool.

makes 2 loaves

Swedish Christmas Rye

"This is a very special bread that Swedish people make over the holidays. The flavor is wonderful.....just a little sweet, but with subtle undertones of citrus and herb."

½ cup cracked wheat
3 tablespoons shortening
¼ cup sugar
¼ cup molasses
1 teaspoon crushed cumin seed
1 teaspoon crushed fennel seed
1½ teaspoons orange zest *(outer orange part grated off)*
2 teaspoons salt
1 cup water, boiling
1 package dry yeast
¼ cup warm water
1 cup milk
1 cup raisins
3½ cups rye flour
3 cups bread flour
2 tablespoons cornmeal
2 tablespoons butter, melted

- In a large bowl place the cracked wheat, shortening, sugar, molasses, cumin, fennel, orange zest and salt. Stir the ingredients together well.
- Pour the 1 cup of boiling water over the mixture and stir it in. Set the bowl aside and let it cool to room temperature.
- In a small bowl place the yeast and the ¼ cup of warm water. Stir them together so that the yeast is dissolved.
- To the molasses mixture add the yeast, milk, raisins and rye flour. Stir them together well.
- Add the bread flour and mix it in so that a moderately stiff dough is formed.
- On a floured surface place the dough and knead it for 10 minutes, or until it is smooth.
- In another large oiled bowl place the dough and turn it so that it is well coated with the oil. Cover the bowl tightly with plastic wrap and set it aside in a warm place.
- Let the dough rise for 2 hours, or until it is double in size.
- Place the dough on a lightly floured surface and punch it down.
- Divide the dough in half and roll out two 10" long loaves.
- Place the loaves on a cookie sheet that has been covered with brown paper and sprinkled with the cornmeal. Let the dough rise for 1 hour, or until it is double in size.
- Preheat the oven to 350°.
- Bake the bread for 50 minutes, or until the bottoms sound hollow when tapped.
- Brush the melted butter on top of the loaves. Let them cool.

makes 2 loaves

Pumpkin Cake with Cream Cheese Icing

"My mother-in-law gave me this recipe and it is excellent. Not only is it quick and easy to make, but it is delicious. People just adore it!"

Pumpkin Cake

1 can pumpkin
2 cups sugar
4 eggs
1 cup vegetable oil
2 cups flour
2 teaspoons baking soda
3 teaspoons ground cinnamon
1 teaspoon salt
Cream Cheese Icing *(recipe follows)*
½ cup walnuts, chopped

- Preheat the oven to 350°.
- In a medium bowl place the pumpkin, sugar, eggs and oil. Beat the ingredients together with an electric mixer so that they are well blended.
- In a large bowl sift together the flour, baking soda, cinnamon and salt.
- Add the pumpkin mixture to the flour mixture, and mix it in well.
- Place the batter in a greased and floured tube pan.
- Bake the cake for 35 minutes, or until a wooden toothpick inserted in the center comes out clean.
- Let the cake cool for 10 minutes and then remove it from the pan. Let the cake cool completely on a wire rack.
- Spread the Cream Cheese Icing on the cake. Sprinkle the walnuts on top.

serves 8 to 10

Cream Cheese Icing

1 8-ounce package cream cheese, softened
2 tablespoons milk *(or as needed)*
1 1-pound box powdered sugar

- In a medium bowl place the cream cheese and milk. Beat them with an electric mixer until they are smooth.
- Add the powdered sugar and beat it in. If necessary, add more milk so that a spreadable, creamy texture is achieved.

frosts 1 cake

Casa Europa

157 Upper Ranchitos Road
Taos, New Mexico 87571
(505) 758-9798
Marcia & Rudi Zwicker, Innkeepers

Just a mile or so off the main routes in Taos is this elegant 200-year-old restored adobe home with its unique European and Southwestern antique furnishings. All rooms have private baths, most have fireplaces, one features a Swedish porcelain stove, another boasts its own Jacuzzi and steam shower, while yet another has a spa bath. A Swedish sauna and hot tub are available to all guests. And don't forget those elegant breakfasts!

Recipes

Almond Cheese Balls

"My husband was looking for a new appetizer recipe, and eventually found this one in an old, old cookbook. Like potato chips, they are so good that you can't eat just one!"

2 cups cheddar cheese, finely grated
¼ cup flour
2 egg whites, beaten stiff
1 cup blanched almonds, coarsely ground
1½ cups vegetable oil

- In a large bowl place the cheese and flour, and mix them together.
- Add the egg whites and gently fold them in so that a dough is formed.
- Spread the almonds on a sheet of waxed paper.
- Roll the dough into 18 individual balls. Roll each ball in the almonds so that it is completely coated.
- In a large skillet place the oil and heat it on medium until it is hot.
- Fry the cheese balls until they are lightly browned on all sides. Serve them hot.

makes 18 balls

Blue Stuffed Mushrooms

"These stuffed mushrooms are just wonderful. Everyone should have a tray of them in the refrigerator for unexpected guests."

4 ounces blue cheese
4 ounces cream cheese
1 tablespoon half & half
16 small mushrooms, stems removed
16 small pecan halves
16 small fresh basil leaves

- In a medium bowl place the blue cheese and cream cheese. Beat them together with an electric mixer so that they are smooth.
- Add the half & half, and beat it in so that the mixture is fluffy.
- Fill the mushroom caps with the cheese mixture.
- Top each one with a pecan half and a basil leaf.

serves 4

Green Chile Cheese Soup

"My 'organic sister' gave me this recipe, and it is so good! The green chile gives the soup a kick and the cheese melts in to make it creamy. If you're not a vegetarian you can add shredded baked chicken. For a perfect light meal, serve this with a good warm bread and a crisp green salad."

1½ teaspoons butter
1½ teaspoons vegetable oil
1 large yellow onion, coarsely chopped
4 cloves fresh garlic, chopped
2 teaspoons ground paprika
3½ cups chicken broth
1½ pounds tomatoes, puréed
4 ounces green chile peppers, roasted, peeled and chopped
2 small potatoes, cut into ½" cubes
¼ teaspoon ground cumin
1 teaspoon fresh cilantro, chopped
½ pound Monterey Jack cheese, cut into 4 pieces

- In a large stockpot place the butter and oil, and heat them on medium until the butter is melted and they are hot. Add the onions and garlic, and sauté them for 5 minutes, or until the onions are translucent.
- Add the paprika, broth, tomatoes, green chile peppers, potatoes, cumin and cilantro. Stir the ingredients together well.
- Reduce the heat to low. Simmer the soup for ½ hour, or until the potatoes are tender.
- Place a piece of cheese on top of each serving.

serves 4

"Taos is a wonderful place to live. It has a nice small town atmosphere, the people are friendly, the climate is not too hot and not too cold, and the skiing is excellent. It's the perfect place to raise our little tyke."

Rudi Zwicker

Easy Creamy Russian Borscht

"When my mother gave me this recipe I remember initially scrunching up my nose in disgust. However, I went ahead and made it, and it was delicious! The miraculous thing is that it is incredibly easy to make, and even non-beet lovers love it."

1	**16-ounce can sliced beets**
4	**teaspoons yellow onions, minced**
1	**teaspoon sugar**
¼	**cup lemon juice, freshly squeezed**
¼	**teaspoon pepper**
½	**teaspoon salt**
¼	**teaspoon fresh dill weed, chopped**
1	**cup sour cream** *(or yogurt)*

- In a food processor place all of the ingredients *(except for the sour cream)*. Blend them together so that they are smooth.
- Add the sour cream and blend it in well.
- Serve the soup cold.

serves 4

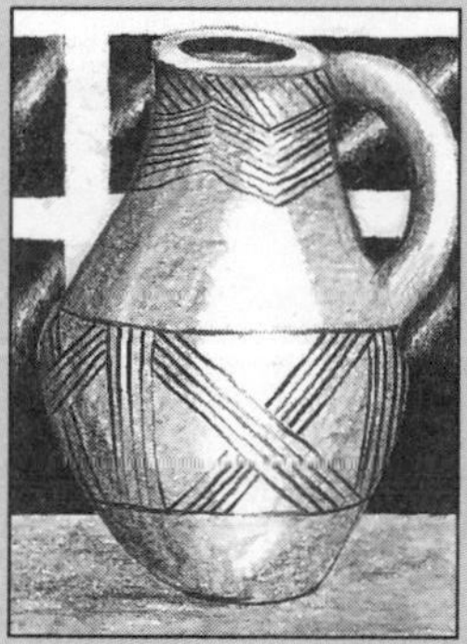

"I was in the restaurant business for twenty years, and in comparison, running a Bed & Breakfast seems easy. It is most enjoyable for me to cook for our guests, make them happy, and perhaps share some of the secrets of Taos."

Marcia Zwicker

Chicken & Cheese Enchiladas

"This is a great recipe for people who don't have a lot of time to cook or shop for specific ingredients. It was given to me by Rudy, a native New Mexican, and she has served it to her family and friends for many years."

1 can cream of mushroom soup
1 can cream of chicken soup
1 8-ounce carton chopped, frozen green chile peppers, thawed
1 15-ounce can chicken broth
1 3-pound chicken, cooked, skin and bones removed, and shredded
1 large yellow onion, chopped
2 cups Monterey Jack cheese, grated
1 dozen corn tortillas

- Preheat the oven to 350°.
- In a large bowl place the mushroom soup, chicken soup, green chile peppers and chicken broth. Stir the ingredients together well.
- Into a large baking dish pour ⅓ cup of the mixture so that the bottom is lightly covered.
- Into another large bowl place the chicken, onions and 1 cup of the cheese. Stir the ingredients together well.
- Down the center of each tortilla, place some of the chicken and cheese mixture. Roll the tortilla up so that the edges overlap.
- Place each enchilada in the baking pan with the seam side down.
- Pour the remaining sauce on top.
- Sprinkle the remaining 1 cup of cheese on top.
- Cover the pan tightly with foil.
- Bake the enchiladas for 30 minutes, or until the cheese is melted and everything is hot.

serves 4 to 6

Green Chile Rice

"My housekeeper is of Spanish heritage, and she gave me this recipe. She tells me that every time she is invited out to dinner and needs to bring a dish, she makes this rice..... and people just gobble it up."

1 cup raw white rice, cooked
1 cup green chile peppers, roasted, peeled and chopped
8 ounces sour cream
1 cup Monterey Jack cheese, grated
1 cup mozzarella cheese, grated
salt *(to taste)*

- Preheat the oven to 350°.
- In a large bowl place all of the ingredients and mix them together well.
- Place the mixture in a greased baking dish.
- Bake it for 35 minutes, or until the cheese is bubbly and everything is hot.

serves 4

"My husband Rudi cooks European for our guests, and I cook American for our family. With these two cultural combinations, together with the influence of the Southwest, we come up with some very interesting dishes."

Marcia Zwicker

Europa Chocolate Mousse Cake

"I am not lying when I tell you that this is one of the yummiest, most richly decadent desserts you will ever taste."

Cake

- **½ pound baking chocolate, melted**
- **¼ cup very strong coffee**
- **¼ cup heavy cream**
- **8 egg yolks**
- **½ cup sugar**
- **1 teaspoon vanilla extract**
- **8 egg whites**
- **¼ cup sugar**
- **Chocolate Mousse** *(recipe follows)*

- Preheat the oven to 350°.
- In a medium bowl place the chocolate, coffee and cream. Beat them with an electric mixer.
- In another medium bowl place the egg yolks, the ½ cup of sugar and the vanilla. Beat them so that the mixture is light and fluffy.
- Pour the egg yolk mixture into the chocolate mixture, and stir them together well.
- In a large bowl place the egg whites and the ¼ cup of sugar. Beat them together with an electric mixer so that the mixture is fluffy.
- With the mixer constantly running, slowly add the chocolate mixture to the egg whites. Beat the ingredients together so that soft peaks *(not too stiff)* are formed.
- Pour the batter into a greased 10" springform pan. Bake it for 10 minutes. Increase the oven temperature to 425°. Continue to bake the cake for 15 minutes more, or until it is firm in the middle.
- Let the cake cool for 1 hour *(the middle will collapse).* Fill in the top with the Chocolate Mousse.

serves 8 to 10

Chocolate Mousse

- **¾ pound semisweet chocolate pieces, melted**
- **¾ cup heavy cream**
- **8 egg whites**
- **¼ cup sugar**
- **1 quart heavy cream, whipped to soft peaks**

- In a large bowl place the chocolate and the ¾ cup of cream, and mix them together well.
- In a medium bowl place the egg whites. While beating them constantly with an electric mixer, slowly add the sugar. Beat the mixture so that stiff peaks are formed.
- Add the egg whites to the chocolate mixture, and gently fold them in. Add the 1 quart of whipped cream and fold it in well. Chill the mousse in the refrigerator.

makes approximately 6 cups

Casa Europa

Chocolate Mint Pie

"For years we went to a restaurant in Boulder, Colorado, and literally suffered through dinner, just to get to this pie. Eventually the restaurant went out of business and I was so upset that the owners kindly gave me the recipe. Don't cheat on the beating time, because that makes all the difference."

1 stick butter, softened to room temperature
1 stick margarine
1½ cups sugar
2 envelopes Chocobake
5 eggs
⅓ teaspoon mint extract
1 9" graham cracker crust

- In a medium bowl place the butter and margarine, and beat them so that they are smooth.
- Add the sugar and beat it in for 5 minutes.
- Add the Chocobake and 1 of the eggs, and beat them in for 5 minutes.
- Add 1 more egg and beat it in for 5 minutes. Add 2 more eggs and the mint extract, and beat them in for 5 minutes. Add the last egg and beat it in for 5 minutes.
- Pour the mixture into the graham cracker crust. Freeze the pie for 2 hours, or until it is hard.

serves 8

Lemon Lime Tart

"Once we were traveling in California and had this dessert at a local restaurant. We absolutely loved it, and so the chef gave us the recipe. It's similar to a lemon meringue pie, but without the meringue."

4 whole eggs
4 egg yolks
1 cup sugar
⅔ cup lemon juice, freshly squeezed
⅔ cup lime juice, freshly squeezed
2 lemons, zested *(outer yellow part grated off)*
2 limes, zested
1½ sticks unsalted butter, cut into chunks
2 Europa Tart Shells *(recipe on page 131)*, **baked**

- In the top of a double boiler place the eggs, egg yolks, sugar, lemon juice, lime juice and zest. Heat the ingredients on low and blend them together well. While stirring constantly, simmer the mixture for 10 minutes, or until it is very thick.
- Remove the mixture from the heat. Add one chunk of butter at a time and stir it in well so that it is melted and the mixture is smooth. Cover the pan and let it cool to room temperature.
- Pour the mixture into the Europa Tart Shells.

makes 2 tarts

Europa Linzer Bars

"In the old days, before I was so busy running a Bed & Breakfast inn, I used to read lots of cookbooks and food magazines for recipe ideas. Now I don't have time, and just use what I already know. This particular recipe came from a reader's request in ***Gourmet*** *magazine. It's a delicious, sophisticated European cookie."*

1 cup butter, softened to room temperature
1 cup brown sugar, packed
½ cup white sugar
1½ cups almonds, toasted and ground
2 eggs, lightly beaten
2 cups flour
1½ teaspoons baking powder
1 teaspoon ground cinnamon
½ teaspoon salt
1½ cups raspberry jam
2 tablespoons powdered sugar

- Preheat the oven to 375°.
- In a large bowl place the butter, brown sugar and white sugar. Blend the ingredients together with an electric mixer so that they are creamy.
- Add the almonds and eggs, and mix them in well.
- In a medium bowl sift together the flour, baking powder, cinnamon and salt. Add them to the butter mixture and mix them in well.
- Place a piece of waxed paper cut to fit in the bottom of a greased medium baking pan.
- Place ⅔ of the dough in the bottom of the pan and press it out to fit. Spread the raspberry jam on top.
- Chill the remaining dough in the refrigerator for 30 minutes, or until it is firm.
- On a lightly floured surface roll out the chilled dough so that it forms a ⅛" thick rectangle. Cut the rectangle into long ½" strips. Arrange them in a lattice pattern on top of the jam.
- Bake the Linzer for 30 minutes, or until it is lightly browned.
- Let the Linzer cool for 10 minutes.
- Sift the powdered sugar on top.
- Cut the Linzer into small bars.

serves 10 to 12

Europa Tart Shell

"Here is a basic sweet shell recipe that can be filled with whatever your heart desires. You need no baking skills to make it successfully."

2⅓ **cups flour**
⅓ **cup sugar**
½ **pound unsalted butter, cut into small pieces**
2 **egg yolks**
2 **tablespoons heavy cream** *(or as needed)*

- In a medium bowl place the flour, sugar and butter. With a pastry blender, cut the ingredients together so that the mixture is crumbly.
- In a small bowl place the egg yolks and 1 tablespoon of the heavy cream, and mix them together well.
- Add the egg yolk mixture to the flour mixture and blend them together so that a smooth ball is formed *(add the remaining 1 tablespoon of cream if necessary).*
- Wrap the dough in plastic wrap and refrigerate it for 1 hour.
- Preheat the oven to 375°.
- On a lightly floured surface roll out the dough to fit a 9" pie plate. Fill it with dry beans to keep it flat.
- Bake the tart shell for 15 minutes, or until it is lightly browned.

makes one 9" tart

"When my husband and I first started out, I was supposed to do all the cooking. For some reason things got turned around, and now he does the cooking and I do the dishes. I prefer it this way, because it's less work!"

Marcia Zwicker

Casita Chamisa

850 Chamisal Road N.W.
Albuquerque, New Mexico 87107
(505) 897-4644
Kit & Arnold Sargeant, Innkeepers

Here in Albuquerque's rural North Valley, near the bosques beside the Rio Grande, the ancestors of the Pueblo Indians built their villages. Later, Spanish settlers established their haciendas in the area. Today's guests at Casita Chamisa may enjoy all the same ambience.....and more. The nineteenth-century adobe house and guest house feature fireplaces, charming furnishings, a greenhouse, flower gardens and access to an indoor heated swimming pool and hot tub. Breakfast on the glass-covered patio is noteworthy for its oven-hot homemade breads and coffee cakes. And how many inns can boast of their own 700-year-old archeological ruins on site?

Recipes

Microwave Baked Apples

"People love baked apples, but the modern day cook seldom makes them for breakfast because they take so long to cook in the oven. That's why this recipe is so great. It's quick, easy to make, and the apples come out perfect every time!"

2 tablespoons butter, softened
¼ cup brown sugar, packed
¼ teaspoon ground cinnamon
4 large baking apples, cored and peeled part way down from the top
2 tablespoons raisins *(optional)*

- In a small bowl place the butter, brown sugar and cinnamon. Mix the ingredients together well.
- Place each apple in a small cereal bowl.
- In the center of each apple stuff some of the filling.
- Sprinkle the raisins on top.
- Cover the bowls with waxed paper and place them in a circular pattern in the microwave.
- Cook the apples on high for 3 to 4 minutes, or until they are tender.

serves 4

"Our Bed & Breakfast sits over ancient Indian pueblo ruins. My wife is an archaeologist, and in the early 1980s when we decided to add a swimming pool and a new wing onto our farmhouse, she conducted an excavation of the site under the sponsorship of the Maxwell Museum of Anthropology."

Arnold Sargeant

Chamisa Puffy Omelette

"I get so many compliments from this dish that it is unbelievable. When I make it I use only three eggs, but the finished product looks enormous because it is all puffed up with air. A good variation is to substitute green chile peppers for the bell peppers."

- 2 **tablespoons butter**
- ½ **cup green bell peppers, seeded and finely chopped**
- 3 **egg yolks**
- 2 **tablespoons milk**
- ¼ **teaspoon baking powder**
- **salt and pepper** *(to taste)*
- 3 **egg whites**
- 1 **tablespoon butter**
- ½ **cup cheddar cheese, grated**

- In a small glass bowl place the 2 tablespoons of butter and the bell peppers. Microwave them on high for 2 minutes. Set the bowl aside.
- In another small bowl place the egg yolks, milk, baking powder, salt and pepper. Blend the ingredients together well.
- In a medium bowl place the egg whites and beat them with an electric mixer on high speed so that stiff peaks are formed.
- Add the egg yolk mixture to the egg whites, and gently fold them in.
- In a 9" glass pie plate place the 1 tablespoon of butter. Microwave it on high for 45 seconds, or until it is melted.
- Place the egg mixture in the pie plate and spread it out evenly. Reduce the microwave power by 50%. Cook the omelette for 3 minutes.
- Lift up the edges with a spatula to allow the uncooked mixture to be exposed. Continue cooking the omelette for 3 more minutes.
- Place the bell pepper mixture and the cheese on ½ of the omelette. Fold the omelette over in half.
- Cook it for another minute, or until the cheese is melted.

serves 3

Sour Cream Biscuits

"This recipe comes from an old, old cookbook I found many years ago. The biscuits are light as a feather and the flavor is excellent. You can use sour milk instead of the sour cream, and they will taste even better."

1 cup flour
½ teaspoon sugar
1½ teaspoons baking powder
¼ teaspoon baking soda
½ teaspoon salt
¼ cup shortening
½ cup sour cream

- Preheat the oven to 450°.
- In a large bowl place the flour, sugar, baking powder, baking soda and salt. Stir the ingredients together well.
- Add the shortening and cut it in with a pastry blender so that the mixture is crumbly.
- Add the sour cream and mix it in so that the ingredients are blended.
- Place the dough on a lightly floured surface. Knead the dough 10 times to make it smooth.
- Roll out the dough so that it is ½" thick.
- Cut out the biscuits with a 2½" round biscuit cutter.
- Place the biscuits on an ungreased cookie sheet. Bake them for 10 minutes, or until they are lightly browned.

makes approximately 16 biscuits

"I think that people who stay at Bed & Breakfast places instead of hotel chains have their own unique culture. Invariably they are bright, interesting, adventurous.....and they make the whole country inn experience worthwhile."

Kit Sargeant

Fruit & Fibre Buttermilk Muffins

"The original recipe for these muffins called for bran cereal, which I thought tasted awful. So I experimented with different types, and finally discovered the Fruit & Fibre cereal to be the perfect thing to use. When the muffins cook, the dried fruits get soft and reconstitute, so you feel like you are eating fresh fruit. The muffins come out best when the dough is first stored in the refrigerator for several days before using. It can be stored for up to a month."

2 eggs, beaten
2 cups buttermilk
2½ teaspoons baking soda
1½ cups sugar
2½ cups flour
½ cup oil
½ 15-ounce box Fruit & Fibre cereal

- Preheat the oven to 400°.
- In a large bowl place the eggs and buttermilk, and mix them together.
- Add the baking soda, sugar, flour and oil, and mix them in. Add the cereal and mix it in.
- Pour the batter into 36 individual greased muffin tins so that they are ⅔ full.
- Bake the muffins for 18 to 20 minutes, or until a wooden toothpick inserted in the center comes out clean.

makes 36 muffins

"People love to discuss the origin of my recipes over breakfast. I can tell the same stories three thousand times, and never get tired of it!"

Arnold Sargeant

Banana Nut Bread

"This recipe works equally well with either bananas or pumpkin. I like to cook the bread in the microwave because it is faster, but the oven works fine also."

2 tablespoons graham cracker crumbs, crushed
1 cup flour
½ cup white sugar
½ cup brown sugar, packed
1½ teaspoons baking powder
½ teaspoon salt
1 cup ripe banana, peeled and mashed
2 eggs
½ cup vegetable oil
½ cup walnuts, finely chopped

- Preheat the oven to 325°.
- Coat the sides of a greased glass loaf pan with the graham cracker crumbs. Line the bottom of the pan with waxed paper and set it aside.
- In a large bowl place the flour, white sugar, brown sugar, baking powder, salt, banana, eggs and oil. Blend the ingredients together with an electric mixer on medium speed so that the dry ingredients are just moistened.
- Add ¼ cup of the walnuts and stir them in.
- Pour the batter into the prepared loaf pan. Sprinkle the remaining walnuts on top.
- Bake the bread for 35 minutes, or until a wooden toothpick inserted in the center comes out clean.
- Remove the bread from the pan and let cool it on a wire rack.

makes 1 loaf

"There is a great intensity involved in owning a Bed & Breakfast. We work seven days a week and do everything ourselves, from the cooking and cleaning to the book work and maintenance. It's really a labor of love!"

Arnold Sargeant

The Dancing Bear

Post Office Box 128
Jemez Springs, New Mexico 87025
(505) 829-3336
Carol Breen & Richard Crosby, Innkeepers

The dramatic red sandstone cliffs of Jemez Canyon form a towering backdrop for the Dancing Bear, where a wall of windows captures the view of the rollicking Jemez River. Although it is just a short drive from Santa Fe and Albuquerque, this is an unexpected and unfamiliar canyon to many travelers. Prehistoric Indian ruins, modern pueblos, an old mission church, fishing, climbing and hiking vie for the visitor's attention. Enjoy a full hot breakfast and then stroll to the nearby Jemez Bath House for a healing soak in the hot mineral waters and a therapeutic massage.

Recipes

Dancing Bear Smoothie

"Both adults and children love this drink, which is super simple to make. Any kind of fresh fruit can be used.....whatever is in season. We find it an excellent way to use up fruit that has gotten too ripe to eat by the piece."

3 cups orange juice
1 cup mixed fruit *(your choice)*
1 banana, peeled

- In a blender place all of the ingredients and blend them on high until they are smooth. Serve the drink well chilled.

serves 4

Jemez River Clam Chowder

"I come from New England and this is an old recipe that has been in my family for generations. Unlike most chowders, this is very light.....but at the same time, it tastes very rich."

1 stick butter
½ cup white onions, finely chopped
1 red bell pepper, seeded and finely chopped
2½ cups potatoes, diced and cooked
1 32-ounce can whole clams *(with liquid)*
2 cups milk
½ cup heavy cream
salt and pepper *(to taste)*

- In a medium saucepan place the butter and heat it on low until it is melted and hot. Add the onions and bell peppers, and sauté them until the onions are translucent. Add the potatoes, clams and milk, and stir them in well. Cook and stir the ingredients for 20 minutes.
- Add the cream, salt and pepper, and stir them in well. Simmer the chowder for 10 minutes, or until it is well heated.

serves 6

"Jemez Springs has a population of 400 and is located in a beautiful river valley surrounded by magnificent high mesas. It is a wonderful, tri-cultural community, and I feel grateful to live here."

Carol Breen

Jemez Glazed Game Hens with Barley Stuffing

"This is the most requested item on our menu. The secret to the delicious taste is the combination of the soy sauce and honey marinade. Sprinkle any extra stuffing around the birds in the plastic bag when you bake them."

Jemez Glazed Game Hens

- ¼ **cup soy sauce**
- 1 **tablespoon honey**
- ¼ **teaspoon garlic powder**
- 2 **Cornish game hens, thawed, rinsed and giblets removed**
- **Barley Stuffing** *(recipe follows)*

- In a small bowl place the soy sauce, honey and garlic powder. Stir them together well.
- Place the hens in a small baking pan. Pour the honey glaze over both the inside and outside of the hens. Cover the pan tightly with foil and place it in the refrigerator.
- While basting the hens occasionally, marinate them for 4 hours.
- Preheat the oven to 350°.
- Stuff the hens with the Barley Stuffing. Place them on a rack inside a plastic baking bag. Place the bag in a shallow baking pan. Follow the instructions on the baking bag box, and bake the hens for 1 hour, or until they are done.

serves 2

Barley Stuffing

- 2 **cups chicken broth**
- ¾ **cup pearl barley**
- ½ **cup piñon nuts** *(pine nuts)*
- 1 **cup fresh mushrooms, coarsely chopped**
- 2 **scallions, finely chopped**
- ¼ **cup soy sauce** *(or to taste)*

- In a small saucepan place the broth and the barley. While stirring frequently, heat them on high until they come to a boil.
- Reduce the heat to low. Simmer the ingredients for 45 minutes, or until the barley is tender and the broth is absorbed.
- Add the piñon nuts, mushrooms, scallions and soy sauce. Stir them in well.

makes approximately 2 cups

Mama Bear's Granola

"I make this granola once a week, and serve it each morning for breakfast. People love it and are always asking for the recipe. Now when they ask, I can tell them it's in this book."

2½ cups rolled oats
½ cup wheat germ
½ cup powdered milk
½ cup soy powder
½ cup shredded coconut
½ cup sesame seeds
½ cup sunflower seeds
½ cup slivered almonds
½ cup honey
½ cup corn oil

- Preheat the oven to 250°.
- In a large bowl place all of the ingredients *(except for the honey and corn oil)* and stir them together well.
- In a small saucepan place the honey and oil. While stirring occasionally, heat them on medium until they are hot.
- While constantly stirring, slowly add the hot honey-oil mixture to the dry mixture, and mix it in well.
- Spread the granola in a very thin layer on cookie sheets.
- Bake it for 30 minutes. Remove the granola from the oven and stir it around.
- Bake it for 30 minutes longer, or until it is lightly browned and firm.

makes 8 cups

Little Bear's Porridge

"One morning a guest told me about this recipe, so I tried it and thought is was just wonderful. I love the way the apple juice sweetens the oats, so that no extra sugar is needed."

1 cup apple juice
1½ cups rolled oats
2 teaspoons ground cinnamon

- In a small saucepan place the apple juice and heat it on low until it is hot. Add the oats and cinnamon, and stir them in well.
- Cover the saucepan and simmer the ingredients for 10 minutes, or until the oats are tender.

serves 2

Eaton House

403 Eaton Avenue
Socorro, New Mexico 87801
(505) 835-1067
Anna Appleby & Tom Harper, Innkeepers

Drivers along I-25 aren't the only ones who follow the path of the Rio Grande: sandhill cranes, hummingbirds, hawks, snow geese and even some whooping cranes follow the river on this main north-south flyway. And wildlife is the lure that brings many visitors to the historic adobe-walled Eaton House in Socorro, built in 1881. Each room has a private bathroom and entrance, and features antique and locally made furniture. Guests may enjoy the full breakfast, or, provided with an "early birder" basket, head out to view the birds and animals.

Recipes

Roman Army Spaghetti with Italian Meatballs

"This recipe comes from my mother, who does not know how to make spaghetti sauce for less than a Roman army. It has been passed down from generation to generation, and seems to improve with age. To get that rich flavor and deep red color you must cook the sauce for a long time."

Roman Army Spaghetti

1 cup olive oil
1/3 cup dried parsley
2 1/2 tablespoons garlic powder
2 1/2 tablespoons dried basil
2 1/2 whole dried bay leaves
1 1/2 teaspoons dried oregano
1 8-ounce can crushed tomatoes
3 12-ounce cans tomato paste
5 1/2 cups water
1/2 teaspoon ground cinnamon
1 tablespoon sugar
1 1/2 teaspoons salt
pepper *(to taste)*
Italian Meatballs *(recipe follows)*
1 1/2 pounds spaghetti, cooked al dente and drained

- In a large stockpot place the oil, parsley, garlic powder, basil, bay leaves and oregano. Heat them on high until the oil is hot and starts to bubble. Sauté and stir them for 5 minutes *(be careful not to burn the herbs)*. Add the crushed tomatoes, tomato paste and water. Stir them in well. Bring the mixture to a boil. Reduce the heat to low and simmer the sauce for 15 minutes *(stir it occasionally)*.
- Add the cinnamon, sugar, salt and pepper, and stir them in.
- Simmer the sauce for 3/4 hour, or until the oil rises to the top *(if the oil doesn't form on top, add 1/3 cup more oil)*.
- Add the Italian Meatballs and simmer them in the sauce for 3 to 4 hours, or until they are done. *(If you make the sauce without the meatballs, simmer it for an extra 2 hours.)*
- Serve the sauce and meatballs with the spaghetti.

serves 8

Italian Meatballs

2 1/4 pounds lean ground beef
1 cup Progresso seasoned bread crumbs
2 eggs, lightly beaten
4 tablespoons dried parsley
1 1/2 teaspoons dried basil
1 1/2 teaspoons garlic powder

- In a large bowl place all of the ingredients and mix them together well. Roll out 20 meatballs with your hands.
- Cook them in olive oil or spaghetti sauce until they are done.

makes 20 meatballs

Eaton House

Blue Corn Piñon Pancakes with Pomegranate Sauce

"The sweet, tart flavor of the Pomegranate Sauce is the perfect complement to the blue corn pancakes, which are deliciously dense and crunchy. Also, the color contrast is quite beautiful."

Blue Corn Piñon Pancakes

- 1 **cup blue cornmeal**
- 1 **cup flour**
- ¼ **cup sugar**
- 2 **teaspoons baking powder**
- 1 **teaspoon baking soda**
- ½ **cup piñon nuts** *(pine nuts)*
- 2 **eggs**
- 2 **cups buttermilk**
- ¼ **cup vegetable oil** *(or as needed)*

- In a medium bowl place the cornmeal, flour, sugar, baking powder, baking soda and piñon nuts. Mix them together well.
- In another medium bowl place the eggs, buttermilk and oil. Whisk them together so that they are well combined.
- Add the egg mixture to the cornmeal mixture, and stir them together so that they are just blended *(do not overmix)*.
- Preheat a greased large skillet so that it is medium hot. Pour ½ cup of batter for each pancake. Cook them for 3 to 4 minutes on each side, or until they are lightly browned and done in the middle.

makes 12 pancakes

Pomegranate Sauce

- ¾ **cup sugar**
- 2 **tablespoons cornstarch**
- 2 **cups pomegranate juice**
- 2 **tablespoons butter**
- 1 **tablespoon lemon juice, freshly squeezed**

- In a medium saucepan place the sugar and cornstarch, and whisk them together well.
- While whisking constantly, slowly add the pomegranate juice. Heat the mixture on medium until it comes to a boil. Cook the sauce for 1 minute, or until it thickens and becomes clear.
- Remove the pan from the heat. Add the butter and lemon juice, and blend them in.

makes approximately 3 cups

Apple Pie Pancake

"These pancakes are a cross between an apple pie and a German pancake. Because they are sweet, I serve them with bacon that is sprinkled with black pepper and then baked in the oven, which is the perfect contrast."

- **5 large eggs**
- **1 cup milk**
- **2 teaspoons vanilla extract**
- **2 tablespoons butter, melted**
- **½ cup flour**
- **1 tablespoon sugar**
- **½ teaspoon baking powder**
- **¼ teaspoon salt**
- **¼ teaspoon ground nutmeg**
- **2 cups Granny Smith apples, peeled and sliced**
- **¾ cup sugar**
- **1 tablespoon ground cinnamon**
- **½ teaspoon ground cloves**
- **¼ teaspoon ground nutmeg**
- **¼ cup unsalted butter**

- Preheat the oven to 425°.
- In a large bowl place the eggs, milk, vanilla and melted butter. Mix them together well.
- Add the flour, the 1 tablespoon of sugar, the baking powder, salt and the first ¼ teaspoon of nutmeg. Beat them together with an electric mixer on high speed until the mixture is foamy. Set the mixture aside.
- In a medium microwave-safe bowl place the apples, the ¾ cup of sugar, the cinnamon, cloves and the second ¼ teaspoon of nutmeg.
- Microwave the ingredients on high for 10 minutes, or until the apples are soft *(occasionally stop the microwave and stir them)*.
- In a medium oven-proof skillet place the unsalted butter. Set the skillet in the oven until the butter is melted. Swirl the butter around so that the pan is well coated.
- Place the apple mixture in the skillet. Pour the egg batter mixture on top.
- Bake the pancake for 15 minutes.
- Reduce the heat to 350°.
- Bake the pancake for 10 minutes more, or until it is browned.
- Remove it from the oven and serve it immediately.

serves 4 to 6

Eaton House

Eaton House Buttermilk Pancakes

"Everyone has a buttermilk pancake recipe, and this is my particular favorite. For a real treat, serve the pancakes with whipped cream and blueberry sauce on top."

2 cups buttermilk
2 eggs, lightly beaten
4 tablespoons safflower oil
2 cups flour
2 tablespoons sugar
4 teaspoons baking powder
1 teaspoon baking soda
1 teaspoon salt

- In a medium bowl place the buttermilk, eggs and oil. Whisk them together well.
- In a large bowl place the flour, sugar, baking powder, baking soda and salt. Mix the ingredients together so that they are well combined.
- Add the egg mixture to the flour mixture, and blend them together so that the batter is smooth.
- Preheat a lightly greased large skillet so that it is medium hot. Pour out ⅓ cup of batter for each 6" pancake. Cook the pancakes for 3 to 4 minutes on each side, or until they are lightly browned and done in the middle.

serves 4

Saucy Blueberry Sauce

"I took a basic recipe for blueberry jam and turned it into a sauce. It's one of the syrups that I serve with my pancakes, and people always want the recipe."

1 pint fresh blueberries, washed
2 cups water
¼ cup sugar
2 tablespoons cornstarch
¼ teaspoon salt
1 tablespoon unsalted butter
2 tablespoons lemon juice, freshly squeezed

- In a medium saucepan place the blueberries and water, and heat them on medium until they are warm.
- In a small bowl place the sugar, cornstarch and salt, and stir them together.
- Add the sugar mixture to the warm blueberries, and blend it in well.
- Cook and stir the sauce until some of the blueberries break and the mixture is thick and clear.
- Remove the pan from the heat.
- Add the butter and lemon juice, and stir them in so that the butter is melted.

makes approximately 2½ cups

Eaton House Scones

"The crystallized ginger gives these scones an unusual, snappy flavor. They are much moister than traditional scones."

⅛ cup milk
⅛ cup honey
4 cups unbleached flour
¼ cup sugar
2 tablespoons baking powder
1 teaspoon salt
1 teaspoon ground ginger
2 sticks butter, softened and cut into small pieces
½ cup crystallized ginger, finely chopped and dredged in flour
½ cup currants, dredged in flour
1 cup milk

- Preheat the oven to 400°.
- In a small saucepan place the ⅛ cup of milk and the honey, and heat them on medium low until the honey is dissolved. Set it aside and keep it warm.
- In a large bowl place the flour, sugar, baking powder, salt and ground ginger. Mix the ingredients together so that they are well combined.
- Add the butter and cut it in with a pastry blender so that coarse crumbs are formed.
- Add the crystallized ginger and currants, and stir them in.
- Add the 1 cup of milk and the warm honey-milk mixture to the flour mixture, and gently mix them in so that a soft ball of dough is formed.
- Place the dough on a lightly floured surface and knead it 5 times.
- Roll it out to form a thick 8" x 8" square.
- Cut the square into quarters, diagonally. Cut each quarter in half to make triangles.
- Place the scones on a lightly greased cookie sheet so that they are 1" apart.
- Bake them for 15 minutes, or until they are lightly browned.

makes 8 scones

"We feel that Socorro is one of the undiscovered gems of New Mexico. The people are friendly and down-to-earth, and the surrounding geographical features are magnificent."

Tom Harper

Simple Mincemeat Squares

"One day a Williams-Sonoma store had samples of these mincemeat squares for the customers to try as an advertisement for their imported English prepared mincemeat. The saleslady was nice enough to get the recipe and send it to me."

- 2½ **cups flour**
- 1 **tablespoon sugar**
- 1 **teaspoon salt**
- 1 **cup shortening**
- 1 **large egg yolk**
- ½ **cup milk**
- 1 **can prepared mincemeat** *(imported English, if possible)*
- 1 **large egg white, lightly beaten**
- 1½ **cups powdered sugar** *(or as needed)*
- 1 **tablespoon lemon juice, freshly squeezed**
- 1 **tablespoon water** *(or as needed)*

- Preheat the oven to 400°.
- In a large bowl sift together the flour, sugar and salt. Add the shortening and cut it in with a pastry blender so that small crumbs are formed.
- In a small bowl place the egg yolk and milk, and whisk them together well.
- Add the egg mixture to the flour mixture, and gently mix it in so that a dough is formed.
- Divide the dough in half.
- On a lightly floured surface roll out each half so that it forms an 11" x 15" rectangle.
- Place one rectangle in the bottom of a baking pan. Spread the mincemeat on top. Gently place the second rectangle on top of the mincemeat. Brush the egg white on top.
- Bake the pastry for 25 minutes, or until it is lightly browned. Let it cool slightly.
- In a small bowl place the powdered sugar and lemon juice, and whisk them together. Add the water if it is needed to make a smooth glaze.
- Drizzle the glaze on top. Cut the pastry into squares.

makes approximately 50 squares

"You ask why do I love what I do? Because right at this moment I am sitting at my desk, looking out the window. The daffodils are in bloom, the sky is clear, and I can see at least 6 different varieties of birds."

Anna Appleby

June's Pie Crust

"Every year during apple season our church has an apple pie fundraiser. June's crust is the best, and she was kind enough to give me the recipe. The vinegar helps to bind the dough together and get rid of the flour taste."

6 cups flour
1 tablespoon salt
1 tablespoon baking soda
4 cups shortening
1 egg plus enough water to make 1 cup
2 tablespoons white vinegar

- In a large bowl place the flour, salt and baking soda. Mix them together well.
- Add the shortening and cut it in with a pastry blender so that the mixture is crumbly.
- In a small bowl place the egg, water and vinegar. Beat them together well.
- Add the egg mixture to the flour mixture and stir them together so that they are just blended *(do not overmix)*.
- Divide the dough into 6 equal parts and roll them into balls. Cover the dough with a damp cloth and refrigerate it for 30 minutes.
- On a lightly floured surface roll out each ball of dough to make a crust that fits a 9" pie pan.

makes three double 9" pie crusts

"I have always loved cooking, and used to bake on weekends as self-therapy for relief from my high-pressure job. The creative aspect is what is especially appealing. I have never found a recipe that I felt could not be improved upon. As Julia Child once said, 'Gourmet means never being able to leave a recipe alone'."

Anna Appleby

El Paradero

220 West Manhattan
Santa Fe, New Mexico 87501
(505) 988-1177
Ouida MacGregor & Thom Allen, Innkeepers

Today it's just a few blocks from the state capitol building, on a quiet side street within walking distance of the shops, galleries and restaurants of Santa Fe. Built around 1800, this structure was originally an adobe Spanish farmhouse. Remodeled and added to over the years, El Paradero is now a charming, rambling building, with rooms that feature folk art and hand-woven textiles as well as modern conveniences. Giant breakfasts are the rule here, with a different entrée and hot homemade breads every day. So stop in and smell the muffins.

Recipes

Pear Ginger Jam

"Ginger and pears go well together, and I use them in pies as well as in jams. You can vary the amount of ginger in this recipe according to taste, but be sure that you use at least two tablespoons."

10 pears, peeled, cored and puréed in a food processor *(to make 4 cups of pulp)*
3 tablespoons fresh ginger root, peeled and grated
1 box pectin
2 tablespoons lemon juice, freshly squeezed
5 cups sugar
6 canning jars and lids

- In a large stockpot place the pear pulp, ginger, pectin and lemon juice. While stirring constantly, heat the ingredients on medium high so that the mixture comes to a rolling boil.
- Add the sugar. While stirring constantly, bring the mixture back to a boil and cook it for 1 minute.
- Remove the pan from the heat. *(If there is foam on the top, stir it into the jam.)*
- Jar the jam according to the manufacturer's instructions.

makes approximately 6 cups

El Paradero Pork Sausage

"While I was living in the Northwest I had a friend who gave me this recipe, along with a food processor, so that I could make it. Now that I live in New Mexico I have added the red chile powder to give it a Southwest twist. It's a nice sausage to serve for a special breakfast."

2 pounds pork butt roast, cut into 1" chunks
1 tablespoon salt
1 teaspoon pepper
1½ tablespoons ground sage
1½ teaspoons red chile powder
½ teaspoon dried oregano
¼ teaspoon dried thyme
¼ teaspoon dried basil

- In a food processor place ¼ of the pork and grind it for 10 seconds. With the processor constantly running, slowly add the remaining pork. Grind it for 30 seconds, or until it is the consistency of ground sausage.
- Place the pork in a large bowl. Add the remaining ingredients and mix them in well with your hands.
- Form the mixture into small patties.
- In a large skillet place the patties. Cook them on medium heat for 4 minutes on each side, or until they are done.

makes approximately 20 patties

Chilled Mango Soup

"This is a generic recipe that will work with any fruit, although I think it's especially good with mango. The yogurt and orange juice are the constants, and should be added according to the consistency you desire."

- **2 cups orange juice**
- **1 cup plain yogurt**
- **1½ cups melon** *(your favorite),* **peeled, seeded and chopped**
- **½ cup ripe peaches, peeled, pitted and chopped**
- **1 ripe banana, peeled**
- **1 ripe mango, peeled and core removed**

- In a blender place the orange juice, yogurt and melon. Blend them together well.
- Add the peaches, banana and mango. Purée the ingredients so that a smooth liquid is formed.
- Chill the soup for 1 hour before serving.

serves 4

Green Chile Dill Quiche

"This recipe was a mistake. One morning my wife was making green chile quiche. She was very sleepy and accidentally dropped an open container of dill weed in the egg mixture. After removing what she could, she went ahead and baked it.....and it tasted better than the original recipe."

- **1 9" prepared pie crust**
- **1 cup cheddar cheese, grated**
- **1 cup Monterey Jack cheese, grated**
- **½ cup scallions, finely chopped**
- **3 eggs, beaten**
- **¾ cup half & half**
- **¾ cup milk**
- **½ cup green chile peppers, roasted, peeled and chopped**
- **1 tablespoon fresh dill weed** *(or 1 teaspoon dried)*
- **salt and pepper** *(to taste)*

- Preheat the oven to 325°.
- In the pie crust layer on the cheddar cheese, Jack cheese and scallions.
- In a medium bowl place the eggs, half & half and milk. Whisk them together well.
- Add the green chile peppers, dill, salt and pepper, and stir them in.
- Pour the mixture into the pie crust.
- Bake the quiche for 30 minutes, or until it is firm.

serves 6 to 8

Banana Oatmeal Pancakes

"I love pancakes and have many different recipes for them. The nice thing about this recipe is that if you use a really ripe banana, the pancakes will be so sweet you won't need to use any syrup. It's a very healthy recipe."

⅔	**cup whole wheat flour**
⅓	**cup sugar**
1	**teaspoon baking powder**
½	**teaspoon baking soda**
¼	**teaspoon salt**
¾	**cup rolled oats**
1	**ripe banana, peeled**
¾	**cup buttermilk**
1	**egg**
2	**tablespoons vegetable oil**

- In a large bowl sift together the flour, sugar, baking powder, baking soda and salt.
- Add the oats and stir them in well.
- In a blender place the banana, buttermilk, egg and oil. Blend them on high speed until they are smooth.
- Add the banana mixture to the flour mixture, and mix them together well. Let the mixture sit for 15 minutes.
- Using a ⅓ measuring cup, pour the batter onto a greased griddle to form pancakes. Cook them for 3 minutes on each side, or until they are brown and done in the middle.

serves 4

"Thomas Jefferson once said, 'Eat breakfast like a king, lunch like a prince and dinner like a pauper.' I completely agree with him and this philosophy is reflected in our reputation for having exceptionally wonderful morning meals."

Thom Allen

Apricot Corn Muffins

"I find that by adding a dried fruit to a basic muffin recipe, the muffins come out really sweet and moist. This recipe is a perfect example."

¼ cup butter, softened
1 cup sugar
1 cup buttermilk
1 egg, lightly beaten
1 teaspoon vanilla extract
½ cup white flour
⅓ cup whole wheat flour
2 teaspoons baking powder
⅔ cup yellow cornmeal
1 cup dried apricots, chopped

- Preheat the oven to 375°.
- In a medium bowl place the butter and sugar. Beat them together with an electric mixer so that they are smooth.
- Add the buttermilk, egg and vanilla. Blend them in well.
- In a large bowl sift together the white flour, wheat flour and baking powder. Add the cornmeal and mix it in.
- Add the buttermilk mixture to the dry ingredients, and mix them together well.
- Add the apricots and gently stir them in.
- Fill 12 individual greased muffin tins with the batter so that they are ⅔ full.
- Bake the muffins for 25 minutes, or until they are lightly browned and done.

makes 12 muffins

"Many years ago we visited Bed & Breakfasts in the British Isles, and thought that owning one in New Mexico would be a wonderful way to earn a living. It was something we could do together, while raising a family at the same time. So for us, home, work and the kids were not separated."

Ouida MacGregor

Cherry Muffins

"I make these in the summertime with fresh cherries. Because of my sweet tooth, I sprinkle a little sugar and almonds on top, which makes them extra delicious!"

2 cups flour
½ cup sugar
1 tablespoon baking powder
½ teaspoon salt
1 cup buttermilk
1 egg, lightly beaten
¾ cup fresh cherries, pitted and chopped
3 tablespoons butter, melted
½ teaspoon almond extract
1 tablespoon sugar
1 tablespoon almonds, sliced

- Preheat the oven to 350°.
- In a large bowl sift together the flour, the ½ cup of sugar, the baking powder and salt.
- In a small bowl place the buttermilk and egg, and whisk them together.
- Pour the egg mixture into the flour mixture, and stir them together.
- Add the cherries, butter and almond extract. Stir them in well.
- Fill 12 individual greased muffin tins with the batter so that they are ⅔ full. Sprinkle the 1 tablespoon of sugar and the sliced almonds on top.
- Bake the muffins for 25 minutes, or until they are lightly browned and done.

makes 12 muffins

"Years ago my wife told me that if I wanted to hang around with her on a permanent basis, I was going to have to learn how to be useful in the kitchen. So she taught me how to cook, and fortunately I found out that I really enjoyed it."

Thom Allen

El Rincón

114 Kit Carson Road
Taos, New Mexico 87571
(505) 758-4874
Nina Meyers & Paul Castillo, Innkeepers

Just a half block from the Plaza in Taos, and across the street from the Kit Carson home, is the 100-year-old adobe that was once the home of La Doña Luz Lucero Martinez, a sister-in-law of the famous – or infamous! – Padre Martinez. The inn, which now boasts a second story constructed in the traditional way, features a variety of rooms, each decorated in a different style, and the works of local artists are displayed throughout the house. Guests may have breakfast on the sunny, flower-filled patio in summer and before the big fireplace in winter.

Recipes

New Mexican Posole

"Posole is a very traditional New Mexican dish, and each family has its own recipe. This one comes from my ex-mother-in-law, and it is just wonderful. Serve it with warm tortillas and a fresh green salad on the side."

2 pounds country style pork ribs
6 dried red chile pods, stems removed
1 32-ounce package fresh posole, rinsed and drained
2 medium yellow onions, quartered
6 cloves garlic, minced
10 cups water

- In a large oiled skillet place the ribs. While turning them occasionally, cook the ribs on medium heat for 20 minutes, or until they are browned. Set them aside.
- In a medium stockpot place the red chile pods and posole, onions, garlic and water. Simmer the ingredients on low heat for 2 hours.
- Add the pork to the posole. Simmer the mixture for 3 hours, or until the meat easily falls off the bone.

serves 6 to 8

El Rincón French Onion Soup

"Thirty-five years ago I lived in Saudi Arabia and had an American girlfriend who was a very good cook. She gave me many excellent recipes, including this one, and I've been using it ever since."

1 stick butter
6 cups yellow onions, finely sliced
6 cups chicken broth
1 cup dry white wine
1 bay leaf
pepper *(to taste)*
1 cup Parmesan cheese *(or to taste),* **freshly grated**
1 cup mozzarella cheese, grated

- In a medium stockpot place the butter and heat it on low until it is melted and hot. Add the onions and sauté them for 10 minutes, or until they are lightly browned *(but not burned).*
- Add the chicken broth, wine, bay leaf and pepper. Stir them in well. Simmer the soup for 2 hours.
- Remove the bay leaf.
- Preheat the oven to 400°.
- Place the soup in individual oven-proof bowls. Sprinkle the two cheeses on top.
- Place the bowls on a flat sheet. Bake them in the oven for 4 minutes, or until the cheese is melted.

serves 4 to 6

El Rincón Gazpacho

"My younger brother and I once spent time in Madrid, Spain, and ate a gazpacho there that was outstanding. When we returned to the States we spent hours trying to re-create it.....and we did a good job! The green chile peppers are my own Southwestern touch."

- 3 **cups chicken broth**
- 2 **cups tomato juice**
- ½ **cup dry white wine**
- ¼ **cup fresh mushrooms, stems removed and finely chopped** *(reserve the stems)*
- ¼ **cup celery, leaves removed and finely chopped** *(reserve the leaves)*
- ⅓ **cup tomatoes, finely chopped**
- ¼ **cup yellow onions, finely chopped**
- 2½ **tablespoons green bell peppers, seeded and finely chopped**
- 2½ **tablespoons red bell peppers, seeded and finely chopped**
- 2½ **tablespoons yellow bell peppers, seeded and finely chopped**
- ¼ **cup green chile pepper, roasted, peeled and finely chopped**
- 3 **cloves garlic, finely chopped**
- 1 **tablespoon fresh chives, finely chopped**

- In a large bowl place the chicken broth, tomato juice and wine. Stir the ingredients together well.
- In a blender place 1½ cups of the broth mixture. Add the reserved mushroom stems and celery leaves. Blend the ingredients together for 30 seconds, or until the mixture is smooth.
- Add the blended mixture to the rest of the broth mixture, and stir it in well.
- Add the rest of the mushrooms and celery, the tomatoes, onions, bell peppers, green chile peppers and garlic. Stir them in well.
- Cover the bowl with plastic wrap and chill the soup in the refrigerator for 2 hours.
- Garnish each serving with the chives.

serves 4 to 6

Pollo Borracho

"Pollo Borracho (drunk chicken) is a South American dish that has become popular in our country. I've been making this recipe for over thirty years, and each time I do something a little bit differently. I'm sure the current version has no resemblance to the original one.....but who cares, as long as it's good!"

½ cup olive oil
6 cloves garlic, minced
1 teaspoon whole peppercorns
6 cups chicken broth
1 cup dry white wine
8 cinnamon sticks
2 cups yellow onions, finely chopped
1 cup green chile peppers, roasted, peeled and finely chopped
1 cup mushrooms, thinly sliced
½ cup pimiento peppers, diced
salt *(to taste)*
4 cups cooked chicken, cut into chunks
1 cup pitted black olives
1 cup stuffed green olives
4 cups cooked brown rice

- In a medium large stockpot place the oil, garlic, peppercorns, chicken broth, wine and cinnamon sticks. Simmer the ingredients on low heat for 2 hours.
- Add the onions, green chile peppers, mushrooms, pimientos and salt. Stir them in well. While stirring occasionally, simmer the ingredients for 1 hour.
- Add the chicken, black olives and green olives. Stir them in well. While stirring occasionally, simmer the mixture for 2 hours. Remove the cinnamon sticks.
- On each of 4 individual plates place the brown rice. Spoon the chicken mixture on top.

serves 4

"My desire to cook is a barometer of my emotional state. If I am depressed, I don't cook at all. But if I'm happy, then I really cook up a storm!"

Nina Meyers

El Rincón Chicken Curry

"I use a lot of curry powder in this dish because it needs to be very spicy. The apricots, raisins and apples are a nice complement to the heat."

- **6 cups chicken broth**
- **3 tablespoons curry powder**
- **3 cups celery, finely chopped**
- **2 cups yellow onions, finely chopped**
- **1 cup apples, peeled, cored and finely chopped**
- **1 cup fresh mushrooms, sliced**
- **½ cup dried apricots, finely chopped**
- **¼ cup raisins**
- **2 whole chicken breasts, cooked, skin and bones removed, and cut into chunks**
- **salt** *(to taste)*
- **4 cups cooked brown rice**

- In a medium stockpot place the chicken broth and curry powder, and stir them together well. Heat them on high until the liquid boils.
- Add the celery, onions, apples, mushrooms, apricots and raisins. Stir the ingredients well. Reduce the heat to low and simmer the mixture for 1 hour.
- Add the chicken and salt, and stir them in well.
- Spoon the mixture on top of the rice.

serves 4

"I was born and raised in Taos, although I spent many of my adult years in different foreign countries. But now I am back to stay for good, and it is the only place on earth I want to be."

Nina Meyers

Crockpot Frijoles

"The native people in New Mexico cook very simply, as exemplified by this recipe. If you look at the ingredients, you might wonder how these beans could taste so good.....but they do! The chicos (dried corn) can be found in the Spanish section of your grocery store."

2 **cups pinto beans, rinsed**
1 **3-ounce bag chicos** *(dried corn)*
1 **medium yellow onion, peeled**
6 **cups water**
salt *(to taste)*

- In a 5-quart crockpot place all of the ingredients. Cook them on low overnight *(covered)*.
- In the morning remove the onion and discard it.
- Mash the beans in the crockpot with a potato masher.
- Turn the crockpot on high. Cook the beans for 4 hours *(without the lid)*. Add the salt and mix it in.

serves 4 to 6

"It is hard for me to write down recipes because I cook from memory and from what is on hand in the kitchen. Every day I make a big pot of something good, and keep it simmering on the stove so that my staff and my family can help themselves as they wish."

Nina Meyers

Four Kachinas Inn

512 Webber Street
Santa Fe, New Mexico 87501
(505) 982-2550 • (800) 397-2564
John Daw & Andrew Beckerman, Innkeepers

This recently completed inn with its own private courtyard is on a quiet residential street within walking distance of the Santa Fe Plaza. The ground floor rooms have individual garden patios and the upstairs room has lovely views of the Sangre de Cristo Mountains. All the rooms have private baths and entrances, handmade furniture and various examples of American Indian art. A unique touch is the guest lounge, an old adobe building outfitted as a Southwestern trading post.

Recipes

Eggplant Parmigiana

"I've been making this dish for many, many years, and it's always a crowd-pleaser. Some recipes for eggplant parmigiana are more complex, but this one is quite easy."

- **2 eggs, beaten**
- **1 large clove garlic, minced**
- **½ teaspoon dried oregano**
- **¼ teaspoon dried basil**
- **1 cup dried bread crumbs, seasoned and crushed**
- **1 large eggplant, sliced into ¼" thick rounds**
- **2 cups olive oil** *(or as needed)*
- **3 cups tomato sauce**
- **½ pound fresh mushrooms, thinly sliced and lightly sautéed**
- **12 ounces mozzarella cheese, thinly sliced**
- **2 ounces Parmesan cheese, grated**

- Preheat the oven to 325°.
- In a medium bowl place the eggs, garlic, oregano and basil. Mix them together well.
- In another medium bowl place the bread crumbs.
- Dip each slice of eggplant first into the egg mixture and then into the bread crumbs, so that it is well coated.
- In a large skillet place the olive oil so that it is ½" deep. Heat it on medium low so that it is hot *(but not smoking)*. Place the eggplant rounds in the skillet and fry them for 2 minutes on each side, or until they are lightly browned and tender *(make sure the oil depth maintains at ½")*.
- Place ½ of the eggplant rounds in a large greased baking pan.
- In this order, layer on ½ of the tomato sauce, mushrooms, mozzarella cheese and Parmesan cheese.
- Use the rest of the eggplant and repeat the layering in the same order.
- Bake the eggplant for 45 minutes, or until the cheese is bubbly and everything is hot.

serves 8

New Mexican Baked Chicken Breasts

"These days everyone feels too guilty to enjoy my fried chicken, so I serve this as a low-fat alternative. It is delicious, and so easy to make."

2 large eggs
1/4 cup salsa *(your favorite)*
1 clove garlic, minced
1 1/2 cups seasoned dried bread crumbs
2 teaspoons red chile powder
2 teaspoons ground cumin
1 teaspoon dried oregano
8 chicken breast halves, skin and bones removed
6 tablespoons olive oil
1 cup sour cream
1 cup salsa
1 large avocado, peeled, pitted and cut into 8 slices
4 scallions, finely chopped

- Preheat the oven to 375°.
- In a medium bowl place the eggs, the 1/4 cup of salsa and the garlic. Mix the ingredients together well.
- In another medium bowl place the bread crumbs, chile powder, cumin and oregano. Stir the ingredients together well.
- Dip each piece of chicken first into the egg mixture and then into the bread crumbs so that each one is well coated.
- Pour the oil into a large baking dish. Place the chicken in the baking dish with the top side down so that it is coated with the oil. Turn the chicken over so that the top side is facing up.
- Bake the chicken for 25 minutes, or until it is done.
- On each of 8 individual plates place one piece of the chicken.
- Top each piece with a dollop of sour cream and some of the 1 cup of salsa.
- Garnish the dish with a slice of avocado and a sprinkling of scallions.

serves 8

Four Kachinas Inn

Old Fashioned Pan Rolls

"Have these rolls baking as your friends arrive for dinner, because they will make the whole house smell good. We serve them for breakfast with plenty of butter and jam."

2	**packages active dry yeast**
½	**cup warm water**
4½	**cups flour**
¼	**cup sugar**
1	**teaspoon salt**
1	**cup butter, melted**
1	**egg, lightly beaten**
1	**cup warm milk**

- In a large bowl place the yeast and water. Let them sit for 15 minutes, or until the mixture is bubbly.
- In a medium bowl place 2 cups of the flour, the sugar and salt. Mix them together well.
- To the yeast mixture add the flour mixture, 5 tablespoons of the butter, the egg and milk. Beat the ingredients together with an electric mixer for 5 minutes.
- While beating constantly, slowly add the remaining 2½ cups of flour.
- Cover the bowl with a cloth and place it in a warm place for 45 minutes, or until the dough is double in size.
- Beat the dough down with your fist.
- Pour ½ of the remaining butter into a medium baking pan. Tilt the pan so that the entire bottom is well coated.
- Drop the dough into the baking pan so that 12 rolls are formed.
- Drizzle the rest of the butter over the rolls.
- Preheat the oven to 425°.
- Cover the pan with a damp cloth and place it in a warm place for 30 minutes, or until the dough is almost double in size.
- Bake the rolls for 15 minutes, or until they are browned.

makes 12 rolls

Potato Cinnamon Buns

"Our repeat guests always insist that we serve these buns. Even our new guests ask for them because they have heard from others how good they are."

1 large potato, boiled, peeled and mashed
1 cup milk
3/4 cup butter, melted
1/4 cup sugar
1/2 teaspoon salt
1/4 cup warm water
1 tablespoon sugar
1 package active dry yeast
4 1/2 cups flour
1 egg
1 teaspoon vanilla extract
1/2 cup brown sugar, packed
1/4 cup sugar
3 teaspoons ground cinnamon
1 cup powdered sugar
2 tablespoons butter, melted
1/8 teaspoon ground cinnamon
1/2 teaspoon vanilla extract
hot water *(as necessary)*

- In a medium saucepan place the potato and milk, and stir them together well.
- Add 4 tablespoons of the butter, the first 1/4 cup of sugar and the salt. Stir the ingredients together over low heat until they are lukewarm. Remove the mixture from the heat and set it aside.
- In a large bowl place the 1/4 cup of warm water, the 1 tablespoon of sugar and the yeast. Stir the ingredients together and let them sit for 15 minutes, or until the mixture is bubbly.
- Add the potato mixture, 2 cups of the flour, the egg and the 1 teaspoon of vanilla. Beat the ingredients together with an electric mixer so that they are well blended.
- While beating constantly, slowly add 2 more cups of the flour so that a dough is formed.
- Place the dough on a heavily floured surface and knead it for 10 minutes, or until it is smooth *(add the remaining flour as necessary)*.
- Place the dough in a large oiled bowl and turn it so that it is well coated with the oil. Cover the bowl with a towel and set it in a warm place for 1 hour, or until the dough is double in size.
- Place the dough on a lightly floured surface and punch it down. Knead it 3 times, or until the air is expelled.
- Roll out the dough to form a 15" x 18" rectangle.
- In a small bowl place the brown sugar, the second 1/4 cup of sugar and the 3 teaspoons of cinnamon. Stir them together well.
- Brush the rectangle with 1/2 of the remaining melted butter. Sprinkle the cinnamon mixture on top.
- Roll the rectangle up so that a log is formed. Slice it into 12 equal pieces.
- Place the pieces on a greased baking pan. Brush the rest of the melted butter on top.

(continued on next page)

- Preheat the oven to 375°.
- Cover the rolls with a cloth and set them in a warm place for 30 minutes, or until they are almost double in size.
- Bake the rolls for 20 to 30 minutes, or until they are richly browned.
- Remove them from the oven and let them cool for 5 minutes.
- In a small bowl place the powdered sugar, the 2 tablespoons of melted butter, the ⅛ teaspoon of cinnamon and the ½ teaspoon of vanilla. Mix them together so that they are smooth *(add the hot water as necessary)*.
- Remove the rolls from the pan and drizzle the icing on top.

makes 12 cinnamon buns

"I'm a self-taught cook and have a natural flair for putting together dishes. Ever since I can remember, whenever I taste a great dish I always have the urge to try it in my kitchen and make it better."

John Daw

Lemon Poppy Seed Muffins

"I got this recipe off the back of a butter box, and they are a favorite at our inn."

- 2 **cups flour**
- ½ **cup sugar**
- 2½ **teaspoons baking powder**
- ½ **teaspoon salt**
- ½ **teaspoon ground nutmeg**
- 5 **tablespoons poppy seeds**
- 1 **lemon, zested** *(outer yellow part grated off)*
- 1 **cup milk**
- 2 **eggs**
- 2 **egg yolks**
- ½ **teaspoon lemon extract**
- ⅓ **cup butter, melted**

- Preheat the oven to 400°.
- In a large bowl place the flour, sugar, baking powder, salt, nutmeg and poppy seeds. Stir the ingredients together well. Add the lemon zest and stir it in.
- In a medium bowl place the milk, eggs, egg yolks and lemon extract. Whisk them together well.
- While whisking constantly, add the butter and blend it in.
- Add the liquid mixture to the dry mixture, and stir them together so that the batter is just moistened, but still lumpy.
- Fill 12 individual greased muffin tins with the batter so that they are ⅔ full.
- Bake them for 15 minutes, or until a wooden toothpick inserted in the center comes out clean.
- Immediately remove the muffins from the tins and let them cool.

makes 12 muffins

"I worked in the social services for most of my life, and find that running a Bed & Breakfast is just another way of serving people. However, now I serve people who are happy and in a good mood, instead of working with those who are burdened.....so it's about ten times as relaxing."

John Daw

Kachina Scones

"I once had a guest from Nashville who told me that these scones were so exquisite that they brought tears to her eyes."

2 cups flour
2 tablespoons sugar
2 teaspoons baking powder
½ teaspoon salt
½ cup butter, softened
1 egg
½ cup half & half
2 tablespoons half & half

- Preheat the oven to 425°.
- In a large bowl place the flour, sugar, baking powder and salt, and mix them together well.
- Add the butter and cut it in with a pastry blender so that coarse crumbs are formed.
- Make a well in the center of the crumbs.
- In a small bowl place the egg and the ½ cup of half & half, and whisk them together well.
- Pour the egg mixture into the well of the crumb mixture. Mix them together with a fork so that a soft dough is formed.
- Place the dough on a lightly floured surface and knead it 3 times.
- Form the dough into a circle that is ¾" thick and 8" in diameter.
- Cut the circle into 8 wedges.
- Place the wedges on a lightly greased cookie sheet.
- Brush the tops with the 2 tablespoons of half & half.
- Bake the scones for 12 minutes, or until they are lightly browned.

serves 4

"I find that running a Bed & Breakfast is every bit as satisfying as being an architect, which was my previous profession. I like being self-employed, meeting new people, and having flexible hours."

Andrew Beckerman

Sour Cream Crumb Cake

"This is a moist, flavorful coffee cake that has a delicious, crumbly topping. It's very quick and easy to make."

1½ cups flour
½ cup white sugar
2 teaspoons baking powder
½ teaspoon baking soda
¼ teaspoon salt
1 cup sour cream
2 eggs, slightly beaten
½ cup butter, melted
1 teaspoon vanilla extract
2 tablespoons flour
2 tablespoons plain dry bread crumbs
2 tablespoons butter
5 tablespoons brown sugar
1 teaspoon ground cinnamon

- Preheat the oven to 350°.
- In a large bowl place the 1½ cups of flour, the white sugar, baking powder, baking soda and salt. Sift the ingredients together.
- In a medium bowl place the sour cream, eggs, melted butter and vanilla. Stir the ingredients together well.
- Add the sour cream mixture to the flour mixture, and stir them together so that the batter is just moistened and lumpy.
- Pour the batter into a greased square baking pan.
- In a small bowl place the 2 tablespoons of flour, the bread crumbs, butter, brown sugar and cinnamon. Cut the ingredients together with a pastry blender so that crumbs are formed.
- Sprinkle the crumbs on top of the batter.
- Bake the cake for 20 minutes, or until the top is browned and the sides pull away from the pan.

serves 4

Four Kachinas Inn

Kachina Cookies

"We serve these cookies with tea every afternoon in the lounge, and our guests just gobble them up. I have been told that they get stuffed into ski parka pockets during the winter for an energy-packed mid-morning snack!"

3½ cups flour
1 teaspoon baking soda
1 teaspoon salt
2 sticks butter, softened
1 cup white sugar
1 cup brown sugar, packed
1 egg
1 cup vegetable oil
1 teaspoon vanilla extract
1 cup rolled oats
1 cup corn flakes, crushed
1 6-ounce package mini chocolate chips
½ cup shredded coconut
½ cup walnuts, finely chopped

- Preheat the oven to 325°.
- In a small bowl place the flour, baking soda and salt. Stir them together well and set the bowl aside.
- In a large bowl place the butter, white sugar and brown sugar. Beat them together with an electric mixer until they are creamy.
- Add the egg and oil, and mix them in well.
- Add the flour mixture and mix it in.
- Add the vanilla, oats, corn flakes, chocolate chips, coconut and walnuts. Stir the ingredients together well.
- Form the dough into 1" balls.
- Place the balls on ungreased cookie sheets and flatten them out slightly with a spatula.
- Bake the cookies for 15 minutes, or until they are lightly browned.
- Let the cookies cool on the sheets for 2 minutes.
- Remove them from the sheets and let them cool completely before storing them.

makes approximately 8 dozen cookies

Four Kachinas Inn

Best of Show Coconut Pound Cake

"This recipe is from an old Junior League of Amarillo cookbook. In 1992 we made it for the Santa Fe County Fair, and it won Best of Show! It is delicious and freezes beautifully."

3 cups flour
2 cups sugar
1 small can evaporated milk with water added to make 1 cup
3 sticks butter, melted
1 teaspoon almond extract
1 teaspoon vanilla extract
5 eggs
7 ounces angel-flake coconut

- Preheat the oven to 325°.
- In a large bowl place the flour and sugar, and mix them together.
- Add the evaporated milk, butter, almond extract and vanilla extract. Beat the ingredients together so that a smooth batter is formed.
- Add 1 egg at a time and blend each one in well.
- Add the coconut and gently fold it in.
- Pour the batter into 4 greased and floured small loaf pans.
- Bake the loaves for 1 hour, or until a wooden toothpick inserted in the center comes out clean.
- Let the loaves cool for 5 minutes. Turn them out onto a wire rack and let them cool completely.

makes 4 small loaves

"We have a dog named Ernie who provides therapy for guests who miss their pets. They snuggle and play with him, and he gives them their 'dog fix'."

Andrew Beckerman

Easy Whiskey Cake

"If you want a fast, easy, delicious dessert, here it is! I don't mind using packaged mixes with fresh ingredients when they come out tasting as good as this cake."

1 package premium yellow cake mix
1 small package instant vanilla pudding
5 eggs, lightly beaten
¾ cup vegetable oil
½ cup bourbon whiskey
½ cup milk
1 cup walnuts
½ cup mini chocolate chips

- Preheat the oven to 350°.
- In a large bowl place the cake mix, pudding, eggs, oil, whiskey and milk. Mix the ingredients together well.
- Add the walnuts and chocolate chips, and mix them in well.
- Pour the batter into a greased and floured bundt pan.
- Bake the cake for 45 minutes to 1 hour, or until a wooden toothpick inserted in the center comes out clean.
- Remove the cake from the oven and let it cool in the pan for 10 minutes.
- Turn it out onto a wire rack to let it cool completely.

serves 8 to 10

"Santa Fe is a very stimulating community. In many ways it reminds me of the San Francisco Bay Area, my previous home, in terms of its cultural richness and natural beauty."

John Daw

The Galisteo Inn

HC 75 Box 4
Galisteo, New Mexico 87540
(505) 466-4000
Wayne Aarniokoski & Joanna Kaufman, Innkeepers • Kirstin Jarrett, Chef

This 240-year-old adobe hacienda is in the magical village of Galisteo, a Spanish colonial outpost founded in 1614, twenty-three miles southeast of Santa Fe. The Southwestern-style rooms include many of the original eighteenth century features. In this serene atmosphere, guests shed today's stresses and relax in a 50-foot lap pool, an outdoor hot tub, an indoor sauna and the surrounding desert. Therapeutic massage, horseback riding and the inn's famous dinners are also available.

Recipes

Skillet Branded Corn Soup

"Full of delicious, subtle tastes, this soup is an excellent vegetarian dish. By searing the corn you get a rich, toasty flavor, which combines with the other ingredients in a most delightful way."

6 fresh ears of corn, husks removed
1 cup yellow onions, thinly sliced
¾ cup red bell peppers, seeded and chopped
1 poblano chile pepper, roasted, peeled and chopped
8 cups vegetable broth
¼ cup lime juice, freshly squeezed
1 teaspoon red chile powder
¼ teaspoon ground cumin
salt and pepper *(to taste)*
½ cup fresh cilantro, coarsely chopped
Avocado Salsa *(recipe follows)*

- In a large cast-iron skillet that is heated on high, place the ears of corn. Sear them so that they are dark on all sides and then remove them. Let them cool. Remove the kernels *(save the cobs)*.
- In a medium bowl place the corn, onions, bell peppers and poblano chile peppers. Set the bowl aside.
- In a large stockpot place the corn cobs and the vegetable broth, and bring them to a boil over high heat. Reduce the heat to low and simmer the ingredients for 5 minutes. Remove the cobs and discard them.
- Add the corn mixture, lime juice, chile powder, cumin, salt and pepper. Stir the ingredients together well. Simmer the soup for 10 minutes.
- Add the cilantro.
- Garnish each serving of soup with a dollop of the Avocado Salsa.

serves 6 to 8

Avocado Salsa

"Fresh, healthy and crunchy, this salsa can be used with any egg, fish, fowl or meat entrée. It's also good with chips, or just spread on a tortilla."

¼ cup red onions, finely chopped
2 Roma tomatoes, seeded and coarsely chopped
1 jalapeño chile pepper, seeded and finely chopped
1 tablespoon lime juice, freshly squeezed
salt and pepper *(to taste)*
2 ripe avocados, peeled, pitted and coarsely chopped

- In a medium bowl place all of the ingredients *(except for the avocados)* and stir them together well.
- Add the avocados and gently toss them in.

makes approximately 2 cups

Tomatillo Rice

"The crunchy texture of the raw vegetables and the tang of the rice vinegar elevate an ordinary brown rice to a brand-new level. When you eat it you will feel its strength and sit up a little straighter!"

2 pounds tomatillos, husks removed, quartered and roasted in a 375° oven for 15 minutes
1 cup red onions, chopped medium
¾ cup red bell peppers, seeded and coarsely chopped
1 cup fresh cilantro, chopped
¼ cup rice vinegar
¼ cup canola oil
1 tablespoon lime juice, freshly squeezed
salt and pepper *(to taste)*
2 tablespoons olive oil
2 cups cooked brown rice

- In a large bowl place the tomatillos, onions, bell peppers, cilantro, vinegar, canola oil, lime juice, salt and pepper. Toss the ingredients together well.
- In a large skillet place the olive oil and heat it on medium until it is hot. Add the tomatillo mixture and sauté it for 2 minutes.
- Add the rice and sauté it until everything is hot.

serves 4

"I get my ideas for recipes by looking at a piece of food and then imagining how to fix it so that I would be happy eating it. I want my food to make me feel good physically, mentally, emotionally and spiritually. I believe that I was born to work with food, just as an artist knows that she was born to paint."

Kirstin Jarrett

Spicy Gazpacho

"This is a wonderful gazpacho that has a rich, smoky, hot flavor of the chipotle chile peppers. If they are available, I will use different colored tomatoes so that the soup looks as good as it tastes."

- **1 32-ounce bottle tomato juice**
- **8 Roma tomatoes, chopped**
- **2 jalapeño chile peppers**
- **1 cucumber, peeled, seeded and chopped**
- **½ medium red onion, chopped**
- **2 cloves garlic**
- **½ bunch fresh cilantro**
- **2 limes, juiced**
- **1 tablespoon juice from chipotle chile peppers in adobo sauce** *(or to taste)*
- **½ teaspoon cayenne pepper** *(or to taste)*
- **½ teaspoon white pepper** *(or to taste)*
- **1 teaspoon salt** *(or to taste)*

- In a food processor, alternately process part of the tomato juice with part of the rest of the ingredients so that a fairly smooth soup is formed.
- Repeat this process until all of the ingredients are incorporated.

serves 8

"We call our chef, Kirstin, the 'Kitchen Angel'. She is the most excellent young person I have ever known, and possesses an extraordinary way with food. We are blessed to have her."

Joanna Kaufman

Chipotle Mashed Potatoes

"Smooth and creamy, with a spicy little bite from the chipotle chile pepper juice, these mashed potatoes are loved by everyone. I leave the skins on for nutrition, and mash the potatoes until there is not a lump left."

- 8 **large baking potatoes** *(skins on)*, **diced medium, boiled and drained**
- ½ **cup sour cream**
- ¼ **cup buttermilk**
- ¼ **cup milk**
- 2 **chipotle chile peppers** *(in adobo sauce)*, **finely chopped**
- **salt and pepper** *(to taste)*
- ½ **cup white cheddar cheese, grated**

- In a large bowl place the potatoes, sour cream, buttermilk, milk, chipotle chile peppers, salt and pepper.
- Mash everything together well.
- Sprinkle the cheese on top.

serves 8 to 10

"Our beautiful and peaceful town of Galisteo has a sense of continuity of time. The buildings are hundreds of years old, everything is handmade, and families have lived here for generations. Even though it is located just twenty minutes from Santa Fe, we feel like we live in another world."

Joanna Kaufman

Roasted Eggplant & Artichoke Lasagna

"This is an exciting, healthy variation of a basic lasagna recipe. People just love its flavor and texture, and the fact that they do not feel full or heavy after having eaten it."

2 medium eggplants, peeled, sliced lengthwise, soaked in salted water and drained
1 pound ricotta cheese
½ pound cottage cheese
½ cup Parmesan cheese, freshly grated
1 cup fresh Italian parsley, chopped
1½ teaspoons red chile flakes
salt and pepper
1 cup artichoke hearts, drained and quartered
½ cup yellow onions, chopped medium
2 tablespoons balsamic vinegar
1 tablespoon fresh garlic, finely chopped
¼ cup olive oil
⅓ cup yellow onions, finely chopped
⅓ cup carrots, finely chopped
⅓ cup celery, finely chopped
2 cloves garlic, finely chopped
12 Roma tomatoes, coarsely chopped
1 tablespoon fresh basil, chopped
1 pound lasagna noodles, cooked al dente and drained

- Preheat the oven to 375°.
- On a cookie sheet place the eggplant slices. Roast them for 15 minutes, or until they are lightly browned. Set the eggplant aside. *(Leave the oven on.)*
- In a medium large bowl place the ricotta, cottage cheese, Parmesan cheese, parsley, red chile flakes, salt and pepper. Blend them together well. Set the bowl aside.
- In a medium bowl place the artichoke hearts, the ½ cup of onions, the vinegar and the 1 tablespoon of garlic. Mix them together. Set the bowl aside.
- In a large skillet place the oil and heat it on medium until it is hot. Add the ⅓ cup of onions, the carrots, celery and the 2 cloves of garlic. Sauté the vegetables for 5 minutes, or until they are tender.
- Add the tomatoes and stir them in. Reduce the heat to low and simmer the ingredients for 5 minutes.
- Add the basil and stir it in.
- Place the mixture in a food processor and purée it until it is smooth.
- In a large oiled baking pan place a small amount of the purée and spread it out evenly on the bottom. In this order, make a layer of ⅓ of the noodles, ½ of the cheese mixture, all of the roasted eggplant, ⅓ of the noodles, the rest of the cheese mixture, the artichokes, the rest of the noodles, and the rest of the purée.
- Cover the pan with foil and bake the lasagna for 30 minutes, or until it is well heated.

serves 8

Chile Seared Salmon in Cucumber Cream with Tomato Relish

"This is an extraordinary, original way to serve salmon. The heat of the red chile and cumin coating is perfectly complemented by the cool Cucumber Cream and the tangy Tomato Relish."

Chile Seared Salmon

- 1 **tablespoon red chile powder**
- 2 **teaspoons ground cumin**
- 2 **teaspoons fresh ground pepper**
- **salt** *(to taste)*
- 8 **6-ounce salmon steaks**
- 1 **tablespoon canola oil**
- **Cucumber Cream** *(recipe follows)*
- **Tomato Relish** *(recipe on next page)*

- In a small bowl place the red chile powder, cumin, pepper and salt. Mix them together well. Sprinkle the spices on both sides of the salmon.
- In a large nonstick skillet place the oil and heat it on medium until it is hot. Sear the salmon for 2 minutes on each side, or until the desired doneness is achieved.
- On each of 8 individual serving plates pour the Cucumber Cream. Place a salmon steak in the center. Place the Tomato Relish on top of the salmon so that it cascades down one side.

serves 8

Cucumber Cream

- 8 **ounces plain yogurt**
- 1½ **cups cucumbers, peeled, seeded and coarsely chopped**
- ½ **cup fresh spinach, washed, deveined and chopped**
- 2 **tablespoons fresh dill weed**
- 1 **tablespoon lemon juice, freshly squeezed**
- ¼ **teaspoon cayenne pepper**
- **salt and fresh ground pepper** *(to taste)*

- In a blender place all of the ingredients and purée them so that they are smooth.

makes approximately 3 cups

Tomato Relish

- **10** **Roma tomatoes, seeded and sliced lengthwise into thin strips**
- **¾** **cup green bell peppers, seeded and thinly sliced**
- **1** **medium cucumber, peeled, seeded and thinly sliced**
- **1** **green chile pepper, seeded and thinly sliced**
- **1** **leek, white part only, thinly sliced**
- **¼** **cup canola oil**
- **2** **tablespoons fresh Italian parsley, chopped**
- **2** **tablespoons fresh dill weed, chopped**
- **2** **tablespoons red wine vinegar**
- **1** **tablespoon Creole mustard**
- **salt and fresh ground pepper** *(to taste)*

- In a medium bowl place all of the ingredients and toss them together well.
- Cover the bowl with plastic wrap and chill it in the refrigerator for 30 minutes.

makes approximately 3 cups

"Perhaps seventy-five percent of the food that I eat consists of what I call 'live food', which essentially means 'uncooked'. This does not mean just eating a raw apple, but rather cutting the apple up and then mixing it in with a lot of other 'live' ingredients. I find this formula keeps me energetic and alert, and aids in digestion."

Kirstin Jarrett

Corn & Green Chile Stuffed Roasted Game Hen

"When I was a little girl I used to get very excited when my father stuffed game hens for our dinner. I would tell him to put all these different ingredients in them, and he was kind enough to humor me. This recipe is a product of my upbringing, and it is wonderful. The corn steams inside the hens, and keeps them moist."

- **1 tablespoon canola oil**
- **1 large yellow onion, diced medium**
- **4 cloves garlic, thinly sliced**
- **12 ears corn, kernels removed**
- **1 pound green chile peppers, roasted, peeled and julienned**
- **1 red bell pepper, seeded and diced medium**
- **1 package cornbread crumbs**
- **1 egg, lightly beaten**
- **¼ cup fresh sage, chopped**
- **¼ cup fresh cilantro, chopped**
- **¼ cup fresh oregano, chopped**
- **½ teaspoon cayenne pepper**
- **½ teaspoon pepper**
- **1 teaspoon salt**
- **8 game hens, washed in cold water, dried, seasoned with salt and pepper inside and out, and lightly oiled on the outside**
- **¼ cup canola oil**

- Preheat the oven to 350°.
- In a large sauté pan place the 1 tablespoon of oil and heat it on medium high until it is hot. Add the onions and garlic, and sauté them for 5 minutes, or until the onions are translucent.
- Add the corn and sauté it for 2 minutes. Remove the pan from the heat. Transfer the mixture to a medium large bowl.
- Add the green chile peppers, bell peppers and cornbread crumbs. Mix them in well.
- Add the egg, sage, cilantro, oregano, cayenne pepper, pepper and salt. Mix everything together.
- Loosely stuff each hen with the mixture.
- To the sauté pan add the ¼ cup of oil and heat it on medium high until it is hot. Sear the hens so that they are golden brown all over.
- Place the hens in a roasting pan.
- Roast them for 30 minutes, or until they are done.

serves 8

Blackened Ribeye with Roasted Vegetable Salsa

"The seasonings on the Blackened Ribeye add a lively, spicy Southwest flavor that is perfectly complemented by the rich, roasted taste of the salsa. You can make this spice mix in larger amounts, and then store it in a jar with a tight-fitting lid for future use on chicken, meat or fish.

Blackened Ribeye

- 1 **tablespoon ground cumin**
- 1 **tablespoon ground dried oregano**
- 1 **tablespoon ground coriander**
- 1 **tablespoon red chile pepper**
- 1 **teaspoon cayenne pepper**
- ½ **tablespoon pepper**
- 2 **tablespoons kosher salt**
- 8 **ribeye steaks**
- 2 **tablespoons canola oil** *(or as needed)*
- **Roasted Vegetable Salsa** *(recipe follows)*

- In a flat bowl place all of the spices and seasonings, and mix them together well. Dredge each steak in the mixture so that it is well coated on both sides.
- In a large heavy skillet place the oil and heat it on medium until it is hot. Sear the steaks on both sides so that the desired doneness is achieved.
- Serve the steaks with the Roasted Vegetable Salsa on top.

serves 8

Roasted Vegetable Salsa

- 4 **ears fresh corn, husked, grilled and kernels removed**
- 1 **green bell pepper, roasted, peeled, seeded and chopped**
- 1 **red bell pepper, roasted, peeled, seeded and chopped**
- 1 **poblano chile pepper, roasted, peeled and chopped**
- 1 **large red onion, peeled, roasted and thinly sliced**
- ½ **cup fresh cilantro, chopped**
- 2 **tablespoons lime juice, freshly squeezed**
- 1 **teaspoon red chile powder**
- **salt and pepper** *(to taste)*

- In a medium bowl place all of the ingredients and toss them together well.

makes approximately 3 cups

Fried Pineapple & Orange Tostada

"Although this is not an overly sweet dish, I serve it for dessert. People are delighted with the presentation, and get a kick out of the unusual treatment of a Mexican tostada."

1 fresh pineapple, peeled, cored and thinly sliced
4 oranges, peeled, sliced into ¼" rounds and seeds removed
4 tablespoons brown sugar
½ teaspoon ground cardamom
½ teaspoon ground cinnamon
2 tablespoons butter *(or as needed)*
8 flour tortillas, cut into wedges
⅓ cup powdered sugar
8 leaves fresh mint, thinly sliced

- Heat a large skillet on medium high until it is hot. Add the pineapple and orange slices so they do not overlap. Sprinkle on the brown sugar, cardamom and cinnamon. Cook the fruit slices until they are browned on one side. Turn the slices over and cook them until the juice is evaporated. Remove the skillet from the heat and set it aside.
- In a medium skillet place some of the butter and heat it on medium until it is melted and hot.
- Fry the tortilla wedges in the butter for 2 minutes on each side, or until they are crisp.
- Spoon the fruit on top of ½ of the wedges. Place another wedge in the fruit so that it stands up.
- Sprinkle on the powdered sugar and mint.
- Place the wedges on 8 individual dessert plates.

serves 8

"We bring pleasure to many people, especially to those who are stressed out from their fast-paced lives. Here at the Galisteo Inn they find tranquillity and peace, and enjoy being pampered, eating excellent food, and feeling their tensions melting away."

Joanna Kaufman

Roasted Banana Sundae with Piñon Chocolate Sauce

"This dessert brings out a childlike delight in even the most sophisticated of restaurant connoisseurs. After all, who can resist a gourmet banana sundae covered with a rich chocolate-nut sauce!"

Roasted Banana Sundae

- 8 **bananas, peeled and sliced in half lengthwise**
- 2 **tablespoons butter, melted**
- 2 **tablespoons pure maple syrup**
- 2 **tablespoons dark rum**
- 8 **scoops vanilla ice cream**
- **Piñon Chocolate Sauce** *(recipe follows)*

- Preheat the oven to 375°.
- In a medium baking pan place the bananas. Pour the butter, syrup and rum on top. Cover the pan with foil and bake the bananas for 10 to 15 minutes, or until the topping is bubbly and hot.
- In each of 8 individual dessert cups place a scoop of the ice cream. Place 2 banana halves in the cup so that they are slightly standing. Pour the Piñon Chocolate Sauce on top.

serves 8

Piñon Chocolate Sauce

- 1 **cup water**
- ¾ **cup sugar**
- 1 **cup Dutch cocoa powder**
- 1 **teaspoon vanilla extract**
- ½ **cup piñon nuts** *(pine nuts)*, **lightly toasted in the oven**

- In a medium saucepan place the water and sugar, and heat them on medium until the sugar is dissolved. While stirring constantly, raise the heat to high and boil the liquid for 1 minute. Remove the pan from the heat.
- Add the cocoa and whisk it in.
- Reduce the heat to medium and return the pan to the stove. Whisk the sauce for 3 to 5 minutes, or until it is smooth.
- Remove the pan from the heat. Add the vanilla and piñon nuts, and stir them in.

makes approximately 3 cups

Grant Corner Inn

122 Grant Avenue
Santa Fe, New Mexico 87501
(505) 983-6678
Louise Stewart & Pat Walter, Innkeepers

As most Santa Fe old-timers know, Colonial mansions have, for at least a century, been as much a part of the streetscape as Pueblo and Territorial-style homes. This recently renovated inn, two blocks from the Plaza, is an exquisite example, beautifully and comfortably decorated with brass and four-poster beds, antique quilts, armoires.....and a rabbit collection. The sumptuous breakfasts are renowned.

Recipes

Lime Jalapeño Hollandaise Sauce

"Tangy from the lime juice and spicy from the jalapeño, this is a Hollandaise Sauce that makes people sit up and take notice."

5 egg yolks
2 teaspoons jalapeño chile peppers, chopped
1 tablespoon lime juice, freshly squeezed
¼ teaspoon salt
1 stick unsalted butter, melted

- In a food processor place the egg yolks, jalapeño chile peppers, lime juice and salt. Purée them together so that they are smooth.
- With the food processor constantly running, slowly add the butter. Purée the mixture for 1 minute, or until it is thick.
- Heat the sauce so that it is warm.

makes approximately 1 cup

Pat's Cranberry Salsa

"I'm a real cranberry lover, and so this salsa is one of my favorite condiments. Serve it instead of a traditional cranberry sauce with a turkey dinner. I even like it on chicken fried steaks!"

2 cups dried cranberries, chopped
1 cup fresh kumquats, thinly sliced
½ cup balsamic vinegar
3 scallions, finely chopped
⅓ cup white onions, finely chopped
½ cup fresh cilantro, chopped

- In a medium bowl place all of the ingredients and stir them together well.
- Cover the bowl and refrigerate the salsa for at least 1 hour.

makes approximately 3½ cups

"As I get older, nutrition becomes more important to me. However, I do not believe in being fanatical about health, as many people seem to be these days. I would rather have a dish with a few extra grams of fat than sacrifice on the taste."

Pat Walter

Pat's Chunky Salsa

"According to our guests, my salsa is world-famous amongst the Bed & Breakfast crowd. The red wine vinegar is the secret to its special flavor."

- **2 large tomatoes, coarsely chopped**
- **½ cup tomato sauce**
- **⅔ cup green chile peppers, roasted, peeled and chopped**
- **⅓ cup yellow onions, finely chopped**
- **3 tablespoons fresh cilantro, finely chopped**
- **2 tablespoons fresh parsley, finely chopped**
- **2 teaspoons red wine vinegar**
- **1 teaspoon lemon juice, freshly squeezed**
- **1 small hot dried red chile pepper, crushed**

- In a medium glass bowl place all of the ingredients. Stir them together well.
- Let the salsa sit at room temperature for 1 hour.

makes approximately 3 cups

Sausage Potato Salad

"Although I've always loved potato salads, I don't like the traditional kind that has a lot of mustard. Instead, I try to come up with more creative versions, such as this recipe, which is especially good because of the sausage."

- **1 pound Italian sausage, cooked, drained and thinly sliced**
- **6 cups potatoes, cooked, cooled and diced medium**
- **1 large cucumber, peeled, seeded and chopped small**
- **2 pimientos, chopped small**
- **3 scallions, minced**
- **1 bunch fresh cilantro, chopped**
- **1 red bell pepper, seeded and chopped**
- **2 teaspoons Dijon mustard**
- **1 cup mayonnaise**
- **½ teaspoon salt** *(or to taste)*

- In a large bowl place the sausage, potatoes, cucumbers, pimientos, scallions, cilantro and bell peppers. Toss them together well.
- In a small bowl place the mustard, mayonnaise and salt, and mix them together.
- Add the dressing to the salad and mix it in.

serves 6 to 8

Sweet Potato Croquettes with Chile Honey Sauce

"Sweet and flavorful, this makes a wonderful side dish for a turkey or wild game entrée. The Chile Honey Sauce drizzled on top really gives these croquettes the crowning touch."

Sweet Potato Croquettes

- 3 **cups fresh bread crumbs**
- ¾ **cup pecans, toasted and crushed**
- 2 **cups sweet potatoes, cooked and puréed**
- ½ **cup flour**
- ⅓ **cup brown sugar**
- 1 **tablespoon butter, melted**
- 1 **teaspoon ground nutmeg**
- 1 **teaspoon ground cinnamon**
- 1 **teaspoon salt**
- 1 **egg yolk, lightly beaten**
- 1 **tablespoon sherry**
- 2 **eggs, lightly beaten**
- 1 **cup vegetable oil** *(or as needed)*
- **Chile Honey Sauce** *(recipe follows)*

- In a large bowl place ½ of both the bread crumbs and pecans. Add the sweet potatoes, flour, sugar, butter, nutmeg, cinnamon, salt, egg yolk and sherry. Beat the ingredients so that the mixture is light.
- Refrigerate it for 2 hours.
- Shape the mixture into patties that are ½" thick and 2" in diameter.
- In a small bowl place the rest of the bread crumbs and pecans, and mix them together.
- Dip each patty first into the beaten eggs and then into the pecan-bread crumb mixture.
- In a large heavy pan place the oil and heat it on medium high until it is hot. Deep-fry the patties for 2 to 3 minutes, or until they are golden brown. Drain them on paper towels.
- Serve the patties with the Chile Honey Sauce on top.

serves 4 to 6

Chile Honey Sauce

- 2 **cups honey**
- ¾ **cup maple syrup**
- ½ **cup orange juice, freshly squeezed**
- 4 **teaspoons orange zest** *(outer orange part grated off)*
- 2 **teaspoons red chile powder** *(or to taste)*

- In a medium saucepan place all of the ingredients. Simmer them for 10 minutes.

makes approximately 3 cups

Cranberry Pumpkin Muffins

"Although these are good muffins all year around, they are especially perfect for the holiday season. The orange color of the pumpkin and the red spots of cranberries make them quite festive looking!"

- **3⅓ cups flour**
- **2 teaspoons baking soda**
- **1 teaspoon baking powder**
- **1 teaspoon salt**
- **2 teaspoons ground cinnamon**
- **1 teaspoon nutmeg**
- **2 cups puréed pumpkin**
- **½ cup milk**
- **⅔ cup oil**
- **2 cups brown sugar**
- **2 eggs, lightly beaten**
- **2½ cups dried cranberries**

- Preheat the oven to 350°.
- In a large bowl place the flour, baking soda, baking powder, salt, cinnamon and nutmeg. Mix the ingredients together and set the bowl aside.
- In a medium bowl place the pumpkin and milk, and blend them together well.
- Add the oil, brown sugar and eggs, and mix them in well.
- While constantly beating, slowly add the egg mixture to the flour mixture so that it is well combined.
- Add the cranberries and stir them in.
- Fill 36 individual paper-lined muffin tins with the batter so that they are ⅔ full.
- Bake the muffins for 40 minutes, or until a wooden toothpick inserted in the center comes out clean.

makes 3 dozen muffins

"I create my recipes strictly based on what I like to eat myself. Luckily, most of our guests like them too!"

Louise Stewart

Orange Liqueur & Poppy Seed Pancakes with B&B Sauce

"This recipe was developed as an entry for a B&B liqueur contest, where the first prize was a trip to Paris. I didn't win, but I think these pancakes are out of this world!"

Orange Liqueur & Poppy Seed Pancakes

1¼ cups flour
1½ tablespoons sugar
1½ teaspoons baking powder
¾ teaspoon salt
2 eggs, lightly beaten
1¼ cups milk
3 tablespoons butter, melted
1 tablespoon B&B liqueur
1 cup poppy seeds
2 oranges, zested *(outer orange part grated off)*
B&B Sauce *(recipe follows)*

- In a medium bowl sift together the flour, sugar, baking powder and salt.
- In a small bowl place the eggs and milk, and whisk them together.
- Add the egg mixture to the flour, and stir it in well.
- Add the butter, B&B liqueur, poppy seeds and orange zest. Stir the ingredients together well.
- Preheat a large oiled skillet so that it is hot.
- Using a ⅓ measuring cup, pour the pancakes into the skillet. Cook them for 3 minutes on each side, or until they are lightly browned. Serve them with the B&B Sauce on top.

serves 4

B&B Sauce

1 cup orange juice, freshly squeezed
1 cup brown sugar
3 tablespoons B&B liqueur
2 tablespoons orange zest

- In a medium saucepan place all of the ingredients. Heat them on medium until they are warm.

makes approximately 2 cups

Baby Greens with Citrus & Southwestern Vinaigrette

"Sweet, tangy and slightly spicy, this is a delightful salad to serve for brunch, or as a first course at an elegant dinner party."

Baby Greens with Citrus

- **2 pounds mixed baby greens, washed and dried**
- **4 large oranges, peeled, sections removed without membrane, and seeded**
- **2 ruby red grapefruits, peeled, sections removed without membrane, and seeded**
- **1 cup pitted green olives, drained**
- **1 medium red onion, very thinly sliced**
- **3/4 cup piñon nuts** *(pine nuts),* **toasted**
- **Southwestern Vinaigrette** *(recipe follows)*

- In a large salad bowl place all of the ingredients *(except for the dressing)* and gently toss them together.
- Add the Southwestern Vinaigrette and toss it in.

serves 6 to 8

Southwestern Vinaigrette

- **1/2 cup white rice vinegar**
- **3 tablespoons orange juice, freshly squeezed**
- **1 tablespoon orange zest** *(outer orange part grated off)*
- **1 clove garlic, pressed**
- **1/2 teaspoon red chile powder**
- **1 teaspoon salt**
- **1 teaspoon white pepper**
- **1 cup olive oil**

- In a food processor place all of the ingredients *(except for the olive oil)* and blend them together.
- With the processor constantly running, slowly dribble in the olive oil.

makes 2 cups

Monterey Tuna Salad

"When our guests want to pack a picnic lunch we make this tuna salad for gourmet sandwiches."

- 2 **6-ounce cans albacore tuna** *(water packed),* **drained**
- 1 **3½-ounce can water chestnuts, drained and chopped**
- 2 **tablespoons fresh cilantro, chopped**
- 1 **bunch fresh dill, chopped**
- 1 **cup mayonnaise**
- 2 **tablespoons lemon juice, freshly squeezed**

- In a medium bowl place all of the ingredients and mix them together well.

makes 4 big sandwiches

"My mother used to cook our family seven-course meals, only everything always came out of a can. I grew up thinking that all cooked vegetables were supposed to look gray. It was only later as a young adult, when I had to cook for myself, that I discovered it was possible to create dishes with fresh foods. Ever since, I've loved cooking!"

Pat Walter

Lamb-Pork Filo Twists with Orzo Pasta & Chipotle Mushroom Sauce

"If you are in the mood to make something that will really dazzle your guests, this is the dish! The presentation is as impressive as the delicious taste."

Lamb-Pork Filo Twists with Orzo Pasta

1 pound ground pork
1 pound ground lamb
1 tablespoon fresh basil, chopped
2 teaspoons fresh garlic, minced
1 teaspoon salt
½ teaspoon pepper
2 tablespoons olive oil
20 sheets filo dough, cut in half
1½ sticks butter, melted
1 pound orzo pasta, cooked al dente and drained
Chipotle Mushroom Sauce *(recipe on next page)*

- Preheat the oven to 375°.
- In a medium bowl place the pork, lamb, basil, garlic, salt and pepper. Mix the ingredients together well with your hands. Form the mixture into 1½" balls.
- In a baking pan place the oil and swirl it around so that the bottom is covered. Place the meatballs in the pan.
- Bake them for 40 minutes, or until they are done. Remove them from the oven and set them aside. *(Leave the oven on.)*
- Brush some of the melted butter on both sides of 3 of the filo dough half-sheets. Stack them together. *(Keep the remaining filo dough covered with a damp cloth.)* Place a meatball in the center of each stack and twist the ends so that they are flared. Lay it on a cookie sheet. Repeat this process for the rest of the meatballs.
- Bake the twists for 25 minutes, or until the dough is lightly browned.
- On each of 6 individual serving plates place the pasta. Place the twists on top. Pour on the Chipotle Mushroom Sauce.

serves 6

"My advice to anyone thinking of starting a Bed & Breakfast is quite simple.....work in one for a year before you make up your mind, because you may be surprised at what you find out!"

Louise Stewart

Chipotle Mushroom Sauce

1 stick butter
4 tablespoons white onions, chopped medium
½ pound fresh shiitaki mushrooms, chopped medium
1 cup beef bouillon
3 chipotle *(or habanero)* **chile peppers, chopped medium**
3 cloves garlic, chopped medium
1 teaspoon liquid smoke
salt and pepper *(to taste)*

- In a small saucepan place the butter and heat it on medium until it is melted and hot.
- Add the onions and sauté them for 5 minutes, or until they are translucent.
- Add the mushrooms and sauté them for 3 minutes, or until they are tender.
- Place the mixture in a food processor. Add the remaining ingredients and purée them so that the mixture is coarse.
- In a medium saucepan place the mixture. While stirring occasionally, heat the sauce on low for 15 minutes.

makes approximately 2 cups

"Santa Fe is the perfect town for our family. The size is ideal, the atmosphere is exciting, and the people are wonderful. Perhaps the only drawback is the abundance of juniper trees, which gives my husband horrendous allergies during the spring when they pollinate."

Louise Stewart

Spicy Stuffed Game Hens with Ancho Chile Pecan Sauce

"I love stuffing game birds with all kinds of different ingredients, and find the combination of fruits and sausage to be particularly delicious. The Ancho Chile Pecan Sauce is the perfect accompaniment, and it can be used with any fowl, lamb or pork."

Spicy Stuffed Game Hens

6 Cornish game hens, rinsed and patted dry
2 cups orange juice, freshly squeezed
1/4 cup yellow onions, chopped
1 teaspoon fresh garlic, minced
6 slices day-old bread, cubed
1 pound ground spicy sausage, cooked and drained
2 tablespoons fresh parsley, minced
1 teaspoon dried sage
1 teaspoon dried thyme
1 stick butter
1/3 cup white onions, chopped
1/2 cup apples, peeled, cored and chopped
1/2 cup pears, peeled, cored and chopped
1/2 cup red seedless grapes
1 stick butter
3 tablespoons Worcestershire sauce
Ancho Chile Pecan Sauce *(recipe on next page)*
Pat's Cranberry Salsa *(recipe on page 187)*

- In a large baking pan place the hens.
- In a small bowl place the orange juice, the 1/4 cup of yellow onions and the garlic. Stir them together and pour the mixture over the hens. Cover the pan with foil and place it in the refrigerator. Marinate the hens for 1 hour.
- Preheat the oven to 425°.
- In a large bowl place the bread, sausage, parsley, sage and thyme. Combine them together.
- In a small saucepan place the first stick of butter and heat it on medium until it is melted and hot. Add the 1/3 cup of white onions and sauté them for 5 minutes, or until they are lightly browned.
- Add the sautéed onions to the bread mixture, and mix them together well. Add the apples, pears and grapes, and stir them in.
- Pour the marinade off the hens into a medium bowl and set it aside.
- Stuff the hens with the bread and fruit mixture.
- In the same small saucepan place the second stick of butter and heat it on medium until it is melted and hot. Add the Worcestershire sauce and stir it in well. Add this mixture to the reserved marinade, and blend them together.
- Pour the liquid over the hens. Cover the baking pan with foil and bake the hens for 10 minutes. Reduce the heat to 350°. While basting the hens frequently, bake them for 1 hour, or until they are done.
- Serve the hens with the Ancho Chile Pecan Sauce on top and Pat's Cranberry Salsa on the side.

serves 6

Ancho Chile Pecan Sauce

- **2 cups chicken broth**
- **5 ancho chile peppers, seeded**
- **5 green chile peppers, roasted, peeled and seeded**
- **3 cloves garlic**
- **1½ teaspoons salt**
- **⅔ cup orange juice, freshly squeezed**
- **¼ cup peanut oil**
- **¼ cup olive oil**
- **3 tablespoons maple syrup**
- **4 teaspoons white wine vinegar**
- **1 cup toasted pecans, chopped**

- In a medium saucepan place the chicken broth, ancho chile peppers and green chile peppers. Heat them on high until they come to a boil. Reduce the heat to low. Cover the saucepan and simmer the ingredients for 10 minutes.
- Add the garlic and simmer the mixture for 5 minutes more.
- In a blender place the mixture and purée it. Add the salt and blend it in.
- Pour the mixture back into the saucepan. Cover the pan and heat it on low for 15 minutes.
- In the blender place the orange juice, peanut oil, olive oil, syrup, vinegar and pecans. Purée the ingredients so that they are smooth.
- Add the puréed mixture to the saucepan, and blend it in well.

makes approximately 4 cups

"I met my husband when he was an art teacher in college and I was a student in his class. First I had to earn my 'A', then via California, we came to Santa Fe and created the Grant Corner Inn."

Louise Stewart

Grandma Stewart's Berry Shortcake

"I grew up with this recipe, which came from the family farm in North Dakota. We had wonderful giant strawberries from the garden and delicious fresh cream from the cow."

3 pints fresh strawberries, washed, dried and sliced
2 pints fresh blackberries, washed and dried
½ cup sugar
1 cup sifted all-purpose flour
¼ cup sugar
2 teaspoons baking powder
1 pinch salt
½ stick unsalted butter, cut into pieces
¼ cup heavy cream
¼ cup milk
1 stick butter, softened
1 pint heavy cream, whipped

- In a medium large bowl place the strawberries, blackberries and the ½ cup of sugar. Toss them together well. Chill them in the refrigerator.
- Preheat the oven to 425°.
- In a large bowl sift together the flour, the ¼ cup of sugar, the baking powder and salt.
- Add the pieces of butter and cut them in with a pastry blender. Add the ¼ cup of heavy cream and the milk, and mix them in.
- Turn the dough out onto a floured surface. Knead it 6 times. Roll out the dough so that it is ⅓" thick. Cut out the biscuits with a floured 2" cutter. Place them on an ungreased baking sheet.
- Bake them for 10 to 15 minutes, or until they are done.
- Slice the cooked biscuits in half. Spread on the softened butter.
- On each of 8 individual dessert plates place one half of a biscuit. Spoon the chilled berries on top. Place the other biscuit half on top. Place more berries on top and then add the whipped cream.

serves 8

"My forte in cooking is to take a very basic recipe and then add one or two surprising ingredients so that the dish takes on an exciting new taste."

Pat Walter

Lemon Spanish Creme Dessert

"This is my mother's recipe that was always a favorite at our family gatherings. It's rather like a 'comfort food'.....something that evokes pleasant memories from the past while you are eating it."

- **2¼ cups milk**
- **½ cup sugar**
- **1 envelope unflavored gelatin**
- **⅛ teaspoon salt**
- **3 egg yolks, lightly beaten**
- **⅓ cup lemon juice, freshly squeezed**
- **2 teaspoons lemon zest** *(outer yellow part grated off)*
- **3 egg whites, beaten stiff**
- **8 fresh strawberries, halved**
- **4 fresh mint sprigs**

- In the top of a double boiler place the milk, sugar, gelatin and salt. While stirring constantly, heat the mixture on medium so that the gelatin dissolves.
- In a medium bowl place the egg yolks. While whisking constantly, slowly add the hot milk mixture. Whisk the mixture so that it is smooth.
- Pour the mixture back into the top of the double boiler. Adjust the heat so that the water is hot, but not boiling. Stir the mixture for 10 minutes, or until it coats a wooden spoon. Remove the sauce from the heat.
- Add the lemon juice and lemon zest, and stir them in well.
- Place the mixture in a large bowl. Cover the bowl with plastic wrap and place it in the refrigerator for 2 hours, or until is thick *(but not set)*.
- Add the egg whites and fold them in.
- Place the mixture in a greased 1 quart mold. Place it in the refrigerator for 4 hours, or until it is firmly set.
- Unmold the custard onto a serving dish. Garnish it with the strawberries and mint.

serves 4 to 6

"Besides socializing with the guests, there are so many diversified aspects to running a Bed & Breakfast, such as decorating a room, creating new recipes, designing ads for promotion, or catering a wedding. There is no way you can be bored!"

Louise Stewart

Hacienda del Sol

109 Mabel Dodge Lane • Post Office Box 177
Taos, New Mexico 87571
Phone (505) 758-0287
John & Marcine Landon, Innkeepers

Once a part of art patroness Mabel Dodge Luhan's estate, this 180-year-old adobe is on acreage that adjoins Taos Pueblo lands, and is a mile north of Taos Plaza. Frank Waters wrote *People of the Valley* in what is now one of the guest rooms. Thick adobe walls, down quilts, kiva fireplaces, handcrafted furniture and original art add to the comfort and period charm. A generous hot breakfast with great coffee completes the picture.

Recipes

Cranberry Glazed Brie

"Many people are not familiar with the flavor and texture of Brie cheese. It is very rich and smooth, and the tart taste of the cranberries is a wonderful complement. Serve this with a tray of crackers for a special occasion."

3 cups cranberries
¾ cup brown sugar, packed
⅓ cup dried currants
½ cup water
⅛ teaspoon dry mustard
⅛ teaspoon ground allspice
⅛ teaspoon ground cardamom
⅛ teaspoon ground cloves
⅛ teaspoon ground ginger
1 2½-pound Brie cheese wheel, top rind cut out with ½" border left
1 apple, cored and thinly sliced
1 pear, cored and thinly sliced

- In a large saucepan place the cranberries, brown sugar, currants, water, mustard, allspice, cardamom, cloves and ginger. Cook and stir the mixture on high heat for 5 minutes, or until most of the cranberries have popped.
- Remove the mixture from the heat and let it cool to room temperature.
- Preheat the oven to 300°.
- Place the Brie on a cookie sheet lined with foil.
- Place the cranberry mixture in the center of the cheese and spread it out to the edges.
- Bake the cheese for 12 minutes, or until it is warm.
- Garnish it with the apple and pear slices.

serves 10 to 12

Cran-Banana Cooler

"Use any kind of fruit juice and fruits that you want with this recipe. It's a delicious thing to serve in the summer."

2 cups cranberry juice, chilled
1 cup milk
1 cup vanilla ice cream
2 tablespoons honey
2 bananas, peeled and cut into pieces

- Place all of the ingredients in a blender and purée them so that they are smooth.

serves 4

Lentil Soup

"The key to the special flavor of this dish is the spinach and Tabasco sauce, which give it a subtle kick. People are always looking for a good lentil soup recipe, and this is one of the best that I have found."

- **¼ cup vegetable oil**
- **3 cups cooked ham, diced medium**
- **1 pound Polish sausage, sliced into ½" thick rounds**
- **1½ cups yellow onions, chopped medium**
- **1 clove garlic, crushed**
- **8 cups water**
- **2 cups celery** *(with leaves)*, **chopped**
- **1 cup tomatoes, peeled and cut into wedges**
- **1 pound lentils, washed**
- **½ teaspoon Tabasco sauce**
- **1 10-ounce package frozen chopped spinach, thawed**

- In a large stockpot place the oil and heat it on medium until it is hot. Add the ham, sausage, onions and garlic. Sauté them for 5 minutes, or until the onions are tender.
- Add the water, celery, tomatoes, lentils and Tabasco sauce. Stir them in well.
- Cover the pot with a lid and reduce the heat to low. Simmer the soup for 2 hours.
- Add the spinach and stir it in.
- Cook the soup for 10 minutes.

makes 4 quarts

"I love to cook, and have an ability to look at a recipe and imagine how it will taste."

Marcine Landon

Western Black Bean Soup

"Black beans may be very healthy, but in my opinion they are not too tasty by themselves. The green chiles and sausage really add a lot of zest to this recipe."

- **2 cups dried black beans, rinsed**
- **6 cups water**
- **8 slices bacon, cut into small pieces and fried** *(reserve the drippings)*
- **1½ cups onions, thinly sliced**
- **1 cup celery, thinly sliced**
- **2 canned green chile peppers, seeded and chopped**
- **2 cloves garlic, crushed**
- **1 bay leaf**
- **1 teaspoon ground cumin**
- **1½ Kielbasa sausages, thinly sliced**

- In a large, heavy stockpot place the beans and water. Bring them to a boil on high heat. Cover the pot, reduce the heat to low and simmer the beans for 2 minutes.
- Remove the pot from the stove and let it sit for 1 hour.
- Add the bacon and drippings to the beans.
- Add the onions, celery, green chile peppers, garlic, bay leaf and cumin. Stir the ingredients together.
- Simmer the beans for 1½ to 2 hours, or until they are tender.
- Add the sausage and stir it in. Remove the bay leaf.
- Cover the pot and simmer the beans for 10 minutes, or until the sausage is heated.

serves 8

"Living in a small town like Taos has one major advantage. Because of its size, there are not a lot of shopping options, so it is easy to make decisions!"

Marcine Landon

Taos Salad

"This is a very old recipe I have been using for a long, long time. It's a tasty vegetarian Southwestern entrée that is both filling and healthy. If you prefer, you can add meat or chicken."

2 cups lettuce, shredded
1 16-ounce can kidney beans, drained
1 cup tomatoes, chopped
½ cup pitted black olives, sliced
1 large avocado, peeled, pitted and mashed
½ cup sour cream
2 tablespoons Italian salad dressing
1 teaspoon dried minced onions
¾ teaspoon red chile powder
⅛ teaspoon pepper
½ cup corn chips, coarsely crushed
½ cup sharp cheddar cheese, grated
¼ cup pitted whole black olives

- In a large bowl place the lettuce, kidney beans, tomatoes and sliced olives. Combine them together well.
- Cover the bowl with plastic wrap and place it in the refrigerator for 30 minutes, or until it is chilled.
- In a medium bowl place the avocado, sour cream, salad dressing, onions, chile powder and pepper. Blend them together well.
- Cover the bowl with plastic wrap and place it in the refrigerator for 30 minutes, or until it is well chilled.
- Place the avocado dressing on the salad and toss it in well.
- Sprinkle the corn chips and cheese on top.
- Garnish it with the whole olives.

serves 4 to 6

"Bo is our pueblo mutt dog, and he plays an important role in greeting our visitors. With his wagging tail and friendly face, he is an expert at getting people to pet him."

John Landon

Old Fashioned Porridge

"I usually get my recipe ideas from food magazines and cookbooks, and then alter them to my taste. This recipe is one such example. It has a very tasty, nutritious, complete quality, which is very satisfying to those who eat it. Sometimes I sprinkle wheat germ on top, which gives the oatmeal a nice crispy texture. It's the perfect thing to serve in the winter."

3 cups water
1⅔ cups rolled oats
2 eggs, lightly beaten
½ cup maple syrup
¼ cup dark molasses
¼ cup brown sugar, packed
⅔ cup raisins
¼ cup walnuts, chopped
½ teaspoon ground cinnamon
½ teaspoon ground ginger
¼ teaspoon ground nutmeg

- Preheat the oven to 350°.
- In a large heavy saucepan place the water. Heat it on high so that it comes to a boil.
- Reduce the heat to medium low. Add the oats. Cook and stir them for 5 minutes.
- In a large oven-proof bowl place the oats and the remaining ingredients. Stir them together well.
- Bake the mixture for 1 hour, or until the porridge is set.

serves 4

"We have a large, friendly cat named TC, which stands for 'Tom Cat', 'Taos Cat', 'Tough Cat' and 'Terrific Cat'. In the morning he goes to the door of each guest's room, and if the door is not locked he unlatches it and goes inside to wake them up."

John Landon

Hot Apple Syrup

"You can use this syrup on any kind of pancakes, although I think it is best with apple. In terms of flavor, it is definitely a class above your usual maple syrup."

1 cup apple juice
¼ cup brown sugar, packed
¼ cup butter
½ teaspoon lemon zest *(outer yellow part grated off)*
¼ teaspoon ground cinnamon
⅛ teaspoon ground nutmeg
2 teaspoons water
1 teaspoon cornstarch

- In a small saucepan place the apple juice, brown sugar, butter, lemon zest, cinnamon and nutmeg. Stir them together and bring them to a boil over high heat.
- Reduce the heat to low and simmer the mixture for 15 minutes.
- In a small bowl place the water and cornstarch. Whisk them together so that they are smooth.
- Add the cornstarch mixture to the apple juice mixture, and bring them to a boil over medium heat. While stirring constantly, cook the mixture for 5 minutes, or until it is just thick.

makes approximately 1½ cups

"Taos is a fascinating town! I love it because of its multi-cultural features and the non-judgmental attitude of its citizens. You can be anything you want to be here, and no one cares. Also, with its relaxed pace and clean air, it is a very healthy place to live."

John Landon

Eggs del Sol

"We make this every week, and it is one of our most frequently requested recipes. You can prepare it the night before, store it in the refrigerator overnight, and then pop it in the oven the next morning."

1	**16-ounce package frozen corn** *(do not thaw)*
½	**cup flour**
12	**eggs, slightly beaten**
1½	**cups cottage cheese**
2	**cups Monterey Jack cheese, grated**
2	**cups cheddar cheese, grated**
½	**cup salsa**
1	**teaspoon baking powder**

- Preheat the oven to 350°.
- In the bottom of a greased 9½" x 11" baking pan place the corn and spread it out.
- In a large bowl place the flour, eggs, cottage cheese, Jack cheese, cheddar cheese, salsa and baking powder. Stir them together well.
- Pour the mixture over the corn.
- Place the small pan in a large baking pan. Add enough water to the large pan so that it is 1" deep.
- Bake the casserole for 1 hour, or until it is set.

serves 6

"John and I both do the cooking. If it's on top of the stove, that's his responsibility.....and if it's inside the oven, that's mine."

Marcine Landon

Del Sol Sloppy Joes

"Thirty-five years ago I bought a Sears & Roebuck electric skillet, and this recipe came from its accompanying cookbook. Old recipes like this are priceless!"

- **2 tablespoons vegetable oil**
- **2 pounds lean ground beef**
- **1 cup yellow onions, finely chopped**
- **1 cup celery, finely chopped**
- **⅓ cup green bell pepper, seeded and finely chopped**
- **2 cloves garlic, minced**
- **2 cups water**
- **½ cup chili sauce**
- **½ cup catsup**
- **4 tablespoons vinegar**
- **2 tablespoons Worcestershire sauce**
- **4 teaspoons brown sugar**
- **2 teaspoons dry mustard**
- **1 teaspoon paprika**
- **1 teaspoon red chile powder**
- **¼ teaspoon pepper**
- **8 hamburger buns, warmed**

- In a large heavy skillet place the oil and heat it on medium until it is hot. Add the beef, onions, celery, bell peppers and garlic. Sauté them for 10 minutes, or until the meat is browned.
- Drain off the excess fat.
- In a small bowl place the remaining ingredients *(except for the hamburger buns)* and whisk them together well.
- Add the mixture to the meat mixture and stir it in well.
- Cover the skillet with a lid and reduce the heat to low. While stirring the mixture occasionally, simmer it for 30 minutes.
- Serve it with the hamburger buns.

serves 8

"Many guests who stay with us come as strangers, but leave as friends."

Marcine Landon

Bacon & Green Chile Corn Bread

"This is a nice alternative to a basic corn bread. The green chile gives it a bite and the bacon adds a pleasing, unexpected flavor."

3 slices bacon, diced
3 tablespoons yellow onion, chopped
1 cup yellow cornmeal
1 cup flour
1 tablespoon baking powder
1 egg, lightly beaten
1 cup milk
1 8-ounce can whole kernel corn, drained
1 4-ounce can mild green chile peppers

- Preheat the oven to 425°.
- In a large cast-iron skillet place the bacon and fry it so that it is crisp. Add the onions and sauté them over medium heat until they are tender. Remove the skillet from the heat and set it aside.
- In a medium bowl place the cornmeal, flour and baking powder. Combine them together.
- In a small bowl place the egg and milk, and whisk them together well.
- Add the egg mixture to the flour mixture, and stir it in well.
- Add the corn and green chile peppers, and stir them in.
- Add the bacon, onions and drippings, and fold them in.
- Place the empty skillet over high heat until it is very hot. Pour the batter into the skillet.
- Bake the corn bread in the oven for 20 minutes, or until it is lightly browned.

serves 10 to 12

"Our inn is located on over one acre of beautiful tree-shaded grounds and has a wonderful country ambiance. It was chosen by **USA Weekend** as one of America's ten most romantic inns."

John Landon

Peach Blackberry Crisp

"I call for frozen fruit in this recipe only because our growing season is so short here in New Mexico. If you have fresh fruit, use two cups for each bag of frozen. I serve this for either breakfast or dessert, and it's always a hit."

3 16-ounce bags frozen peach slices, thawed and cut into ½" pieces
1 16-ounce bag frozen blackberries, thawed
½ cup flour
½ cup brown sugar, packed
1½ cups Quaker 100% natural cereal
⅓ cup butter, melted

- In a medium casserole dish place the peaches and blackberries. Cover the dish with a lid and chill it in the refrigerator overnight.
- Drain off the excess liquid.
- Preheat the oven to 300°.
- In a medium bowl place the flour, brown sugar and cereal. Stir them together well.
- Add the butter and stir it in so that it is well combined.
- Sprinkle the mixture on top of the chilled fruit.
- Bake the crisp for 30 minutes, or until it is bubbly and hot.

serves 4

"Some of our guests are fascinated by what we do for a living. They fantasize about what they believe to be the ideal occupation. Of course, if they stay with us for more than a few days, reality starts to sink in, and they begin to realize that it is not quite as glamorous as it seems.....especially when they see us washing dishes and cleaning rooms!"

Marcine Landon

Gooey Cake with Coconut Pudding Icing

"This recipe has been in my family for over thirty years, and everyone always loves it. Although it's not a pretty cake, it tastes really yummy and is very gooey and fun to eat."

Gooey Cake

2 cups flour, sifted
1½ cups sugar
2 teaspoons baking soda
2 eggs, slightly beaten
1 16-ounce can fruit cocktail
Coconut Pudding Icing *(recipe follows)*

- Preheat the oven to 300°.
- In a large bowl sift together the flour, sugar and baking soda.
- Add the eggs and fruit cocktail, and stir them in.
- Pour the batter into a greased 9" tube pan.
- Bake the cake for 1 hour, or until a wooden toothpick inserted into the center comes out clean.
- Let the cake cool for 10 minutes.
- Remove it from the pan, place it on a wire rack and let it cool completely.
- Frost the cake with the Coconut Pudding Icing.

serves 8

Coconut Pudding Icing

1 cup powdered sugar
½ cup butter
½ cup evaporated milk
1 egg yolk
1 cup coconut, shredded
½ cup walnuts, finely chopped
1 tablespoon vanilla extract

- In a medium heavy saucepan place the sugar, butter, milk and egg yolk. While stirring constantly, bring the mixture to a boil. Cook the mixture for 2 minutes.
- Add the coconut, nuts and vanilla. Stir them in well.
- Remove the icing from the heat and let it cool for 10 minutes before frosting the cake.

frosts 1 cake

Hacienda de Placitas

491 Highway 165
Placitas, New Mexico 87043
(505) 867-3775
François & Carol Orfeo

North of Albuquerque, in the small historic village of Placitas in the Sandia Mountains, is a landmark estate, locally known as "the windmill house." This exquisite hacienda, combining European and Spanish colonial influences, provides forever views and enchanted sunsets. In addition to the main villa, there are two complete guest houses, one an authentic log cabin. The artist-owners maintain an art-antique gallery, and offer a terraced pool, Jacuzzi-exercise room and large meeting-reception spaces. Their gourmet breakfasts are memorable.

Recipes

Crab-Stuffed Zucchini

"Many years ago when I was a single mother I had this dear sweet lady who looked after my children while I went to work. She had an enormous garden, and in the summer she would show up each day with her little red wagon filled to the brim with zucchini. This recipe is a result of my effort to cope with her bounty, and it is a real favorite. Serve it as an appetizer, entrée or side dish."

2 tablespoons butter
4 medium zucchini, sliced in half lengthwise, pulp removed and chopped, and the outer halves reserved
¼ cup scallions, finely chopped
1 clove garlic, finely chopped
8 ounces crab meat, cleaned
½ cup mayonnaise
½ cup Swiss cheese, grated
1 8-ounce package cream cheese, softened
½ cup seasoned dry bread crumbs
4 teaspoons butter, melted

- Preheat the oven to 350°.
- In a medium skillet place the 2 tablespoons of butter, and heat it on medium until it is melted and hot. Add the zucchini pulp, scallions and garlic. Sauté them for 5 minutes, or until the scallions are tender.
- Remove the pan from the heat and set it aside.
- In a large skillet place the zucchini halves with the cut side down. Add enough water to cover the bottom to ¼" deep. Heat it on medium high so that it boils. Cover the skillet with a lid and cook the zucchini for 5 to 7 minutes, or until they are tender. Remove them from the water and pat them dry.
- In a medium baking pan place the squash halves with the hollow side up.
- In a medium bowl place the reserved zucchini pulp mixture, the crab meat, mayonnaise, Swiss cheese and cream cheese. Combine them well.
- Fill the zucchini halves with the mixture.
- In a small bowl place the bread crumbs and the 4 teaspoons of butter, and combine them together well.
- Sprinkle the crumb mixture on top of the stuffed zucchini.
- Bake the zucchini for 25 minutes, or until the tops are lightly browned.

serves 8

Country French Cassoulet François

"This is a delicious, hearty peasant-style dish that my French husband likes to make. If a more soup-like consistency is desired, add extra white wine during the last forty minutes of baking. A good cabernet and thickly sliced bread as accompaniments are a must!"

½ pound pork sausage, crumbled
½ pound Polish sausage, sliced
½ pound lean boneless pork, cubed
½ pound lean boneless lamb, cubed
⅓ cup yellow onions, finely chopped
2 cloves garlic, minced
2 15-ounce cans navy beans
½ cup dry white wine
1 small white onion, peeled and left whole
2 whole cloves
1 medium carrot, cut in half lengthwise
1 rib celery
1 sprig fresh cilantro
1 bay leaf
½ teaspoon pepper, freshly ground
salt *(to taste)*
1 cup dried bread crumbs, crushed
2 tablespoons butter, melted

- Preheat the oven to 325°.
- In a large skillet place the sausages, pork, lamb, chopped onions and garlic. Cook them on medium high so that the meat is browned and the onions are tender. Drain off the excess fat *(reserve 2 tablespoons)*.
- Add the beans and wine, and stir them in.
- Place the mixture in a medium casserole dish.
- Stud the whole white onion with the cloves. Place it in the casserole.
- Add the carrots, celery, cilantro and bay leaf.
- Cover the casserole and bake it for 45 minutes.
- Remove the whole onion, carrots, celery, cilantro and bay leaf.
- Add the pepper and salt, and stir them in.
- In a small bowl place the bread crumbs and butter, and combine them well. Sprinkle the bread crumbs on top of the beans.
- Bake the casserole for 40 minutes, or until the top is browned.

serves 8

Vegetarian Black Bean Chili

"I owe this recipe to my children, who developed it because of their health conscious concerns. If you are not a bean eater, you can leave them out and it still tastes delicious. I like to serve it with grated cheese, a dollop of sour cream and some sliced jalapeños."

1 medium eggplant, cut into ½" cubes
1 tablespoon coarse salt
½ cup olive oil
1⅓ cups yellow onions, chopped
2 small zucchini, cut into ½" cubes
2 small yellow summer squash, cut into ½" cubes
1 yellow bell pepper, seeded and cut into ½" pieces
1 green bell pepper, seeded and cut into ½" pieces
1 red bell pepper, seeded and cut into ½" pieces
5 cloves garlic, chopped
1 28-ounce can peeled tomatoes, drained and chopped
1 cup vegetable broth
3 tablespoons red chili powder
1 tablespoon dried basil
1 tablespoon dried oregano
1 teaspoon pepper
½ teaspoon crushed red pepper
salt *(to taste)*
1 16-ounce can black beans *(with liquid)*
1 tablespoon lemon juice, freshly squeezed

- In a small bowl place the eggplant and coarse salt, and toss them together. Let the eggplant sit for 1 hour so that the bitterness is drawn out. Rinse the eggplant cubes well under water and pat them dry.
- In a large skillet place ¼ cup of the olive oil and heat it on medium until it is hot. Add the onions, squash, bell peppers and garlic. Sauté them for 5 to 7 minutes, or until they are just tender.
- In a medium skillet place the remaining ¼ cup of olive oil and heat it on medium until it is hot. Add the eggplant and sauté it for 10 minutes, or until it is just tender.
- In a large stockpot place all of the heated ingredients. Add the tomatoes, vegetable broth, chili powder, basil, oregano, pepper, crushed red pepper and salt. While stirring occasionally, simmer the ingredients on low heat for 30 minutes.
- Add the black beans and lemon juice, and stir them in well.
- Simmer the chili for 20 minutes.

serves 8

Souffléd Eggs & Shrimp Orfeo with Easy Hollandaise Sauce

"While this dish is superb for any meal of the day, it is probably the most special when served for breakfast. By adding the mayonnaise and water to the eggs, and whisking them in a copper bowl, the eggs gain volume and have a soufflé quality."

Souffléd Eggs & Shrimp Orfeo

- **4 eggs**
- **¼ cup water**
- **¼ cup mayonnaise**
- **1½ tablespoons butter**
- **2 croissants, halved lengthwise**
- **1 cup** *(2 ounces)* **popcorn shrimp**
- **4 slices Swiss cheese**
- **Easy Hollandaise Sauce** *(recipe follows),* **heated**

- Preheat the oven to 350°.
- In a medium bowl *(preferably copper)* place the eggs, water and mayonnaise. Whisk the ingredients together until the mixture is frothy and lemon colored.
- In a medium large skillet place the butter and heat it on medium low until it is melted and hot. Add the egg mixture and cook it so that the bottom begins to set. Lift it up so that the uncooked eggs run underneath. Fold the omelette in half. Cut it into 4 pieces.
- Place each omelette piece on top of a croissant half. Place ¼ of the shrimp and a slice of cheese on top.
- Bake the omelettes in the oven for 3 minutes, or until the cheese is melted. Serve them with the Easy Hollandaise Sauce on top.

serves 4

Easy Hollandaise Sauce

- **1 stick butter**
- **1 9-ounce package commercially prepared Hollandaise mix**
- **¼ cup mayonnaise**
- **1½ cups milk**

- In a small saucepan place the butter and heat it on medium until it is melted and hot. Add the Hollandaise mix and stir it in. Remove the pan from the heat.
- Add the mayonnaise and milk, and stir them in.
- Return the pan to the heat. While stirring constantly with a wire whisk, bring the mixture to a gentle boil. Reduce the heat to low. Simmer and stir the sauce for 1 minute, or until the mayonnaise is blended in well.

makes approximately 2 cups

Hacienda de Placitas Plum Liqueur

"Because my husband has a tremendous sweet tooth, he is indirectly responsible for my creation of this recipe. At first we tried peaches, nectarines and peaches, but nothing worked as well as the plums. For some reason, they made the liqueur smoother. If you put this in a fancy bottle, it makes a perfect gift."

3 pounds plums, halved and pitted
4 cups sugar
4 cups vodka

- In a gallon-size screw-top glass jug place all of the ingredients. Screw the lid on tightly and invert the jug.
- Let it sit for 24 hours. Turn the jug upright and let it sit for another 24 hours.
- Repeat this process until all of the sugar is dissolved.
- Store the liqueur in a cool dark place for 2 months.
- Strain the liqueur through a cheesecloth.
- Pour the mixture into decorative containers.

makes 2 quarts

"I believe the worst part about running a Bed & Breakfast is saying goodbye to our guests. They are so open and friendly that we quickly become bonded to them. When they leave we share a warm farewell, but feel a sadness just the same."

Carol Orfeo

Carolnata Caponata

"This has a delicious combination of different flavors, with the capers, eggplant, green and black olives, and cilantro. It's great for a side dish or as an appetizer with pita bread. Serve it either warm or cold."

- **½ cup olive oil**
- **1 28-ounce can peeled and chopped tomatoes** *(with juice)*
- **1½ pounds eggplant, peeled and cubed**
- **2 green bell peppers, seeded and chopped medium**
- **1½ cups yellow onions, chopped medium**
- **3 cloves garlic, finely chopped**
- **⅓ cup red wine vinegar**
- **3 tablespoons sugar**
- **3 tablespoons tomato paste**
- **2 tablespoons capers**
- **½ cup pimiento-stuffed green olives, drained and thickly sliced**
- **½ cup pitted black olives, drained and thickly sliced**
- **¼ cup fresh cilantro, chopped**
- **2 teaspoons dried mixed Italian herbs**
- **1 teaspoon salt**
- **½ teaspoon pepper, freshly ground**
- **½ cup piñon nuts** *(pine nuts)*

- In a large heavy saucepan place the olive oil and heat it on medium until it is hot. Add the tomatoes, eggplant, bell peppers, onions and garlic. Sauté the ingredients for 5 minutes.
- Reduce the heat to low and simmer the mixture for 15 minutes, or until the vegetables are tender.
- Add the vinegar, sugar, tomato paste, capers, green olives, black olives, cilantro, Italian herbs, salt and pepper. Stir them in well. Cover the saucepan with a lid and simmer the ingredients for 15 minutes more.
- Add the piñon nuts and stir them in.

serves 8 to 10

"As a native of Paris, France, I have always been involved in both cooking and painting. To me, they are both art forms. Instinctively I know how to do each one, but can't really explain to others how I do it. Just as each painting is unique, so is each dish that I make.....even if it is a basic recipe I have made a hundred times before."

François Orfeo

Infamous Pancakes

"These days so many of our guests are health conscious, and so I like to take recipes that sound delicious and then alter them slightly to make them more nutritious. The response has been very enthusiastic!"

1½ cups ricotta cheese
½ cup plain yogurt
1¼ cups Granny Smith apples, peeled, cored and finely chopped
½ teaspoon salt
2 tablespoons honey
1 teaspoon lemon juice, freshly squeezed
½ teaspoon ground cinnamon
1 tablespoon piñon nuts *(pine nuts)*
1 tablespoon sunflower seeds
½ cup blueberry dry pancake mix
½ cup whole wheat flour
4 egg yolks, beaten
4 egg whites, beaten stiff
4 tablespoons butter *(or as necessary)*

- In a large bowl place all of the ingredients *(except for the egg yolks, egg whites and butter)* and combine them together well.
- Add the egg yolks and mix them in.
- Add the egg whites and gently fold them in.
- In a large skillet place 2 tablespoons of the butter and heat it on medium until it is melted and hot. Using a ⅓ measuring cup, pour the pancakes into the skillet. Fry them for 3 minutes on each side, or until they are browned *(add more butter as it is needed)*.

serves 4

"As a Frenchman I did not grow up eating spicy foods.....so even though I love New Mexico, I must admit I do not love its green chile."

François Orfeo

Plum au Flan

"Rather than just serving fresh fruit juices for breakfast, I try to incorporate the fruit into more interesting recipes. This is a rich and scrumptious dish that is also excellent as an entrée or dessert."

- **1 Walnut Quiche Crust** *(recipe follows)*
- **2 pounds ripe plums, halved and pitted**
- **⅔ cup white sugar**
- **⅓ cup brown sugar**
- **1 teaspoon ground cinnamon**
- **3 egg yolks**
- **1½ cups sour cream**

- Preheat the oven to 400°.
- In the Walnut Quiche Crust place the plums with the cut side down.
- In a small bowl place the white sugar, brown sugar and cinnamon, and mix them together. Sprinkle the sugar mixture over the plums. Bake the plums for 15 minutes.
- In a medium bowl place the egg yolks and sour cream, and whisk them together well. Pour the sour cream mixture over the plums.
- Bake the flan for 30 minutes more, or until the custard is puffy and lightly browned.
- Remove the flan from the oven and let it cool for 20 minutes, or until it is set.

serves 8

Walnut Quiche Crust

"By putting walnuts in this quiche crust you turn it from something ordinary into something extra special."

- **2 cups flour, sifted**
- **2 tablespoons sugar**
- **½ teaspoon salt**
- **¼ teaspoon baking powder**
- **1 stick butter, softened**
- **½ cup walnuts, ground**

- In a large bowl sift together the flour, sugar, salt and baking powder.
- Add the butter and cut it in with a pastry blender so that fine crumbs are formed.
- Add the walnuts and mix them in well.
- Place the mixture in a 12" quiche pan. Firmly press it into the bottom and up the sides of the pan.

makes 1 crust

Piñon Apple Pie

"Several years ago I took a trip to Hawaii and was served this pie at a local restaurant. After returning home I tried to re-create it, and finally came up with this recipe. The pie is very traditional with the cinnamon and apples, but the pineapple juice gives it a wonderful additional dimension."

1½ cups pineapple juice
¾ cup sugar
7 medium cooking apples, peeled, cored and sliced
3 tablespoons cornstarch
1 tablespoon butter
½ teaspoon vanilla extract
¼ teaspoon salt
1 9" prepared pie crust, baked
¼ cup piñon nuts *(pine nuts)*

- In a large saucepan place 1¼ cups of the pineapple juice and all of the sugar. Heat and stir them on medium so that the mixture comes to a boil. Add the apples and stir them in. Reduce the heat to low. Cover the saucepan and simmer the apples for 3 minutes, or until they are tender *(not too soft)*. Remove the apples from the syrup with a slotted spoon and set them aside.
- In a small bowl place the cornstarch and the remaining ¼ cup of pineapple juice, and whisk them together so that they are blended. Add the liquid to the syrup.
- Cook and stir the mixture on medium until it is thick and bubbly. Remove it from the heat.
- Add the butter, vanilla and salt, and stir them in well.
- Let the mixture cool for 10 minutes.
- Pour ½ of the mixture into the prepared pie crust. Place the apples on top. Spoon the remaining mixture on top of the apples.
- Let the pie cool completely. Sprinkle the piñon nuts on top.

serves 8

"We don't have time to travel because we are so busy running our inn.....so we travel through the adventures of our guests. They give us the energy we need to keep going."

François Orfeo

Hacienda Vargas

Post Office Box 307
Algodones, New Mexico 87001
(505) 867-9115
Julia & Pablo DeVargas, Innkeepers

Just a few miles north of Albuquerque and south of Santa Fe, but in a different world, is Algodones, once an overnight stop on the Chihuahua Trail. This tranquil small village has an atmosphere quite different from its big-city neighbor's bustle. The site of the hacienda was a stagecoach stop and an Indian trading post, and includes an adobe chapel. Each guest bedroom has a kiva fireplace, private entrance, and New Mexican antique furniture. In addition to serving a full breakfast, the owners also will prepare outdoor family celebrations for up to 200 people.

Recipes

Cuban Black Beans

"My black beans are world famous! They have a slight sweet-sour taste, which is very Cuban. Traditionally they are served on a bed of white rice, with a little olive oil dribbled on top."

- 2½ **pounds black beans, cooked** *(reserve the liquid)*
- 3 **cups green bell peppers, seeded and chopped medium**
- 3 **cups yellow onions, chopped medium**
- 2 **cups olive oil**
- 2 **small jars pimientos**
- 2 **teaspoons sugar**
- **salt and pepper** *(to taste)*
- ⅓ **cup white vinegar**

- In a large stockpot place the beans and their liquid. Set the pot aside.
- In a food processor place the bell peppers and onions, and blend them so that they are finely ground.
- In a large skillet place 1 cup of the olive oil. Heat it on medium until it is hot. Add the onion mixture and sauté it for 10 minutes.
- Add 1 jar of the pimientos and sauté them for 5 minutes.
- Remove 1 cup of the beans from the pot and mash them.
- Add the sautéed mixture and mashed beans to the rest of the beans, and stir them together well.
- Add the sugar, salt and pepper, and stir them in. Simmer the ingredients on low for 1 hour.
- Add the remaining olive oil and pimientos, and the vinegar. Gently stir them in.
- While stirring occasionally, simmer the mixture for 1 hour, or until it is thick.

serves 12 to 16

"My father was French, my mother was half Spanish and half Italian, and I used to live in Cuba. So my cooking has many ethnic influences. I love to make up recipes and combine my favorite flavors into a brand-new dish. If possible, I always use lots of spices and garlic."

Julia DeVargas

New Mexico Vegetable Medley

"One day when I had to supply a vegetable dish for a wedding reception, I started throwing together everything that I had in the refrigerator. The dish turned out to be a big hit and I've been making it ever since."

- ½ **cup olive oil**
- 1 **green bell pepper, seeded and diced**
- 1 **red bell pepper, seeded and diced**
- 1 **yellow bell pepper, seeded and diced**
- 2 **cups fresh mushrooms, sliced**
- ½ **cup scallions, chopped**
- ½ **cup fresh cilantro, chopped**
- ½ **cup white wine**
- 1½ **tablespoons lemon juice, freshly squeezed**
- **salt and pepper** *(to taste)*

- In a large skillet place the oil and heat it on medium until it is hot. Add all of the bell peppers and sauté them for 3 minutes.
- Add the mushrooms, scallions and cilantro, and stir them in well.
- Add the wine, lemon juice, salt and pepper. Sauté the ingredients for 3 minutes, or until the vegetables are tender but still crisp *(do not overcook)*.

serves 6 to 8

Pasta Salad Olé

"Here is a recipe that I came up with just by using ingredients that I had on hand. It's one of my most successful creations to date."

- 1 **8-ounce can pitted black olives, drained**
- ½ **cup honey Dijon mustard**
- ½ **cup peppercorn salad dressing** *(your choice)*
- 1 **teaspoon garlic powder**
- 1½ **teaspoons salt**
- ½ **teaspoon red chile powder**
- 2 **tablespoons Parmesan cheese, freshly grated**
- 2 **cups Cilantro Sauce** *(recipe on page 226)*
- 1 **24-ounce package rottelle pasta, cooked al dente and drained**

- In a large bowl place all of the ingredients *(except for the pasta)* and stir them together well.
- Add the pasta and toss it well. Serve the salad chilled.

serves 10 to 12

Kika's Scramble

"Kika is both my chef and my sister-in-law. One morning she was making this recipe, which originally called for bread crumbs. Discovering that we were out, she decided to use stove-top stuffing instead, and the dish turned out to be twice as good."

¼ cup butter
¼ cup flour
1 cup milk
1 cup half & half
1 pound mild cheddar cheese, grated
¼ teaspoon dried thyme
¼ teaspoon dried basil
20 eggs, hard-boiled, peeled and thinly sliced
1 pound bacon, cooked, drained and crumbled
¼ cup fresh parsley, finely chopped
2 cups buttered stove-top stuffing, heated

- Preheat the oven to 350°.
- In a medium saucepan place the butter and heat it on medium until it is melted. Add the flour and whisk it in so that a smooth paste is formed.
- While stirring constantly, add the milk and half & half. Stir them in until the sauce thickens.
- Add the cheese, thyme and basil, and stir them in until the cheese is melted. Remove the sauce from the heat and set it aside.
- In a greased medium casserole arrange ½ of the eggs on the bottom. In this order, layer on ½ of the bacon, parsley and cheese sauce. Repeat the layering with the remainder of these ingredients.
- Sprinkle the stuffing on top.
- Bake the casserole for 30 minutes, or until everything is hot.

serves 8 to 10

"Northern New Mexico is a very magical place. Anyone who spends time here eventually feels its peace and tranquillity. For some, this is a very emotional experience. I witness the transformation in our guests. They may arrive tense, but they always leave happy."

Pablo DeVargas

Chicken Cilantro

"I have a Mexican friend from California who showed me how to make this recipe. His family owns quite a few restaurants and he is a very good cook. It's one of my favorite dishes because it is both simple and delicious."

¼ cup olive oil
8 chicken breast halves, skin and bones removed
salt and pepper to taste
Cilantro Sauce *(recipe follows),* **heated**

- In a large skillet place the oil and heat it on medium until it is hot. Place the chicken breasts in the skillet and sprinkle them with the salt and pepper. Sauté the breasts for 5 minutes on each side, or until they are just done.
- On a large serving dish place the chicken. Pour the Cilantro Sauce on top.

serves 8

Cilantro Sauce

"This is a very versatile sauce that can be served with pasta, beef or seafood. Once I used it in place of a hollandaise sauce with eggs benedict, and it was a big hit!"

1 pint heavy cream
1 cup fresh cilantro, chopped
1 cup scallions, chopped
5 cloves garlic
1 jalapeño chile pepper *(or to taste)*

- In a food processor place all of the ingredients and blend them together so that a smooth sauce is formed.

makes approximately 3 cups

Hacienda Shrimp

"This shrimp is excellent with pasta and a light cream or butter sauce. It's also good cold, on top of a green salad."

¼ cup butter
20 jumbo shrimp, peeled and deveined
¼ cup fresh cilantro, chopped
2 tablespoons fresh garlic, finely chopped
1 tablespoon lime juice, freshly squeezed
salt and pepper *(to taste)*

- In a large skillet place the butter and heat it on medium until it is melted and hot. Add the shrimp and sauté them for 2 minutes, or until they just begin to turn pink. Add the cilantro, garlic, lime juice, salt and pepper. Sauté the mixture for 5 minutes, or until the shrimp are pink.

serves 4 to 6

Sopaipillas de Vargas

"I am not a native New Mexican, and so making sopaipillas seems hard to me. But Kika, my chef, thinks they are the simplest things in the world to make. In any case, they taste delicious and are well worth the effort. Poke a hole in them and squeeze the honey inside."

2 **cups flour**
1 **teaspoon baking powder**
½ **teaspoon salt**
2 **tablespoons shortening**
¾ **cup warm water**
2 **cups shortening** *(or as needed)*

- In a medium bowl place the flour, baking powder and salt. Stir the ingredients together. Add the 2 tablespoons of shortening and cut it in with a pastry blender so that coarse crumbs are formed. Make a well in the center of the crumbly mixture. Pour the water into the well and mix it in with a fork.
- On a floured surface place the dough and knead it until it is smooth. Cover the dough with a damp cloth and set it aside for 20 minutes.
- On a lightly floured surface roll out the dough so that it forms a ⅛" thick square. Cut the square into twenty-four 4" squares.
- In a large heavy skillet melt enough of the 2 cups of shortening so that it is 2" deep. Heat the skillet on medium until the shortening is hot. Fry the squares in the oil for 1 minute on each side, or until they are lightly browned. Drain the sopaipillas on paper towels.

makes 2 dozen

Jule's Rice Pudding

"This is a Cuban recipe that was passed down to me by my grandmother. The only tricky part is not letting the pudding burn while you are cooking it."

½ **cup raw white rice**
1½ **cups water**
1 **lime rind** *(green and white part removed from the fruit)*
1 **cinnamon stick**
4 **cups milk**
1 **cup sugar**
1 **teaspoon vanilla extract**
¼ **teaspoon salt**
1 **teaspoon ground cinnamon**

- In a large saucepan place the rice, water, lime rind and cinnamon stick. Stir and cook the mixture on medium heat until it comes to a boil. Reduce the heat to low. Cover the saucepan with a lid and simmer the rice for 35 minutes, or until it is soft.
- Add the milk, sugar, vanilla and salt. While stirring very often, cook the pudding for 1 hour, or until it thickens *(do not let it burn)*.
- Remove the lime rind and cinnamon stick. Sprinkle the ground cinnamon on top of each serving.

serves 8 to 10

Hacienda Vargas

Inn of the Animal Tracks

707 Paseo de Peralta
Santa Fe, New Mexico 87501
(505) 988-1546
Daun Martin, Innkeeper

They say that each of the rooms at this unusual inn has an animal spirit as its patron. Guests may enjoy queen-size platform beds, hardwood floors and special views of gardens, trees, New Mexico skies, and perhaps local wildlife, from rooms with names like Whimsical Rabbit, Soaring Eagle and Gentle Deer. Imaginative full breakfasts are served in the dining room or on the patio, depending on the season. Guests can walk only three blocks west to the Plaza, and return at 4:30 pm for the special afternoon tea.

Recipes

Baba Eggplant Dip

"This is a wonderful Mid-Eastern dip that is tasty, low in calories and healthy. People always love it, and most have no idea that they are eating eggplant. I usually serve it with pita bread or crackers."

1	**large eggplant**
3	**tablespoons plain yogurt**
3	**cloves garlic** *(or to taste)*, **chopped**
3	**scallions, chopped**
2	**tablespoons fresh cilantro, chopped**
2	**tablespoons sesame seeds**
1	**tablespoon lemon juice, freshly squeezed**
½	**teaspoon cayenne pepper**
	salt and pepper *(to taste)*
1	**tablespoon sesame seeds**

- Preheat the oven to 350°.
- Pierce the eggplant in several places with a fork. Place it in a pie pan.
- Bake it for 1 hour, or until it is soft.
- Scrape out the pulp.
- In a food processor place the eggplant pulp and the rest of the ingredients *(except for the 1 tablespoon of sesame seeds)*. Purée them together so that they are smooth.
- Place the dip in a bowl and chill it for 1 hour.
- Sprinkle the 1 tablespoon of sesame seeds on top.

makes approximately 2 cups

"I've been an innkeeper for over fifteen years. Like any business you own, it's very hard work. But the rewarding part is that you get to interact with people when they are at their best. And, as I always say, it certainly beats being a telephone rep!"

Daun Martin

Cucumber Dill Salad

"I'm a sucker for dill, and so I really love this recipe. By slicing the cucumbers paper thin and draining out their liquid with the salt, you raise this vegetable to a level far above the common, thickly sliced salad cucumber. Be sure to use a good quality oil and tarragon vinegar."

6 long, thin cucumbers, peeled and sliced paper thin
½ cup salt *(or as needed)*
1½ tablespoons fresh dill, finely chopped
1 tablespoon tarragon vinegar
¾ teaspoon white pepper
1½ teaspoons sugar
3 tablespoons vegetable oil

- In a shallow baking dish place a layer of the cucumbers. Sprinkle on some salt. Repeat this process with the rest of the cucumbers. Let them sit in a cool place for 2 hours so that the liquid is drawn out.
- Place the cucumbers in a colander and rinse them thoroughly. Pat them dry with paper towels.
- Place the cucumbers in a medium bowl.
- In a small bowl place the dill, tarragon, vinegar, white pepper, sugar and oil. Whisk the ingredients together well. Pour the dressing over the cucumbers and toss it in.
- Cover the cucumbers with plastic wrap and chill them in the refrigerator.

serves 4 to 6

Prosperous Cabbage

"It's an old Southern tradition to serve this dish on New Year's Day, along with some black-eyed peas. The belief is that if you eat it, then you will have a prosperous year and make lots of money. Don't be afraid of the combination of cabbage and cheese, because it's great!"

1 stick butter
1 head green cabbage, thinly sliced
½ cup yellow onions, thinly sliced
¼ teaspoon paprika
salt and pepper *(to taste)*
2 cups sharp cheddar cheese, grated

- In a large stockpot place the butter and heat it on medium until it is melted and hot. Add the cabbage and onions, and sauté them so that the cabbage is just translucent.
- Sprinkle on the paprika, salt and pepper, and toss them in.
- Sprinkle on the cheese. Cover the pot with a lid and remove it from the heat. Let it sit until the cheese is melted.

serves 4 to 6

Breakfast Chilaquillas

"Chilaquillas is a Mexican dish consisting of layers of tortilla chips, cheese, beans, salsa and other tasty ingredients. This particular version came out of my head. The spiciness is determined by the salsa that you use. Also, you can add green chile peppers for extra flavor and heat."

16 eggs, slightly beaten
1 cup salsa
1 cup milk
8 flour tortillas
1 16-ounce can refried beans *(or see page 111 for homemade recipe)*
1½ 16-ounce cans whole kernel corn, drained
1½ cups sour cream
2 cups salsa
2 cups cheddar cheese, grated

- Preheat the oven to 350°.
- In a medium large bowl place the eggs, the 1 cup of salsa and the milk. Mix them together well.
- In a medium greased baking pan place ½ of the tortillas. Spread ½ of the beans on top.
- In this order, layer on ½ of the corn, sour cream, salsa and cheese. Pour ½ of the egg mixture on top.
- Spread the rest of the beans on top of the remaining tortillas. Place them on top of the egg mixture. Repeat the layering process with the rest of the ingredients.
- Place the pan in a large baking pan. Add enough water to the large pan so that it is 1" deep.
- Bake the chilaquillas for 45 minutes, or until the eggs are set.

serves 8

"Sometimes my guests arrive tired and cranky, so I have my dog Barney calm them down. He's a huge, mixed breed, and people can't help but smile when they see him. He understands his role, and is a master at making people happy, expecially with the little teddy bear he always carries in his mouth."

Daun Martin

Soft Scones with Cream Topping

"These are large scones that are not too sweet. I serve them to my guests at afternoon tea, when, in my opinion, they do not need something that gives them a sugar rush."

- **3 cups flour**
- **⅓ cup sugar**
- **2½ teaspoons baking powder**
- **½ teaspoon baking soda**
- **¾ teaspoon salt**
- **¾ cup butter, softened**
- **1 cup buttermilk**
- **¾ cup raisins**
- **1 teaspoon lemon zest** *(outer yellow part grated off)*
- **1 tablespoon heavy cream**
- **2 tablespoons sugar**
- **¼ teaspoon ground cinnamon**

- Preheat the oven to 425°.
- In a large bowl place the flour, the ⅓ cup of sugar, the baking powder, baking soda and salt. Stir them together with a fork.
- Add the butter and cut it in so that coarse crumbs are formed.
- Add the buttermilk, raisins and lemon zest, and stir them in so that the batter is just moist.
- Form the dough into a ball.
- Place the dough on a floured surface and knead it 20 times. Roll it out to form a circle that is ½" thick.
- In a small bowl place the heavy cream, the 2 tablespoons of sugar and the cinnamon. Whisk them together well.
- Brush the dough with the cream topping and cut it into 16 pie-shape wedges.
- On a greased cookie sheet place the wedges.
- Bake them for 12 minutes, or until the tops are lightly browned.

makes 16 scones

Inn of the Animal Tracks

Caramel Custard Pudding

*"I love to use the **Joy of Cooking** cookbook, and this is one of its recipes that I have altered slightly. Be very, very careful when you add the scalded milk to the dissolved sugar, because the sugar is extremely hot and can burn you. Use heavy hot pads."*

1 cup sugar
¼ cup hot water
3 cups half & half, scalded
1 cup milk
4 tablespoons cornstarch
2 eggs, lightly beaten
2 teaspoons vanilla extract

- In a large cast-iron pot place the sugar and hot water. Stir them together just once. Heat the mixture on medium high so that the sugar dissolves and turns a caramel color. Slowly add the scalded half & half and stir it in *(be careful because it will foam and spatter).*
- In a small bowl place the milk and cornstarch. Whisk them together so the cornstarch dissolves.
- While stirring constantly, add the milk to the sugar mixture. Cook and stir the ingredients for 5 minutes, or until the mixture is slightly thickened. Remove the pot from the heat and set it aside.
- In a large bowl place the eggs. While stirring constantly, add the hot mixture to the eggs, 1 tablespoon at a time. When you have added approximately 1 cup of the hot mixture, add the remainder all at once.
- Pour the mixture back into the large saucepan. Heat it on medium and stir it constantly for 5 minutes, or until it is thick.
- Remove the pudding from the heat. Pour it into a large bowl and let it cool. Add the vanilla and stir it in.

serves 4

Daun's Raspberry Pie

"When I serve this for my guests, there is never anything left in the pan. The recipe is simple, and it's a great way to use up any surplus of berries you may have."

6 cups fresh raspberries
1 cup sugar
4 tablespoons cornstarch
2 tablespoons lemon juice, freshly squeezed
1 9" pie crust, baked
1 cup heavy cream, whipped and sweetened

- In a food processor place 3 cups of the berries, the sugar and cornstarch. Purée them together.
- Place the mixture in a large saucepan. While stirring occasionally, heat it on low for 10 minutes, or until it is thick. Add the remaining 3 cups of berries and the lemon juice, and stir them in.
- Let the mixture cool. Pour it into the pie crust and top it with the whipped cream.

makes one 9" pie

Annie's Chocolate Cake with Chocolate Buttercream Frosting

"This is the number one requested recipe by my guests. The frosting really gives you a sugar and caffeine jolt. Whenever I owe someone a favor, I bake this cake for them."

Annie's Chocolate Cake

2 cups flour
2 cups sugar
1 cup cocoa powder
2 teaspoons baking soda
1 teaspoon salt
1 cup vegetable oil
2 eggs, lightly beaten
1 teaspoon vanilla extract
2 cups strong coffee, cooled
Chocolate Buttercream Frosting *(recipe follows)*

- In a large bowl place the flour, sugar, cocoa, baking soda and salt. Combine the ingredients together well.
- Add the oil, eggs and vanilla. Beat them in well. While constantly stirring, slowly add the coffee.
- Pour the batter into a greased bundt pan.
- Bake the cake for 30 minutes, or until a wooden toothpick inserted in the center comes out clean.
- Invert the cake onto a serving plate and let it cool.
- Frost the cake with the Chocolate Buttercream Frosting.

serves 8 to 10

Chocolate Buttercream Frosting

5 cups powdered sugar
½ cup butter, softened
¾ cup cocoa powder
strong coffee *(as necessary)*

- In a medium bowl place the powdered sugar, butter and cocoa. Beat them together with an electric mixer so that they are creamy.
- While stirring constantly, slowly add the coffee until the frosting is spreadable.

frosts 1 cake

Buttermilk Lemon Pound Cake

*"I got this recipe from **Fannie Farmer's Cookbook** and altered it slightly for the high elevation of Santa Fe. The cake is not overly sweet, but you can make it richer by serving it with whipped cream."*

3 cups flour
½ teaspoon baking soda
½ teaspoon baking powder
1 teaspoon salt
1 cup butter, softened to room temperature
2 cups sugar
4 eggs, room temperature
1 teaspoon lemon juice, freshly squeezed
1 cup buttermilk
1 tablespoon lemon zest *(outer yellow part grated off)*
¼ cup powdered sugar

- Preheat the oven to 350°.
- In a large bowl place the flour, baking soda, baking powder and salt. Combine the ingredients together. Set the bowl aside.
- In another large bowl place the butter and beat it with an electric mixer so that it is creamy. While constantly beating, slowly add the sugar and blend it in well.
- Add the eggs and lemon juice, and beat them in so that the butter is light and fluffy.
- Add ½ of the flour mixture to the egg mixture, and beat it in well.
- In a small bowl place the buttermilk and lemon rind, and stir them together.
- Add ½ of the buttermilk mixture to the batter and blend it in well.
- Add the remaining flour and buttermilk mixture to the batter. Beat them in so that the batter is smooth.
- Pour the batter into a greased bundt pan.
- Bake the cake for 1 hour, or until a wooden toothpick inserted in the center comes out clean.
- Let the cake cool for 10 minutes.
- Invert the cake onto a serving plate. Sprinkle the powdered sugar on top.

serves 8

La Posada de Chimayó

Post Office Box 463
Chimayó, New Mexico 87522
(505) 351-4605
Sue Farrington, Innkeeper

An old adobe home and guest house invite travelers to this historic northern New Mexico village located on the High Road to Taos. The community is famous for its fine Rio Grand-style Spanish weaving and for its remarkable church, the Santuario de Chimayó, sometimes known as the Lourdes of America. This is a peaceful center for day trips to Taos, Santa Fe, several Indian pueblos and archaeological ruins. Ample breakfasts satisfy even the heartiest eaters.

Recipes

Peanut Butter Stuffed Jalapeños

"I got this recipe from a guest who once regaled us with it at our breakfast table. I simply didn't believe her until I tried it. For some reason, the chemistry of peanut butter and jalapeños together produces an excellent taste that is not too hot."

5 jalapeño chile peppers, sliced lengthwise and seeds removed

5 tablespoons peanut butter *(your favorite)*

- Fill each jalapeño pepper half with the peanut butter.

makes 10 appetizers

Salsa Fresca

"A salsa like this is common to almost every table in old México. You can serve it with chips, tacos, eggs, soups or meats. To me, it is one of the most versatile condiments in the world."

1 cup tomatoes, chopped

⅓ cup white onions, finely chopped

2 serrano chile peppers, seeded and finely chopped

1 tablespoon lime juice, freshly squeezed

2 teaspoons fresh cilantro, finely chopped

salt *(to taste)*

- In a medium bowl place all of the ingredients and mix them together. Cover the bowl with plastic wrap and chill it in the refrigerator for 30 minutes.

makes approximately* 1½ *cups

Huevos Revueltos a la Mexicana

"This is a classic Mexican breakfast which includes salsa ingredients mixed in with scrambled eggs. You can serve the eggs with refried beans, cheese and warm tortillas. A lot of people like to put everything in a tortilla, roll it up and then eat it."

2 tablespoons vegetable oil

½ cup tomatoes, chopped medium

¼ cup white onions, chopped medium

2 serrano chile peppers, seeded, and chopped small

10 eggs, beaten with 2 tablespoons water

¼ teaspoon salt

- In a medium skillet place the oil and heat it on medium until it is hot. Add the tomatoes, onions and serrano chile peppers. Sauté them for 2 minutes, or until the onions are translucent.
- Add the eggs and salt. Stir them occasionally for 5 minutes, or until they are firm.

serves 4

All-in-One-Pot Breakfast

"One evening some unexpected guests showed up, and all that I had in the kitchen was eggs, potatoes, sausage and cheese. I developed this recipe out of desperation, and it has been a standard ever since."

- 1 **tablespoon canola oil**
- 5 **cups potatoes** *(skins on),* **diced**
- 1 **pound ground sausage**
- 12 **eggs, lightly beaten**
- 2 **cups Monterey Jack cheese, grated**

- In a large cast-iron skillet place the oil and heat it on medium high until it is hot. Add the potatoes and sausage, and sauté them until they are cooked.
- Add the eggs and sauté them until they are done. Sprinkle the cheese on top.
- Place the skillet under the broiler for 3 minutes, or until the cheese is lightly browned.

serves 6 to 8

Chimayó Sausage Popover

"This is a delicious breakfast dish that is especially good if served with applesauce and scrambled eggs."

- ½ **pound ground sausage, cooked** *(reserve 2 tablespoons of the grease)*
- ½ **cup flour**
- 3 **eggs, lightly beaten**
- ½ **cup milk**
- ⅛ **teaspoon salt**

- Preheat the oven to 400°.
- In a medium pie pan place the sausage and reserved grease.
- In a small bowl place the flour, eggs, milk and salt. Beat them together well.
- Pour the batter on top of the sausage. Bake it for 45 minutes, or until it is puffy and lightly browned. Serve it immediately.

serves 4

"Chimayó is a beautiful, small rural community. It is made up of clusters of tiny neighborhoods, each one with its own name. My inn is in the area called 'El Rincon de los Trujillos', which means 'corner of the Trujillo family'."

Sue Farrington

Chicken with Sour Cream Sauce

"This is a very easy, basic recipe that can be embellished according to your taste. Fresh herbs, garlic and paprika are all good additions to the sauce. I like to serve it with rice and a green salad."

1 3-pound chicken, quartered
2 teaspoons salt
2 teaspoons pepper
1½ cups sour cream

- Preheat the oven to 350°.
- In a medium baking pan place the chicken. Sprinkle it with the salt and pepper.
- Cover the pan with foil and bake the chicken for 1 hour, or until it is done.
- Remove the chicken and place it on a warm platter. Drain off most of the grease from the pan. Add the sour cream and stir it in.
- Place the pan on the stove and heat it on low. While stirring and scraping the bottom of the pan, heat the sauce.
- Pour the sauce over the chicken.

serves 4

"There are several reasons why I enjoy my work. First, I make a terrible employee, and by running a Bed & Breakfast I can be my own boss. Second, I find guests to be just delightful.....they are bright, interesting and lively. It's important that the breakfast table be square or round (not elongated), so that everyone can share in the conversation."

Sue Farrington

La Posada de Taos

309 Juanita Lane • Post Office Box 1118
Taos, New Mexico 87571
(505) 758-8164
Nancy & Bill Swan, Innkeepers

This secluded adobe compound, just 2½ blocks from the Taos Plaza, bills itself as a "bed and hearty breakfast" inn. Word of mouth.....literally!.....has attracted many new guests to the delightful hacienda just to enjoy the breakfast. Fireplaces or wood-burning stoves, ceiling fans, and a secluded courtyard add to the charm of the guest accommodations.

Recipes

Tomatillo Sauce

"I brought this recipe back from a wonderful woman in San Miguel de Allende, México. I call it my 'Anglo Sauce' because it is mild, with just a slight hint of heat."

2 pounds tomatillos, peeled
4 serrano chile peppers, coarsely chopped
3 cups chicken broth
5 cloves garlic
1 small yellow onion, quartered
½ teaspoon cornstarch, mixed with ½ teaspoon water
¼ cup fresh cilantro, chopped

- In a medium saucepan place the tomatillos, serrano chile peppers and chicken broth. Bring the mixture to a boil over medium heat. Cook it for 15 minutes. Remove the saucepan from the heat.
- Remove the vegetables with a slotted spoon and place them in a food processor. Add the garlic and onions.
- Purée the ingredients so that the mixture is smooth.
- Add the purée to the liquid in the saucepan. Add the cornstarch and stir it in well. Cook the sauce until it thickens.
- Let the sauce cool completely.
- Add the cilantro and stir it in.

makes approximately 5 cups

"I'm the world's biggest fan of Taos.....I could sell it to anyone! Not only do I love the melding of the Indian, Spanish and Anglo cultures, but I also find the people to be intriguing. People are not who they seem to be. The restaurant cook may be a former stockbroker, the waiter may be a published author, and the shop clerk may be a doctor of psychology."

Bill Swan

Author's note: While writing this chapter, ownership of the inn changed to Bill and Nancy Swan. The previous owner, Sue Smoot, is responsible for the following recipes: *Sunshine Poppyseed Dressing, La Posada Gazpacho, Ceviche,* and *Frosted Banana Walnut Cake.*

La Posada Salsa

"My niece and I created this recipe about a month after I moved to New Mexico. The chile powder and cumin give it a subtle, more complex flavor than that of a typical fresh salsa. This is delicious with breakfast burritos."

- ½ **tablespoon vegetable oil**
- 8 **jalapeño chile peppers, chopped small**
- ¼ **cup yellow onions, chopped small**
- ½ **cup red chile powder**
- 1 **teaspoon fresh cumin, ground**
- 2 **cloves garlic, minced**
- 1 **28-ounce can tomatoes** *(with juice),* **chopped**
- 1½ **tablespoons lime juice, freshly squeezed**
- **salt** *(to taste)*
- ¼ **cup fresh cilantro, chopped**

- In a medium skillet place the oil and heat it on medium until it is hot. Add the jalapeño chile peppers and onions, and sauté them for 5 minutes, or until they are cooked but still crisp.
- Add the chile powder and cumin, and sauté them for 5 minutes.
- Add the garlic and tomatoes, and stir them in well. Simmer the ingredients for 5 minutes.
- Add the lime juice and salt, and stir them in.
- Remove the mixture from the heat. Add the cilantro and stir it in.

makes approximately 1 quart

"If you are a grumpy person who doesn't like to talk until after ten o'clock in the morning, then the Bed & Breakfast experience may not be for you. But usually even the most hard-core grumbler is won over by our warmth and ambiance."

Nancy Swan

Salsa Verde

"A versatile and easily made sauce, this is excellent with eggs, burritos, seafood, chicken or beef."

6 tablespoons vegetable oil
3 green chile peppers, roasted, peeled and chopped
1 cup green bell peppers, seeded and coarsely chopped
¾ cup yellow onions, coarsely chopped
4 cups chicken broth
4 cumin seeds, ground
3 tablespoons fresh parsley, chopped
½ cup cornstarch, dissolved in 1 cup cold water

- In a medium skillet place the oil and heat it on medium until it is hot. Add the green chile peppers, bell peppers and onions. Sauté them for 5 minutes, or until the onions are translucent.
- In a food processor place the sautéed vegetables, chicken broth, cumin and parsley. Purée them for 30 seconds.
- Place the mixture in a medium saucepan. Simmer it on low heat for 15 minutes.
- Add the cornstarch and stir it in.
- Cook the salsa for 5 minutes, or until it thickens.

makes approximately* 1½ *quarts

Sunshine Poppy Seed Dressing

"This is a delicious dressing that has a particular affinity for a freshly prepared grapefruit and avocado salad."

1½ cups sugar
2 teaspoons dry mustard
2 teaspoons salt
⅔ cup vinegar
3 tablespoons onion juice
2 cups vegetable oil
3 tablespoons poppy seeds

- In a medium bowl place the sugar, mustard, salt and vinegar. Stir them together well.
- Add the onion juice and whisk it in.
- While whisking constantly, slowly add the oil.
- Add the poppy seeds and whisk the dressing for 3 minutes.
- Chill the dressing before using it.

makes approximately* 3½ *cups

La Posada Gazpacho

"This is an excellent gazpacho that I have refined over the years. It's light, refreshing, and takes only a few minutes to prepare."

- 2 **16-ounce cans Progresso peeled tomatoes**
- ½ **cucumber, peeled, seeded and chopped**
- ½ **cup green bell peppers, seeded and coarsely chopped**
- ⅓ **cup salad oil**
- ¼ **cup wine vinegar**
- 1 **tablespoon onions, grated**
- 2 **cups tomato juice**
- 1 **tablespoon Worcestershire sauce**
- 1 **tablespoon Tabasco sauce** *(or to taste)*
- **salt and pepper** *(to taste)*

- In a food processor place the tomatoes, cucumbers and bell peppers. Pulse them so that they are chopped small.
- Place the mixture in a large bowl. Add the remaining ingredients and stir them in.
- Chill the soup in the refrigerator.

serves 8

"I am always fascinated by our guests. They have such diversified lives and come from all over the world.....and here they show up on my doorstep! It's a great pleasure to get to know them, and to help them enjoy their stay in our beautiful New Mexico."

Nancy Swan

Ceviche

"I'm really crazy about this dish.....it is just fabulous! I got the recipe in 1952 from the owner of our honeymoon hotel in Acapulco. It has a lot of different ingredients, and each one must be included for the success of the dish."

- **1 pound fresh whitefish, cut into ¼" cubes**
- **3 tablespoons lime juice, freshly squeezed**
- **1 tablespoon lemon juice, freshly squeezed**
- **Roma Sauterne wine** *(as needed)*
- **1 cup yellow onions, finely chopped**
- **5 scallions, finely chopped**
- **1 28-ounce can whole tomatoes, chopped**
- **1 8-ounce can tomato sauce**
- **½ cup salad peppers, finely chopped**
- **½ cup fresh cilantro, finely chopped**
- **2 tablespoons large capers**
- **1 tablespoon Tabasco sauce**
- **1 teaspoon dried oregano**
- **1 teaspoon fresh sweet basil, chopped**
- **1 teaspoon ground coriander**
- **3 tablespoons olive oil**

- In a large enamel pan place the fish. Pour the lime and lemon juices on top. Add enough of the Roma Sauterne wine to cover the fish.
- Cover the pan tightly with foil and place it in the refrigerator for 24 hours.
- Add the remaining ingredients *(except for the olive oil)* and stir them in well .
- Cover the pan tightly and place it in the refrigerator for up to 10 days.
- Add the olive oil and stir it in well.

serves 10 to 12

"Taos has a strange phenomenon referred to by the locals as 'The Hum'. It is a mysterious sound that is heard by many of the area residents. Of unknown origin, it is an enigma to all."

Bill Swan

Mexican Quiche

"This is a very simple and easy recipe that always gets rave reviews. Serve it with some sour cream and scallions on top, and a red salsa on the side."

15 eggs, beaten
½ cup flour
1 pint cottage cheese
½ pound cheddar cheese, grated
½ pound Monterey Jack cheese, grated
1 7-ounce can green chile peppers, chopped
1 teaspoon baking powder

- Preheat the oven to 350°.
- In a large bowl place all of the ingredients and beat them together well.
- Place the mixture in a greased medium baking pan.
- Bake the quiche for 30 minutes, or until a knife inserted in the center comes out clean.

serves 10 to 12

Cactus Quiche

"Cactus is a wonderful tasting food.....it's like a cross between a green chile pepper and a green bell pepper. But because most people have never heard of eating cactus, I don't tell my guests that it is in this quiche until after they have finished eating it. You should see how surprised they are!"

1 can cactus slices
2 tablespoons red onions, very thinly sliced
1 cup Swiss Gruyere cheese, grated
⅓ cup cottage cheese
5 eggs
¼ teaspoon white pepper

- Preheat the oven to 350°.
- In the bottom of a greased casserole place the cactus slices. Place the onions and cheese on top.
- In a food processor place the cottage cheese, eggs and white pepper. Blend them together so that they are creamy.
- Pour the egg mixture on top of the casserole ingredients.
- Bake the quiche for 30 minutes, or until it is set.

serves 4

Egg & Sausage Strata

"Whenever I serve this for breakfast, there is not a morsel left. It is one of our most frequently requested recipes."

6 slices bread, crusts removed, and one side buttered
1 pound bulk pork sausage, cooked and drained
1½ cups sharp cheddar cheese, grated
6 eggs, beaten
2 cups half & half
1 teaspoon salt
½ teaspoon dry mustard

- In a greased 13" x 9" x 2" baking dish place the bread slices with the buttered side up. Sprinkle the sausage on top. Sprinkle on the cheese.
- In a medium bowl place the eggs, half & half, salt and dry mustard, and beat them together. Pour the mixture over the cheese.
- Cover the dish with foil and refrigerate it overnight.
- Remove the dish from the refrigerator 30 minutes before you are ready to bake it.
- Preheat the oven to 350°.
- Bake the strata for 35 minutes *(covered)*.
- Remove the foil.
- Bake it for 10 minutes more, or until it is set.
- Remove the strata from the oven and let it sit for 10 minutes.

serves 8 to 12

"As innkeepers who serve breakfast to hundreds of different people, we have learned to be extremely flexible about the food we serve. Many people have special dietary requirements, so instead of altering our usual recipes, we make up special dishes just for them."

Nancy Swan

Herbed Biscuits

"Many people expect something sweet for breakfast, such as coffee cake or cinnamon rolls. These biscuits are a nice compromise, because although they contain a small amount of sugar, they basically are loaded with rich flavors of different herbs."

3 cups flour
1/3 cup sugar
2 tablespoons baking powder
1 teaspoon baking soda
1 teaspoon salt
1/2 cup shortening
1/2 cup butter, cold
2 tablespoons olive oil
1/2 cup celery leaves, finely chopped
1/3 cup yellow onions, finely chopped
2 cloves garlic, minced
2 tablespoons fresh dill, chopped
2 tablespoons fresh parsley, chopped
2 teaspoons fresh thyme, ground
2/3 cup buttermilk
1/3 cup heavy cream

- In a food processor place the flour, sugar, baking powder, baking soda and salt. Process the ingredients for 10 seconds.
- In a large bowl place the flour mixture. Add the shortening and butter, and cut them in with a pastry blender so that coarse crumbs are formed.
- Cover the bowl with plastic wrap and place it in the refrigerator for 4 hours *(or overnight)*.
- In a small skillet place the oil and heat it on medium until it is hot. Add the celery leaves, onions and garlic. Sauté them for 5 minutes, or until the onions are translucent.
- Add the dill, parsley and thyme, and stir them in.
- Preheat the oven to 375°.
- Remove the skillet from the heat and let the mixture cool for 10 minutes.
- Add the onion mixture to the chilled crumb mixture and mix it in well.
- In the center of the crumb-herb mixture, form a well. Pour the buttermilk into the well. Mix it in with a fork so that the dough is just moistened.
- On a lightly floured surface roll out the dough so that it is 1/2" thick.
- Using a 2" glass, cut the biscuits out. Place them on a cookie sheet so that they barely touch each other. Brush the cream on top.
- Bake the biscuits for 15 minutes, or until they are browned.

makes 24 biscuits

Easy Lemon Poppy Seed Bread

"This is my favorite recipe for a bread because it is easy to make, it freezes beautifully, and it tastes just heavenly. When people ask me for the recipe I am almost embarrassed to give it to them because it is so ridiculously simple."

1 package lemon cake mix
1 package instant lemon pudding
4 eggs
4 tablespoons poppy seeds
½ cup vegetable oil
1 cup hot water
½ cup sugar
1 large lemon, juiced

- Preheat the oven to 350°.
- In a large bowl place all of the ingredients *(except for the sugar and lemon juice)* and mix them with an electric mixer for 4 minutes.
- Pour the batter into two greased medium loaf pans.
- Bake the bread for 40 to 50 minutes, or until a wooden toothpick inserted in the center comes out clean.
- Remove the bread loaves from the pans and set them on a wire rack.
- In a small bowl place the sugar and lemon juice, and mix them together. Spoon the mixture on top of the bread.
- Brush on the glaze to cover the top of the bread.

makes 2 loaves

"Owning a successful Bed & Breakfast is a marvelous ego builder, because not only do we get an endless supply of compliments, we also have people who come back for ten years in a row. It's then that we know we are doing something right."

Nancy Swan

Banana Crunch Loaf

"This is a delicious bread that freezes very well. It has a nice texture because the top and bottom are crunchy and the middle is moist."

1 cup sugar
½ cup butter, softened
2 eggs
1 cup bananas, peeled and mashed
½ teaspoon vanilla extract
½ cup sour cream
2 cups sifted flour
1 teaspoon baking soda
1 teaspoon baking powder
¼ teaspoon salt
1 cup sugar
1 cup pecans, chopped
1 teaspoon ground cinnamon

- Preheat the oven to 350°.
- In a large bowl place the first cup of sugar and the butter, and cream them together.
- One at a time, add the eggs and beat them in.
- Add the bananas, vanilla and sour cream, and mix them in well.
- In a medium bowl sift together the sifted flour, baking soda, baking powder and salt.
- Fold the dry mixture into the creamed mixture so that it is just moistened.
- In another medium bowl place the second cup of sugar, the pecans and cinnamon. Mix them together.
- Sprinkle ½ of the pecan topping in the bottom of 3 greased medium loaf pans. Spoon the batter on top. Sprinkle the rest of the topping on top.
- Bake the loaves for 45 minutes, or until a wooden toothpick inserted in the center comes out clean.

makes 3 loaves

Frosted Banana Walnut Cake

"Delicious and moist, this cake always gets a standing ovation from my guests. The slight broiling of the frosting before serving gives it the crowning touch."

- ¾ **cup butter, softened**
- 1½ **cups white sugar**
- ½ **cup sour milk** *(or buttermilk)*
- 1 **cup ripe bananas, peeled and mashed**
- 2 **eggs, slightly beaten**
- 1 **teaspoon vanilla extract**
- 1¾ **cups flour**
- 1 **teaspoon baking soda**
- ½ **teaspoon salt**
- 1 **cup walnuts, chopped**
- ½ **cup butter**
- 1 **cup brown sugar**
- ⅓ **cup milk**

- Preheat the oven to 350°.
- In a large bowl place the ¾ cup of butter and the white sugar. Beat them together with an electric mixer so that they are creamy.
- Add the sour milk, bananas, eggs and vanilla. Blend them in well.
- In a medium bowl sift together the flour, baking soda and salt.
- Add the banana mixture to the flour mixture, and combine them together.
- Add the nuts and stir them in well.
- Place the batter in a greased 13" x 9" baking pan.
- Bake the cake for 35 minutes, or until a wooden toothpick inserted in the center comes out clean.
- In a small saucepan place the ½ cup of butter and the brown sugar. While stirring constantly, heat them on medium low until the butter is melted and the brown sugar dissolves.
- Add the milk and stir it in well. Bring the mixture to a boil and cook it for 2 minutes.
- Spread the frosting on top of the cake.
- Preheat the oven to broil.
- Place the cake under the broiler for 3 minutes, or until the frosting glazes *(be careful not to burn it)*.

serves 8 to 10

Little Tree

Post Office Box 1100-255
Taos, New Mexico 87571
(505) 776-8467
Charles & Kay Giddens, Innkeepers

Ten miles northeast of Taos, off the road to Taos Ski Valley, is this peaceful inn dedicated to the trees of northern New Mexico. Although this is a new adobe building, it has been constructed in the old style, complete with walled courtyard, kiva fireplaces, a rambling portal, and ceilings beamed with vigas (tree-trunk beams) and latillas (crosswise saplings). Heated tile floors, handcrafted furniture and works of art complete the decor. Health-conscious gourmet breakfasts are included in the price; the starry skies are free.

Recipes

Breakfast Pasta

"I don't tell our guests that I am going to serve them pasta for breakfast, because if I did they would look at me askance. But if I bring this dish out unannounced, in all politeness they will take a taste, and then they are hooked!"

- **1 tablespoon olive oil**
- **2 cloves garlic, chopped small**
- **1 cup mushrooms, thinly sliced**
- **⅓ cup scallions, thinly sliced**
- **1 tablespoon butter**
- **1 tablespoon olive oil**
- **8 ounces spaghettini, cooked al dente and drained**
- **6 eggs, lightly beaten**
- **½ cup Parmesan cheese, freshly grated**
- **2 tablespoons fresh parsley, chopped**
- **1½ teaspoons fresh basil, chopped**
- **2 Roma tomatoes, chopped**
- **pepper** *(to taste)*

- In a small skillet place the first tablespoon of olive oil and heat it on medium until it is hot. Add the garlic and mushrooms, and sauté them for 3 minutes. Add the scallions and sauté them for 1 minute. Remove the skillet from the heat and set it aside.
- In a large skillet place the butter and the second tablespoon of olive oil, and heat them on medium until the butter is melted and they are hot. Add the pasta and stir it in. Add the eggs and ½ of the Parmesan cheese. Stir them in until the eggs begin to form curds on the pasta.
- Add the mushroom mixture, parsley and basil. Stir them in well.
- Add the tomatoes and pepper, and gently stir them in.
- Sprinkle the remaining Parmesan cheese on top of each serving.

serves 4

Border Chili

"This is an old recipe from southern Texas. It originally called for cabrito (goat) and suet (lard), but I substituted beef and eliminated the fat. It's one of those dishes that might sound uninteresting, but actually tastes fantastic."

- **2 pounds lean ground beef, browned**
- **1 quart water**
- **2 tablespoons chili powder**
- **8 cloves garlic, chopped**
- **1 tablespoon cumin seeds, ground**
- **1 teaspoon dried oregano**
- **1 tablespoon cornstarch, dissolved in ¼ cup water**

- In a large kettle place all of the ingredients *(except for the cornstarch)*. Cover it tightly with a lid. Cook the chili on low for 3 hours.
- Add the dissolved cornstarch and stir it in so that the chili thickens.

serves 6

Taos Stuffed Chicken Breast

"This is a great recipe for chicken. It has a good texture, the meat comes out tender, and despite the length of this recipe, it is easy to make."

- **1 tablespoon olive oil**
- **4 tablespoons piñon nuts** *(pine nuts)*
- **3 cloves garlic, chopped**
- **½ cup green chile peppers, roasted, peeled and chopped**
- **¼ cup scallions, finely chopped**
- **½ teaspoon dried oregano**
- **6 6-ounce boneless chicken breasts, skins removed, and flattened to ¼" thick**
- **6 tablespoons feta cheese, crumbled**
- **1 cup flour**
- **salt and pepper** *(to taste)*
- **1 egg**
- **1 tablespoon water**
- **4 tablespoons dried bread crumbs, finely crushed**
- **4 tablespoons yellow cornmeal**
- **4 tablespoons Parmesan cheese, freshly grated**
- **6 tablespoons butter** *(or as needed)*

- In a medium skillet place the olive oil and heat it on medium until it is just warm. Add the piñon nuts and garlic, and sauté them for 3 minutes. Add the chile peppers, scallions and oregano, and sauté them for 2 minutes. Remove the skillet from the heat and let the mixture cool.
- In the center of each chicken breast place some of the mixture. Sprinkle 1 tablespoon of the feta cheese on top of the filling. Fold the ends of the breast up toward the center and secure them with a wooden toothpick. Place the chicken on a platter and refrigerate it for 1 hour.
- In a pie plate place the flour, salt and pepper. Stir them together. Set the plate aside.
- In a small bowl place the egg and water, and whisk them together well. Set the bowl aside.
- In another pie plate place the bread crumbs, cornmeal and Parmesan cheese. Stir them together well. Set the plate aside.
- Dredge each rolled piece of chicken first in the flour, next in the egg wash and last in the bread crumb mixture.
- In a large heavy skillet place the butter and heat it on medium low until it is melted and hot. Add the chicken and sauté it for 5 to 8 minutes on each side, or until it is just done.

serves 6

"As a former trial lawyer, I had projects go on for years with no resolution. But when I cook, I have an immediate result.....and that is very, very satisfying."

Charles Giddens

Nut Grain Griddle Cakes

"These are a cross between johnnycakes and regular pancakes, with the addition of walnuts to give them extra texture and taste."

1	**cup whole wheat flour**	2	**cups buttermilk**
½	**cup stone-ground cornmeal**	1	**egg, lightly beaten**
¾	**teaspoon baking soda**	2	**tablespoons canola oil**
½	**teaspoon baking powder**	2	**tablespoons molasses**
½	**teaspoon salt**	1	**cup walnuts, chopped**

- In a large bowl place the flour, cornmeal, baking soda, baking powder and salt. Mix the ingredients together.
- In a medium bowl place the buttermilk, egg, oil and molasses. Mix them together well.
- Add the buttermilk mixture to the flour mixture, and mix them together.
- Add the walnuts and stir them in.
- Preheat a lightly oiled griddle so that a drop of water sizzles on its surface. Pour small amounts of the batter onto the griddle. Cook the pancakes for 3 minutes on each side, or until they are lightly browned.

serves 4

"I started cooking when I was about ten years old. Both of my parents worked, so when I came home from school I had the kitchen to myself. I used the original **Joy of Cooking** cookbook and made everything in the dessert section."

— Kay Giddens

Seven Grain Biscuits

"These biscuits are healthy, tasty, and remarkably light in texture. You can find the seven grain in any health food store."

- 1/4 **cup seven grain**
- **warm water** *(as needed)*
- 1 **egg, lightly beaten**
- 4 **tablespoons canola oil**
- 3/4 **cup buttermilk**
- 1 3/4 **cups flour**
- 2 **teaspoons baking powder**
- 1/4 **teaspoon baking soda**
- 1/2 **teaspoon salt**

- Preheat the oven to 400°.
- In a small bowl place the seven grain. Add enough water to cover it. Let it sit so that the water is absorbed.
- In a medium bowl place the egg, oil and buttermilk. Whisk them together well.
- In a large bowl place the flour, baking powder, baking soda and salt. Stir them together well.
- Add the seven grain and the egg mixture to the dry ingredients, and mix them together well.
- Place the dough on a floured surface and knead it 5 times. Roll out the dough so that it is 1/2" thick. Cut out the biscuits with a floured biscuit cutter. Place them on a flat sheet.
- Bake the biscuits for 15 minutes, or until they are lightly browned and a wooden toothpick inserted in the center comes out clean.

makes approximately 8 large biscuits

"I fell in love with the architecture of Taos. The smooth, thick roundness of the adobe buildings seemed to me the way all buildings ought to be."

Charles Giddens

Charles's Little Tree Cookies

"I think a lot of oatmeal cookies are rather boring, so I came up with this recipe that includes two of my favorite things.....chocolate and walnuts. These cookies are so good that they disappear as fast as I can make them!"

2 sticks margarine, softened
1¼ cups brown sugar
½ cup white sugar
2 eggs, lightly beaten
2 tablespoons milk
2 teaspoons vanilla extract
1¾ cups flour
½ teaspoon baking soda
¼ teaspoon salt
2½ cups rolled oats
2 cups mini semisweet chocolate chips
1 cup walnuts, chopped

- Preheat the oven to 350°.
- In a medium large bowl place the margarine, brown sugar and white sugar. Beat them together until the mixture is light.
- Add the eggs and beat them in.
- Add the milk and vanilla, and beat them in.
- Add the flour, baking soda and salt. Mix them in well.
- Add the oats, chocolate chips and walnuts. Mix them in.
- On a greased cookie sheet drop tablespoons of the batter.
- Bake the cookies for 10 minutes, or until they are done.

makes approximately 36 cookies

"My wife taught me how to cook. At first I was very intimidated, but she convinced me that if I could read, then I could follow a recipe. And if I could follow a recipe, then I could cook. And she was right!"

Charles Giddens

Open Sky

Route 2, Box 918 • Turquoise Trail
Santa Fe, New Mexico 87505
(505) 471-3475
Babette Miller, Innkeeper

Nine miles south of Santa Fe, on the famed Turquoise Trail, is a rural version of Santa Fe style. This renovated adobe is set on ten acres of land and boasts endless views in all directions. Guest rooms are furnished in Southwestern style and have access to a country courtyard. After a delectable continental breakfast, guests may head north to the sophistication of Santa Fe or south along the Turquoise Trail to the no-longer-ghost towns of Cerrillos, Madrid and Galisteo.

Recipes

Grandma's Brandy Slush

"This is so good on a hot afternoon! My grandma used to make huge batches of it in the summer and keep it frozen in the deep freeze. Because of the alcohol it stays slushy, and you can remove what you need at the time. Each person can add the lemon-lime soda to his glass according to his taste."

9½ cups water
3 cups brandy
2 cups sugar
1 12-ounce can frozen orange juice
1 6-ounce can frozen lemonade
1 6-ounce can frozen limeade
4 cans lemon-lime soda *(or to taste)*

- In a 5-quart container place all of the ingredients *(except for the soda)* and mix them together well.
- Chill the mixture in the refrigerator for 3 days *(stir it occasionally)*.
- Place the mixture in the freezer for 2 hours, or until it becomes slushy.
- Place the mixture in a large serving bowl. Add the soda and mix it in.

serves 20 to 25

Shrimp Dip

"I make this dish for parties and always get enthusiastic compliments, if not requests for the recipe. It's quite rich, but people don't seem to care when they eat it!"

8 ounces cream cheese, softened
1 small can shrimp, drained and chopped
⅓ cup yellow onions, finely chopped
3 stalks celery, finely chopped
2 tablespoons mayonnaise
1 teaspoon lemon juice, freshly squeezed
¼ teaspoon Tabasco sauce

- In a medium bowl place all of the ingredients and blend them together well.
- Cover the bowl with plastic wrap and chill it in the refrigerator for 1 hour before serving.

makes approximately 2 cups

German Potato Salad

"This is my grandmother's excellent recipe. I used to watch her make it, and she would say to add 'a little of this' and 'a little of that'.....and so I never got the exact quantities for the ingredients. This version is not quite as good as hers, but it's as close as I can get!"

½ pound bacon, cut into 1" pieces
¾ cup sugar
2 tablespoons flour
3 tablespoons vinegar
2 cups water
salt *(to taste)*
5 cups potatoes, cooked, peeled and thinly sliced

- In a large skillet place the bacon and cook it on medium so that is slightly crispy.
- Add the sugar and stir it in. Add the flour and stir it in well.
- Add the vinegar and water, and stir them in well. Bring the mixture to a boil. While constantly stirring, boil the mixture for 3 minutes.
- Add the salt and stir it in.
- In a large bowl place the potatoes. Pour the bacon mixture over the potatoes and stir it in well *(if there is extra dressing you may freeze it)*.
- Serve the salad warm.

serves 8

"I retired as a teacher early in life, and needed to find a way to earn a living. I bought this fabulous old home outside of Santa Fe, and as I was remodeling it, realized that it would be perfect for a Bed & Breakfast. It turned out to be very successful and I couldn't be happier with my life."

Babette Miller

John's Prize Winning Chili

"My brother-in-law John made this for a chili cook-off in Laramie, Wyoming, and it won first prize. I forced him to write down all the ingredients, which was hard for him to do because he likes to cook from the cuff. In my opinion, it's the best chili in the country."

3 tablespoons vegetable oil
1 pound ground beef
1 pound stew meat, cut into ½" pieces
5 bratwurst, cooked and sliced into ¼" rounds
1 28-ounce can whole tomatoes
1½ cups red onions, chopped medium
½ cup white onions, chopped medium
1 cup green bell peppers, seeded and chopped medium
¼ cup green chile peppers, roasted, peeled and chopped medium
5 cloves garlic, finely chopped
1 jalapeño chile pepper, chopped
1 teaspoon pepper
½ teaspoon ground cumin
½ teaspoon dried oregano
¼ teaspoon paprika
¼ teaspoon red chile powder
1 ancho chile *(or to taste),* **crumbled**
2 15-ounce cans red kidney beans
1 12-ounce can white beans
1 15-ounce can pinto beans

- In a large stockpot place the oil and heat it on medium until it is hot. Add the ground beef, stew meat and bratwurst. Sauté them for 10 to 15 minutes, or until they are browned.
- Add the remaining ingredients *(except for the beans)* and stir them in well. Reduce the heat to low and simmer the chili for 2½ hours.
- Add the beans and stir them in. Simmer the chili for 30 minutes.

serves 8 to 10

"My philosophy of cooking includes using the highest quality ingredients possible, and never ever skimping on doing what is needed to make the food taste good."

Babette Miller

Moussaka

"This is one of my all-time favorite recipes. It tastes better than any moussaka I've had in any Greek restaurant, so now I never even order it because I'm so spoiled. Unlike in most casseroles, the different tastes are clean and distinct and do not merge together."

1½ cups fresh steamed vegetables *(your favorites)*
2 tablespoons dried bread crumbs
2 tablespoons butter
1⅓ cups yellow onions, chopped
½ pound ground beef
1 small can tomato paste
1 cup white wine
1 teaspoon white pepper
1 teaspoon salt *(to taste)*
1 cup Parmesan cheese, freshly grated
3 tablespoons butter
4 tablespoons flour
2¾ cups milk
½ teaspoon ground nutmeg
½ teaspoon salt
2 eggs

- Preheat the oven to 350°.
- In a lightly greased large casserole dish place the vegetables. Sprinkle the bread crumbs on top. Set the dish aside.
- In a medium skillet place the 2 tablespoons of butter and heat it on medium until it is melted and hot. Add the onions and sauté them for 5 minutes, or until they are lightly browned.
- Add the beef and sauté it until it is done.
- Add the tomato paste, wine, white pepper and the 1 teaspoon of salt. Stir them in well. Reduce the heat to low and simmer the ingredients for 10 minutes.
- Place the meat mixture on top of the bread crumbs in the casserole dish. Sprinkle ½ of the Parmesan cheese on top. Set the dish aside.
- In the same skillet place the 3 tablespoons of butter and heat it on medium until it is melted and hot. Add the flour and stir it in well.
- Add the milk and whisk it in. While stirring constantly, bring the mixture to a gentle boil.
- Add the nutmeg and the ½ teaspoon of salt, and stir them in.
- Remove the pan from the heat. While whisking constantly, add the eggs one at a time.
- Pour the white sauce over the Parmesan cheese in the casserole dish. Sprinkle the remaining Parmesan cheese on top.
- Bake the moussaka for 20 minutes, or until it is lightly browned and everything is hot.

serves 6

Chicken Alfredo

"Rich and delicious, this chicken is perfect to serve for a special company dinner or when you are not worried about calories."

2 cups dried bread crumbs, finely ground
½ cup Parmesan cheese, freshly grated
1 tablespoon dried parsley
1 egg
1 tablespoon water
¼ teaspoon salt
4 6-ounce boneless chicken breasts, skins removed, and pounded to ¼" thick
½ cup Monterey Jack cheese, grated
½ pint half & half
¼ cup Parmesan cheese, freshly grated

- Preheat the oven to 350°.
- In a small bowl place the bread crumbs, the ½ cup of Parmesan cheese and the parsley. Mix them together.
- In another small bowl place the egg, water and salt. Beat them together.
- Dip each piece of chicken first into the egg batter and then into the bread crumbs so that it is well coated.
- Place the chicken in a lightly greased baking dish.
- Sprinkle the Jack cheese on top.
- Add the half & half.
- Sprinkle on the ¼ cup of Parmesan cheese.
- Bake the chicken for 30 minutes, or until it is done.

serves 4

"The people who stay at my Bed & Breakfast inn tend to be looking for peace and solitude, rather than for tourist attractions. They enjoy the quiet beauty of the countryside, and are not as interested in the hubbub of shops and restaurants."

Babette Miller

Cranberry Nut Bread

"I usually make this bread over the holidays, both to serve to my guests and to give as gifts to my friends. It's one of those moist breads that gets moister and better with time."

- **2 cups flour**
- **1 cup sugar**
- **1½ teaspoons baking powder**
- **½ teaspoon baking soda**
- **½ teaspoon salt**
- **¼ cup shortening**
- **1 egg, beaten**
- **¾ cup orange juice, freshly squeezed**
- **1 teaspoon orange zest** *(outer orange part grated off)*
- **½ cup walnuts, chopped**
- **2 cups fresh cranberries, chopped**

- Preheat the oven to 350°.
- In a large bowl sift together the flour, sugar, baking powder, baking soda and salt.
- Add the shortening and cut it in with a pastry blender so that coarse crumbs are formed.
- In a small bowl place the egg, orange juice and orange zest. Stir them together.
- Add the egg mixture to the crumb mixture, and stir them together so that the dough is just moistened.
- Add the walnuts and cranberries, and fold them in.
- Place the batter in a greased loaf pan. Spread it around so that there is more batter toward the sides than in the middle.
- Bake the bread for 1 hour, or until a wooden toothpick inserted in the center comes out clean.
- Remove the bread from the pan and let it cool on a wire rack.

makes 1 loaf

"My grandmother was a fabulous cook and taught me how to make her recipes when I was growing up. However, she would never tell me the exact proportions or measurements for things, and so I never learned to make her dishes as good as hers. Sometimes I think she did this on purpose, so her recipes would be secret."

Babette Miller

Fruit Pizza

"My sister, who is an excellent cook, gave me this recipe. It's unique because it is a sweet pizza made out of cookie dough, with fruit on top. People are always surprised when they first try it, because they don't expect it to taste so good. It is beautiful to look at, and will look different each time you make it, depending on the kind of fruit you use."

1 roll prepared sugar cookie dough
1 8-ounce package cream cheese, softened
⅓ cup sugar
2 kiwis, peeled and thinly sliced
8 strawberries, cored and thinly sliced
1 cup green grapes, halved
1 small can mandarin oranges, drained
1 cup orange juice, freshly squeezed
¼ cup lemon juice, freshly squeezed
¼ cup water
1 cup sugar
3 tablespoons cornstarch

- Preheat the oven to 350°.
- Roll out the cookie dough so that it fits a 12" pizza pan. Place the dough on the pan.
- Bake it for 12 minutes, or until it is lightly browned.
- Remove it from the oven and let it cool completely. *(Turn off the oven.)*
- In a small bowl place the cream cheese and the ⅓ cup of sugar, and blend them together so that they are creamy.
- Spread the mixture evenly on top of the cookie crust. Arrange the fruit pieces on top in an attractive pattern.
- In a medium saucepan place the orange juice, lemon juice, water, the 1 cup of sugar and the cornstarch. While stirring occasionally, bring the ingredients to a boil over medium heat. Boil the glaze for 2 minutes, or until it is thick.
- Remove the saucepan from the heat and let the glaze cool for 10 minutes.
- Drizzle the glaze on top of the fruit.

serves 6

Orange Street Inn

3496 Orange Street
Los Alamos, New Mexico 87544
(505) 662-2651
Susanne & Michael Paisley, Innkeepers

High on the spectacular Pajarito Plateau, nestled against the Jemez Mountains, this inn features elegant style and comfort. Guests may listen to the sighing pines, breathe the champagne air and enjoy a full breakfast prepared by one of the owners who is a teacher of gourmet cooking. Prehistoric Indian ruins and awe-inspiring geological wonders are just minutes away from the front door.

Recipes

Huevos Los Alamos Grande with Corn Crêpes

"Our guests find this dish to be a wonderful introduction to the popular New Mexican flavors of chile, corn and egg. It is a much more subtle and elegant variation of the traditional Huevos Rancheros."

Huevos Los Alamos Grande

4 eggs, lightly beaten
¼ cup sour cream
¼ teaspoon ground turmeric
½ teaspoon onion powder
¼ teaspoon salt
¼ teaspoon white pepper
¼ cup sharp cheddar cheese, grated
2 tablespoons green chile peppers, roasted, peeled and chopped
2 tablespoons salsa
2 tablespoons unsalted butter
1 tablespoon unsalted butter
4 Corn Crêpes *(recipe follows)*
½ cup sour cream

- In a medium bowl place the eggs and the ¼ cup of sour cream, and whisk them together well.
- Add the turmeric, onion powder, salt and white pepper. Whisk them in.
- Add the cheese, green chile peppers, salsa and the 2 tablespoons of butter. Mix them in.
- In a medium skillet place the 1 tablespoon of butter and heat it on medium until it is melted and hot. Add the egg mixture and allow a thin cooked layer to form on the bottom. Turn and mix the eggs with a spatula. Cook the eggs until they are just done *(not dry or hard)*.
- Place the eggs in the crêpes and roll them up. Garnish each serving with a dollop of sour cream.

serves 4

Corn Crêpes

4 eggs
¾ cup milk *(or as needed)*
½ cup all-purpose flour
½ cup corn flour
1 cup corn kernels, puréed
4 tablespoons butter *(or as needed)*

- In a medium bowl place the eggs and milk, and whisk them together well.
- Add the all-purpose flour, corn flour and puréed corn. Mix the ingredients together so that the batter is the consistency of heavy cream *(add more milk if necessary)*.
- In a crêpe pan place some of the butter and heat it on medium until it is melted and hot. For each crêpe add ¼ cup of the batter and tilt the pan so that the batter spreads out all over the bottom. Cook the crêpe for 1 minute. Flip it over and cook it for 30 seconds longer. *(The crêpes may be frozen.)*

makes 8 crêpes

Mushroom Tarragon Crêpes

"This is one of my most treasured recipes. The sweet vermouth is the secret to the rich flavor of the mushroom filling, and the tarragon crêpes are the perfect complement."

Mushroom Filling

4 tablespoons unsalted butter
½ pound mushrooms, sliced
2 tablespoons flour
¼ teaspoon sage
¼ teaspoon salt
¼ teaspoon white pepper
½ cup milk
1 cup sour cream
1 tablespoon sugar
¼ cup sweet vermouth
8 Tarragon Crêpes *(recipe on next page)*
4 tablespoons butter, melted
½ cup sour cream
8 mint leaves

- In a large skillet place the butter and heat it on medium until it is melted and hot. Add the mushrooms and sauté them for 5 to 8 minutes, or until they are dark in color.
- Add the flour and stir it in so that it absorbs all of the liquid. Cook and stir it for 2 minutes.
- Add the sage, salt and white pepper, and stir them in.
- Add the milk and the 1 cup of sour cream, and stir them in. Cook the mixture so that it thickens.
- Add the sugar and vermouth, and mix them in.
- Cook the filling for 2 minutes.
- Cover the pan with a lid and remove it from the heat. Let it cool slightly.
- Place some of the mixture down the center of each Tarragon Crêpe and then roll it up.
- Place a dollop of the ½ cup of sour cream on top and garnish it with a mint leaf.
- Serve the crêpes immediately.

serves 4

Tarragon Crêpes

½ **cup milk**
1 **teaspoon dried tarragon**
2 **eggs**
½ **cup milk** *(or as needed)*
1 **cup all-purpose flour**
¼ **teaspoon salt**
1 **cube unsalted butter, melted**

- In a small saucepan place the first ½ cup of milk and bring it to a simmer *(do not boil)*. Add the tarragon and set the pan aside.
- In a medium bowl place the eggs and the second ½ cup of milk, and whisk them together.
- Add the warm milk and whisk it in.
- Add the milk mixture to the flour and salt, and mix it in so that the batter is smooth and the consistency of heavy cream *(add more milk if necessary)*.
- In a crêpe pan place some of the butter and heat it on high until it is hot. For each crêpe, add ¼ cup of the batter and cook it for 1 minute. Flip it over and cook it for 30 seconds.

makes approximately 6 crêpes

"While some inns might be remembered for their architectural beauty, we are remembered for our friendliness."

Susanne Paisley

Breakfast Monte Cristo Sandwiches

"Desperation is often the mother of invention. In this case, I suddenly had a much larger crowd for breakfast than anticipated, and my pantry was nearly empty. However, there were some french toast supplies left over from the morning before, and so I came up with this recipe. It went over so well with the guests that I now offer it as a regular dish on our breakfast menu."

8 eggs
1 cup milk
1 teaspoon Schillings Fines Herbs
¼ teaspoon onion powder
1 teaspoon ground turmeric
1 teaspoon sugar
1 teaspoon salt
1 teaspoon pepper
8 slices English muffin bread *(or sourdough bread)*
2 tablespoons vegetable oil *(or as needed)*
4 slices smoked turkey
4 slices Muenster cheese
1 cup sour cream
1 teaspoon fresh dill, chopped

- In a large bowl place the eggs, milk, Fines Herbs, onion powder, turmeric, sugar, salt and pepper. Mix everything together well.
- Add the bread slices and soak them until they almost fall apart.
- In large skillet place the vegetable oil and heat it on medium until it is hot. Add the bread slices and cook them until they are golden brown on one side.
- Remove 4 of the slices and set them aside.
- Turn the remaining slices over in the skillet so that the cooked side is facing up. Place a slice of both the turkey and cheese on top of each piece.
- Place the cooked side of the remaining bread slices on top of the cheese, with the uncooked side facing up.
- Flip the sandwiches over and cook the other sides until they are golden brown.
- Cut each sandwich into 4 wedges.
- In a small bowl place the sour cream and dill weed, and mix them together.
- Place a dollop of sour cream on top of each wedge.

serves 4

Orange Street Inn

French Toast Extraordinaire

"The combination of sour cream, brown sugar, rum, and onion powder in this recipe produces a delicious, unusual taste. This dish will satisfy all but the biggest of eaters!"

- **8 eggs**
- **¼ teaspoon ground turmeric**
- **¾ cup sour cream**
- **¼ cup milk**
- **¼ teaspoon onion powder**
- **½ teaspoon nutmeg**
- **¼ teaspoon white pepper**
- **¼ teaspoon salt**
- **¼ cup brown sugar**
- **¼ teaspoon rum extract** *(or brandy)*
- **8 thick slices whole wheat French bread, left unwrapped overnight to dry out**
- **2 tablespoons vegetable oil** *(or as needed)*
- **4 tablespoons butter, melted**
- **1 cup fruit preserves** *(or as needed),* **heated**
- **2 tablespoons powdered sugar** *(or as needed)*

- In a large bowl place the eggs and turmeric, and whisk them together.
- In a small bowl place the sour cream and milk, and whisk them together. Add the mixture to the eggs, and whisk it in well.
- Add the onion powder, nutmeg, white pepper, salt, brown sugar and rum extract. Mix the ingredients together well.
- Add the bread slices and soak them until they almost fall apart.
- In a large skillet *(or griddle)* place the oil and heat it on medium until it is hot. Fry the bread slices on one side until they begin to bulge on top.
- Brush on the melted butter and flip the slices over.
- Fry them until the center is the consistency of pudding *(but not runny)*.
- Garnish each piece with the fruit preserves. Sprinkle on the powdered sugar.

serves 8

"Michael and I have found that running a Bed & Breakfast is the perfect way for us to earn a living. We are together all day long, and yet we each have our own areas of responsibility so we don't get in each other's way."

Susanne Paisley

Yogurt Biscuits

"One morning I was making biscuits and discovered that I was out of buttermilk. So I used yogurt instead, and found the flavor to be excellent. If you use vanilla yogurt instead of plain, and ½ whole wheat flour instead of all white, you can make delicious scones from this recipe."

3 cups flour
3 tablespoons sugar
1 tablespoon baking powder
2 teaspoons baking soda
¼ teaspoon onion powder
1½ sticks unsalted butter, cut into small pieces
1 large egg
1 egg yolk
1½ cups plain yogurt

- Preheat the oven to 350°.
- In a large bowl place the flour, sugar, baking powder, baking soda and onion powder. Mix them together well.
- Add the butter and cut it in with a pastry blender so that pea-size crumbs are formed.
- In a small bowl place the egg, egg yolk and yogurt, and whisk them together well.
- Add the egg mixture to the dry mixture, and stir it in with a fork.
- Dust your hands with flour. Knead the mixture in the bowl until everything is well combined and the dough is smooth and pliable.
- On a floured board form the dough into a circle that is ¾" thick.
- Cut out biscuits that are 2" in diameter *(try a wine glass)*. Place them on a greased baking sheet.
- Bake the biscuits for 25 minutes, or until they are nicely browned.

makes approximately 12 biscuits

"Through my experience in teaching gourmet cooking for the University of New Mexico at Los Alamos, I have learned the importance of simple recipes that communicate unfamiliar, yet enchanting, flavors."

Michael Paisley

Ratatouille Paisley

"We love ratatouille, and during the height of zucchini season in our garden, we eat it until we are practically speaking French. In this recipe I've juggled the spices to produce a delicate sweet and sour flavor."

- ½ **cup olive oil** *(or as needed)*
- 2 **medium yellow onions, thinly sliced**
- 1 **large eggplant, peeled and diced into ½" pieces**
- 4 **medium zucchini, diced into ½" pieces**
- 1 **small red bell pepper, seeded and julienned**
- 4 **cloves garlic, minced**
- 4 **tomatoes, skinned, seeded and diced**
- ½ **cup fresh basil** *(or 2 tablespoons dried),* **chopped**
- 1 **teaspoon Worcestershire sauce**
- 1 **tablespoon soy sauce**
- ¼ **cup balsamic vinegar**
- 3 **tablespoons sugar**
- **salt and pepper** *(to taste)*

- In a large wok place some of the oil and heat it on high until it is very hot. Add the onions and stir-fry them until they begin to brown. Remove them and set them aside. Repeat this process individually for the eggplant, zucchini and bell peppers.
- Reduce the heat to medium. Add the garlic and stir-fry it until it begins to brown.
- Add the tomatoes and basil, and cook them until they are hot.
- Add the rest of the cooked vegetables, the Worcestershire sauce, soy sauce, vinegar and sugar. Stir them in gently.
- Simmer everything for 5 minutes.
- Season the ratatouille with the salt and pepper.

serves 6 to 8

"To be successful in this business you must have a nurturing nature and you absolutely must be a 'people person'."

Susanne Paisley

Calabacitas Soup

"On Sunday mornings I make a big pot of this soup and then eat it all week long. The spicy flavor comes from the darkly broiled chicken coated with the New Mexico Spice."

- 4 **cups chicken broth**
- 2 **medium yellow onions, thinly sliced**
- 2 **medium potatoes, diced into ¼" cubes**
- 1 **zucchini, diced into ¼" cubes**
- 4 **tablespoons olive oil** *(or chicken fat)*
- 4 **tablespoons flour**
- 4 **chicken thighs, coated with New Mexico Spice** *(recipe on next page),* **broiled and meat diced small**
- 2 **cups canned sweet corn** *(with juice)*
- 1 **8-ounce can mild green chile peppers, diced**
- 1 **cup sour cream**
- **salt and pepper (to taste)**
- ½ **bunch fresh cilantro, chopped**

- In a large stockpot place the chicken broth, onions, potatoes and zucchini. Bring the ingredients to a boil and then simmer them for 15 minutes, or until the potatoes begin to soften.
- In a small saucepan place the oil and heat it on medium until it is hot. Add the flour and stir it in until a golden brown roux is formed.
- To the stockpot add the broiled chicken, corn and green chile peppers. Bring the ingredients to a boil.
- Add the roux and stir it in so that the liquid thickens.
- Add the sour cream, salt and pepper, and stir them in.
- Remove the soup from the heat.
- Garnish each serving with the cilantro.

serves 6 to 8

"Wildlife is abundant in this part of the country, and our guests have excitedly spotted elk, coyote, black bear, and even the rare golden eagle with its eight-foot wing span."

Michael Paisley

New Mexico Spice Mix

"I make up a large batch of this to store in my cupboard and then use it liberally to season soups, stews, meat, chicken and fish. It is especially good for broiling or barbecuing because it holds up well under high temperatures."

- ½ **cup mild red chile powder**
- ½ **cup dried oregano**
- ¼ **cup garlic powder**
- ¼ **cup onion powder**
- 2 **tablespoons sugar**
- 2 **tablespoons salt**

- Mix all of the ingredients together well and store them in a jar with a tight lid.

makes 1¾ cups

"I like to take a basic recipe that everyone knows and then change some of the ingredients so that it becomes a brand-new dish. My favorite recipes are those that are easy to make and have a lot of pizzaz."

Michael Paisley

Zucchini Muffins

"I find it fascinating how grated zucchini melds into the fabric of a muffin or bread loaf, and seems to almost disappear. Eventually I doubled the amount used in this recipe, and the taste and texture hardly changed at all."

2 cups all-purpose flour
1 teaspoon baking soda
1 teaspoon baking powder
1 teaspoon salt
2 teaspoons ground cinnamon
1 teaspoon ground nutmeg
2 eggs
1 cup brown sugar
1½ teaspoons vanilla extract
¾ cup vegetable oil
2 cups zucchini, grated
1 cup raisins, cooked in apple juice or brandy until softened, and drained
1 cup pecans, chopped

- Preheat the oven to 375°.
- In a large bowl place the flour, baking soda, baking powder, salt, cinnamon and nutmeg. Whisk everything together well.
- In a medium large bowl place the eggs, and whisk them.
- Add the brown sugar and whisk it in.
- Add the vanilla and oil, and whisk them in well.
- Add the zucchini, raisins and pecans, and mix them in well.
- Add the zucchini mixture to the flour mixture, and fold it in so that it is just incorporated.
- Place the batter in 12 individual greased muffin tins so they are ⅔ full.
- Bake the muffins for 20 minutes, or until the tops are springy and a wooden toothpick inserted in the center comes out clean.

makes 12 muffins

"My love of cooking comes from my father, who made fantastic dishes, and my grandmother, who cooked huge quantities of food quite effortlessly."

Michael Paisley

Coconut Chocolate Chip Muffins

"The inspiration for these muffins came to me at a time when I was suffering from a sweet-tooth attack, and just had to have something decadent. The result was deadly delicious."

2 cups all-purpose flour
½ cup sugar
½ teaspoon baking powder
¼ teaspoon baking soda
¼ teaspoon salt
2 large eggs
1 cup plain yogurt
¾ cup vegetable oil
½ cup coconut milk
2 cups shredded coconut *(sweetened)*
1 cup mini chocolate chips

- Preheat the oven to 375°.
- In a large bowl place the flour, sugar, baking powder, baking soda and salt. Mix them together well.
- In a medium bowl place the eggs, yogurt, oil and coconut milk. Whisk them together well.
- Add the coconut and chocolate chips, and mix them in.
- Add the wet mixture to the dry mixture, and carefully fold it in so that the dry ingredients are moist.
- Place the batter in 12 individual greased muffin tins so that they are ⅔ full.
- Bake the muffins for 20 to 25 minutes, or until a wooden toothpick inserted in the center comes out clean.

makes 12 muffins

"We want our Bed & Breakfast to exude 'Style', with a capital 'S'! One way we try to accomplish this is by our devoted attention to detail in every aspect of the inn's operation."

Susanne Paisley

McGraham Tipsy Cake with Pudding Frosting

"One day when I was preparing to teach an Irish Cooking Class for the University, I couldn't find the recipe for the advertised Tipsy Cake, as outlined in the course guide. In a panic, I came up with this creation, and luckily it came out fantastic. One word of warning.....if you let the cake soak in the liquor too long, it will indeed tip over on itself!"

McGraham Tipsy Cake

2 cups flour
2 teaspoons baking powder
½ teaspoon ground cardamom
¼ teaspoon salt
¾ cup butter, softened
¾ cup sugar
2 eggs
1 teaspoon vanilla extract
¾ cup milk
½ cup apple juice
½ cup orange juice, freshly squeezed
¼ cup brandy
¼ cup honey
Pudding Frosting *(recipe on next page)*

- Preheat the oven to 375°.
- In a large bowl place the flour, baking powder, cardamom and salt. Mix them together well.
- In a medium bowl place the butter and sugar. Whip them together so that they are creamy.
- Add the eggs and vanilla, and whip them until the mix is fluffy.
- In small amounts, alternately add and stir the egg mixture and the milk into the flour mixture.
- Pour the batter into two 8" greased and floured cake pans.
- Bake the cake for 20 to 30 minutes, or until a wooden toothpick inserted in the center comes out clean.
- Remove the cakes from the pans and set them on a rack.
- In a small saucepan place the apple juice, orange juice, brandy and honey. Heat and blend them together.
- Pour the liquid into a large shallow dish. Quickly immerse both sides of one of the cakes in the liquid.
- Place it on a serving plate and frost it with the Pudding Frosting.
- Dip both sides of the other cake in the liquid, and place it on top of the first cake.
- Frost the second layer. Serve the cake warm.

serves 8 to 10

Pudding Frosting

- ¼ **cup butter**
- ¼ **cup flour**
- ¼ **cup applesauce**
- ½ **cup sugar**
- **2 egg yolks**
- ¼ **cup brandy**
- **1 cup milk**

- In a small saucepan place the butter and heat it on medium low until it is melted and hot. Add the flour and stir it in for 5 minutes *(do not let it brown)* to make a roux.
- In a medium saucepan place the applesauce, sugar and egg yolks. Stir them together well.
- Add the roux and blend it in.
- While gradually increasing the heat, slowly add and stir in the brandy and milk so the frosting is the consistency of a heavy pudding.

frosts 1 cake

"I cannot cook worth beans! Even though I can follow a recipe to the letter, it never comes out good, and I cannot tell you why. Michael, on the other hand, has a magical gift with food. He can turn an ordinary dish into something extraordinary."

Susanne Paisley

Preston House

106 Faithway Street
Santa Fe, New Mexico 87501
(505) 982-3465
Signe Bergman, Innkeeper • Olive Paradis, Manager

Victorian ambience and Southwestern charm share the spotlight with a garden cottage at Preston House just four blocks from the Santa Fe Plaza. The turn-of-the-century mansion and Queen Anne-style garden cottage have been lovingly restored by the artist-owner, who has also added adobe guest house rooms. The inn is an ideal base for those who visit Santa Fe on business, with conference space and audiovisual and office equipment available, and catered meals an option.

Recipes

Champagne Jelly

"Here is a great way to use up leftover champagne that has gone flat."

- 2 **cups champagne** *(flat)*
- 3 **cups sugar**
- 1 **2¾-ounce package Certo liquid fruit pectin**
- 4 **8-ounce jelly jars, sterilized**

- In the top of a double boiler place the champagne and sugar. Stir them together over boiling water for 4 minutes, or until the sugar is dissolved.
- Remove the pan from the heat.
- Immediately add the Certo and stir it in so that it is well blended.
- Fill each jar to ½" from the top.
- Seal the jars according to the instructions.

makes four 8-ounce jars of jelly

"I opened my Bed & Breakfast in 1981, with the intention of trying it out for a maximum of two years. But the experience turned out to be so profitable and so much fun that I've continued on ever since, with no plans to retire."

Signe Bergman

Green Chile Cornmeal Muffins

"These muffins have a delightful sweet and hot flavor that many people find to be pleasantly surprising. Either yellow or blue cornmeal may be used."

1¼ cups flour
¾ cup cornmeal
¼ cup sugar
1 tablespoon baking powder
½ teaspoon salt
1 cup sour cream
½ teaspoon baking soda
1 egg, lightly beaten
¾ cup cheddar cheese, grated
1 7-ounce can green chile peppers, chopped

- Preheat the oven to 350°.
- In a large bowl place the flour, cornmeal, sugar, baking powder and salt. Mix the ingredients together.
- In a medium bowl place the sour cream and baking soda, and stir them so that the mixture is frothy.
- To the flour mixture add the sour cream, egg, cheddar cheese and green chile peppers. Mix the ingredients together so that they are well combined *(if the mixture is too thick, add a small amount of milk)*.
- Fill 24 individual greased muffin tins with the batter so that they are ⅔ full.
- Bake the muffins for 25 minutes, or until they are light brown and a wooden toothpick inserted in the center comes out clean.

makes 24 muffins

"I love Santa Fe for many reasons.....the mountains, the clear air, the architectural style, the cultural opportunities.....but most of all I love it for the people. They are creative, intelligent, warm, and make it very easy for a single woman to be accepted."

Signe Bergman

Irish Soda Bread

"This is a basic Irish bread recipe that is slightly sweet because of the raisins and sugar. It's lovely any time of day, along with a cup of hot tea."

3½ cups flour
½ cup sugar
½ teaspoon baking soda
2 teaspoons baking powder
1 teaspoon salt
2 teaspoons caraway seeds
2 large eggs, slightly beaten
1 pint sour cream
1 cup raisins, soaked in warm water until softened and drained

- Preheat the oven to 350°.
- In a large bowl place the flour, sugar, baking soda, baking powder, salt and caraway seeds. Mix the ingredients together well. Add the eggs and sour cream, and fold them in so that they are just combined *(do not overmix)*. Add the raisins and gently fold them in.
- Place the dough in a greased and floured 8" round cake pan. Even out the top of the batter with a floured spatula. With a knife, cut an 'X' across the dough.
- Bake the bread for 1 hour, or until it is lightly browned on top.
- Immediately remove the bread from the pan and wrap it in a dampened cloth. Place the bread on a wire rack and let it cool.

makes 1 loaf

Preston House Shortbread

"The almond extract gives this shortbread an additional yummy taste. We serve it with afternoon tea and people just gobble it up."

1¼ cups flour
3 tablespoons sugar
1 stick butter, cut into pieces
½ teaspoon vanilla extract
½ teaspoon almond extract

- Preheat the oven to 325°.
- In a medium bowl place the flour and sugar, and mix them together. Add the butter and cut it in with a pastry blender so that fine crumbs are formed. Add the vanilla and almond extracts, and mix them in.
- Form the dough into a ball. Knead it until it is smooth.
- On an ungreased cookie sheet place the dough ball. Pat it with your fingers so that an 8" circle is formed. Scallop the edge. Prick the dough with a fork. Cut the dough into 12 wedges *(do not separate them)*.
- Bake the shortbread for 25 to 30 minutes, or until the edges are lightly browned. Re-cut the wedges. Let them cool on a wire rack.

serves 6

Pecan Coffeecake

"Originally this recipe came from ***Better Homes & Gardens****, and over the years it has gone through some changes, all for the better. The rum, sour cream and pecans are what make it so delicious."*

- **1 cup pecans, finely chopped**
- **⅓ cup brown sugar**
- **1 teaspoon ground cinnamon**
- **2½ cups all-purpose flour**
- **1 cup sugar**
- **1 tablespoon baking powder**
- **½ teaspoon salt**
- **½ cup butter**
- **3 eggs, beaten**
- **1 8-ounce carton sour cream**
- **⅓ cup milk**
- **1 teaspoon vanilla extract**
- **2 cups apples, peeled and finely chopped**
- **1 cup powdered sugar**
- **2 tablespoons hot water**
- **¼ teaspoon rum flavoring**

- Preheat the oven to 350°.
- In a greased 10" bundt pan, sprinkle ½ cup of the pecans evenly on the bottom. Set the pan aside.
- In a small bowl place the remaining pecans, brown sugar and cinnamon. Mix the ingredients together and set them aside.
- In a medium bowl place the flour, sugar, baking powder and salt. Add the butter and cut it in with a pastry blender so that coarse crumbs are formed. Make a well in the center of the crumbs.
- In another medium bowl place the eggs, sour cream, milk and vanilla. Stir them together so that they are blended.
- Pour the sour cream mixture into the well of the crumb mixture. Mix them together so that the crumbs are just moistened *(do not overmix)*. Add the apples and fold them in.
- Remove 1 cup of the batter and add it to the brown sugar and pecan mixture to make the filling. Stir the ingredients together so that they are well blended.
- Into the bundt pan place ½ of the plain batter. Spoon the filling on top. Gently pour the remaining plain batter on top of the filling.
- Bake the cake for 45 to 50 minutes, or until a wooden toothpick inserted near the center comes out clean.
- Cool the cake in the pan on a wire rack for 10 minutes. Invert the cake onto a serving plate. Remove the bundt pan and let the cake cool for 15 minutes more.
- In a small bowl place the powdered sugar, hot water and rum flavoring. Beat the ingredients together with an electric mixer on medium speed. Slowly add more water if necessary so that a smooth creamy mixture is achieved.
- Drizzle the icing over the cake.

serves 8

Preston House

The Best Blueberry Muffins

"The nutmeg is what gives this recipe that extra something in taste. Frozen blueberries work better than fresh, only because they don't bleed their color as much."

½ cup butter, softened
1 cup sugar
2 eggs
1 teaspoon vanilla extract
2 teaspoons baking powder
¼ teaspoon salt
1½ cups frozen blueberries
2¼ cups flour
½ cup milk
1 tablespoon sugar
½ teaspoon nutmeg

- Preheat the oven to 375°.
- In a medium bowl place the butter and the 1 cup of sugar. Beat them together with an electric mixer on medium to high speed for 2 minutes, or until the mixture is creamy and fluffy.
- Add the eggs one at a time, and blend each one in thoroughly.
- Add the vanilla, baking powder and salt. Mix the ingredients together.
- Add the blueberries and gently mix them in.
- Alternately add small amounts of the flour and milk, and lightly stir them together so that the flour is barely moistened.
- Fill 12 individual greased muffin tins with the batter so that they are ⅔ full.
- Sprinkle the 1 tablespoon of sugar and the nutmeg on top.
- Bake the muffins for 30 minutes, or until they are lightly browned.

makes 12 muffins

"I truly love to eat sweet things, and I think this is why I have come to be a good baker. Unfortunately, my sweet tooth has caused both my husband and me to suffer in the size of our waistlines!"

Olive Paradis

Preston Bread Pudding

"We have been making this pudding for years here at the inn, and the recipe is constantly being altered, according to who is in the kitchen."

- **6 eggs**
- **2½ cups sugar**
- **1 tablespoon ground cinnamon**
- **1 tablespoon ground nutmeg**
- **1 tablespoon vanilla extract**
- **½ cup butter, melted**
- **4½ cups milk**
- **6 cups white bread, crusts removed, and cubed**
- **1 cup pecans, coarsely chopped**
- **1 cup raisins**

- Preheat the oven to 350°.
- In a large bowl place the eggs and beat them with an electric mixer on high speed until they are frothy.
- Add the sugar, cinnamon, nutmeg, vanilla and butter. Mix the ingredients together well.
- Add the milk and bread cubes, and stir them in. Let the bread soak for 15 minutes.
- Add the pecans and raisins, and stir them in well.
- Pour the batter into a 13" x 9" greased baking pan.
- Bake the pudding for 45 minutes, or until it is set.

serves 6 to 8

"Smokey is our cat, and he is the official resident greeting committee. Repeat guests who get to know Smokey often invite him to sleep on their beds at night. He's very friendly and loves people."

Signe Bergman

Breakfast Apple Pie

"The corn flakes in the bottom of the pie are the secret to this recipe. They soak up the juices from the apples and sugar, so the top crust comes out drier and flakier. People always want to know the recipe."

¾ cup flour
½ cup sugar
½ cup butter, cut into small pieces
5 large apples, quartered, peeled, cored and thinly sliced
½ cup sugar
1 teaspoon ground cinnamon
1 9" unbaked pie shell
1½ cups corn flakes

- Preheat the oven to 425°.
- In a medium bowl place the flour, the first ½ cup of sugar and the butter. Cut the butter into the flour with a pastry blender so that the mixture is well blended and crumbly. Set the topping mixture aside.
- In a large bowl place the apples, the second ½ cup of sugar and the cinnamon. Toss the ingredients together so that all of the apples are coated.
- Sprinkle the corn flakes in the bottom of the pie shell. Place the apples on top. Sprinkle the topping evenly over the apples.
- Bake the pie for 10 minutes.
- Reduce the heat to 350°.
- Bake the pie for 35 minutes more, or until the apples are tender.

serves 6 to 8

"Many new Bed & Breakfast owners make the mistake of not hiring enough people to help them, and so they burn out after one or two years. It's important to understand from the beginning how much work it is, and to be sure to reserve enough time for yourself."

Signe Bergman

Preston House Cookies

"Initially this was a plain chocolate chip cookie recipe. The addition of the white chocolate elevates the flavor to another level and makes them truly gourmet."

2 cups flour
2½ cups rolled oats, coarsely blended
½ teaspoon salt
½ teaspoon baking powder
1 teaspoon baking soda
1 cup butter
1 cup white sugar
1 cup brown sugar
2 large eggs
1 teaspoon vanilla extract
6 ounces semisweet chocolate chips
1 ounce plain Hershey bar, grated
1½ cups walnuts, chopped
6 ounces white chocolate, coarsely chopped

- Preheat the oven to 375°.
- In a medium bowl place the flour, oats, salt, baking powder and baking soda. Mix the ingredients together well and set them aside.
- In a large bowl place the butter, white sugar and brown sugar. Beat the ingredients together with an electric mixer on medium speed until they are creamy.
- Add the eggs and vanilla, and beat them in well.
- Add the creamy mixture to the flour mixture, and blend it in well.
- Add the chocolate chips, grated Hershey bar, walnuts and white chocolate. Stir them in so that the ingredients are well blended.
- Roll the dough into 1" balls.
- Place them 2" apart on a greased cookie sheet.
- Bake the cookies for 10 minutes, or until they are lightly browned.

makes approximately 4 dozen cookies

Applesauce Spice Streusel Bread

"I love the texture of this bread, which is both moist and crunchy at the same time. The streusel topping is excellent, and can be sprinkled on top of muffins as well."

4 cups flour
1½ teaspoons baking soda
1½ teaspoons baking powder
1 teaspoon ground cinnamon
1 teaspoon ground allspice
½ teaspoon ground nutmeg
½ teaspoon salt
2 cups sugar
2 cups applesauce
⅔ cup vegetable oil
4 tablespoons milk
4 eggs
1½ cups walnuts, chopped
½ cup brown sugar
⅔ cup walnuts, chopped

- Preheat the oven to 350°.
- In a large bowl place the flour, baking soda, baking powder, cinnamon, allspice, nutmeg and salt. Mix the ingredients well and then set them aside.
- In another large bowl place the sugar, applesauce, oil, milk, eggs and the 1½ cups of walnuts. Mix the ingredients together.
- Add the liquid mixture to the flour mixture, and mix it in well.
- Pour the batter into 2 greased loaf pans.
- In a small bowl place the brown sugar and the ⅔ cup of walnuts, and mix them together well. Sprinkle the mixture on top of the loaves.
- Bake the bread for 1 hour, or until the loaves are golden brown.

makes 2 loaves

"It is a true joy to work at the Preston House. Signe is a wonderful boss, and the staff and guests are like one big happy family. We have lots of hugs and good vibrations."

Olive Paradis

Rugelach Cookies

"This is the best cookie in the world! It is extra rich because of the cream cheese in the dough. To be more frugal, yogurt can be substituted."

2 sticks margarine, softened
1 8-ounce package cream cheese, softened
2½ cups all-purpose white flour
¼ teaspoon salt
1 cup raisins, chopped
1 cup walnuts, finely chopped
¾ cup sugar
1 tablespoon ground cinnamon
½ cup raspberry jelly

- In a large bowl place the margarine and cream cheese, and beat them together well with an electric mixer. With the mixer constantly running on medium speed, gradually add the flour and salt.
- Form the dough into a ball. Wrap it in plastic wrap and refrigerate it for 1 hour.
- Preheat the oven to 375°.
- In a medium bowl place the raisins, walnuts, sugar and cinnamon. Mix the ingredients together and set them aside.
- Divide the refrigerated dough into 5 equal pieces and shape them into balls.
- On a floured surface roll out each ball into a 9" circle.
- Spread the jelly thinly on top of each circle.
- Sprinkle ½ cup of the raisin-sugar mixture evenly on top of each circle.
- Cut each circle into 10 wedges.
- Starting at the wide end, roll up each wedge and then pinch the ends to seal it.
- On a lightly greased baking sheet place the cookies and bake them for 15 to 20 minutes, or until they are lightly browned.
- Cool them on a wire rack.

makes 50 cookies

"The main reason why I love my occupation is that each day is different, with endless new challenges. Fortunately, I have an excellent staff to help me meet them!"

Signe Bergman

Chocolate Raspberry Cheesecake

"We try to make things that are outrageously delicious, and this cheesecake is one of those dishes. It is not something to eat every day, but just when you are in the mood to splurge."

1½ cups Oreo cookies, finely crushed
2 tablespoons butter, melted
4 8-ounce packages cream cheese, softened
1 cup sugar
1 cup sour cream
1 tablespoon vanilla extract
4 eggs
1 6-ounce package semisweet chocolate chips, melted
⅓ cup raspberry preserves
1 6-ounce package semisweet chocolate chips
¼ cup whipping cream
1 small package fresh raspberries

- In a small bowl place the cookie crumbs and butter, and mix them together well.
- Place the cookie mixture in a 9" springform pan. Press the crumbs into the bottom of the pan so that a firm crust is formed. Set the pan aside.
- Preheat the oven to 425°.
- In a large bowl place 3 of the packages of cream cheese and the sugar. Beat them together with an electric mixer on medium speed so that they are well blended.
- Add the sour cream and vanilla, and blend them in well.
- Add one egg at a time to the batter and blend each one in *(do not overbeat)*.
- Pour the batter onto the crust.
- In a medium bowl place the remaining package of cream cheese and the melted chocolate. Beat the ingredients together with an electric mixer on medium speed so that they are well blended.
- Add the raspberry preserves and mix them in well.
- Place rounded tablespoons of the chocolate-cream cheese batter on top of the plain batter.
- Bake the cheesecake for 10 minutes. Reduce the heat to 250°. Bake it for 1¼ hours more, or until the center is firm.
- Loosen the cake from the pan by running a knife around the inside rim. Let the cake cool completely. Remove the rim of the pan.
- In a small saucepan place the second package of chocolate chips and the whipping cream. Heat them on low so that the chocolate is melted and the mixture is smooth.
- Spread the chocolate on the top and sides of the cooled cake.
- Place the fresh raspberries on top.

serves 10

Preston House

The Red Violet Inn

344 North 2nd Street
Raton, New Mexico 87740
(505) 445-9778 • (800) 624-9778
Ruth & John Hanrahan, Innkeepers

This stately red brick Victorian home, built in 1902, is within walking distance of Raton's downtown historical district and beguiling antique shops. Here in the far north of New Mexico at the bottom of the high pass that leads into Colorado, the Victorian era seems still to live. The inn's guest rooms feature such items as four-posters and brass beds, and selections from the owners' collection of antique bowls, pitchers and chamber pots are on display throughout the house.

Recipes

Our Lentil Soup

"Lentil soup is always delicious and healthy, and this particular version is especially good. As with many soups or stews, you can add whatever vegetables you have in the refrigerator."

3 quarts chicken broth
1 pound lentils, washed and drained
½ cup brown rice
4 tablespoons vegetable oil
1⅓ cups yellow onions, chopped medium
2 stalks celery, chopped
1 cup carrots, chopped
2 cups potatoes, peeled and cubed small
3 cloves garlic, chopped
1 quart hot water
1 16-ounce can whole tomatoes, crushed
¼ teaspoon paprika
¼ teaspoon dried parsley
¼ teaspoon dried basil
salt and pepper *(to taste)*

- In a large stockpot place the chicken broth, lentils and rice. Simmer the ingredients on low heat for 1½ hours.
- In another large stockpot place the oil and heat it on medium until it is hot. Add the onions, celery, carrots, potatoes and garlic. Sauté them 5 minutes, or until the onions are tender.
- Add the hot water and stir it in. Reduce the heat to low and simmer the vegetables for 15 minutes.
- Add the lentil and rice mixture, tomatoes, paprika, parsley, basil, salt and pepper.
- Simmer the soup for 10 minutes, or until everything is hot.

serves 8

"We wanted the name of our inn to be one that people would remember. There is no such thing as a red violet.....but there definitely is a Red Violet Inn!"

John Hanrahan

Cold Watermelon Soup

"Years ago I ordered this soup at an inn in Gold Hills, Colorado. It was really good, so I asked the owner for the recipe. He wouldn't give it out, but he did tell me what the ingredients were. I came home and eventually figured out the proportions."

- **1½ cups sugar**
- **1 cup water**
- **2 slices lime**
- **1 whole vanilla bean**
- **4 1" thick slices watermelon, rinds and seeds removed**
- **3 cups cold white wine** *(or white grape juice)*

- In a medium saucepan place the sugar, water, lime slices and vanilla bean. Bring the mixture to a boil over medium heat. While stirring occasionally, cook the mixture for 10 minutes.
- Remove the slices of lime and vanilla bean, and discard them.
- In a food processor place the watermelon and sugar sauce, and purée them so that they are smooth.
- Place the mixture in a medium bowl. Cover the bowl with plastic wrap and chill it in the refrigerator for 1 hour.
- Add the wine and stir it in.

serves 8

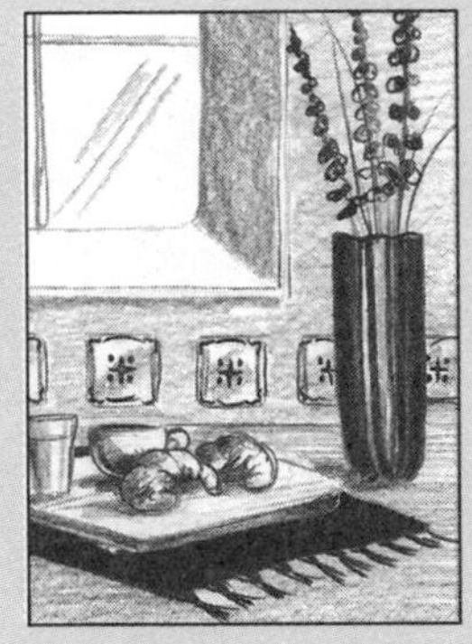

"I've always enjoyed cooking and reading cookbooks. I was a librarian, and my station was next to the cookbook stacks. When the work was slow I spent hours poring over the recipes. Today I have an extensive cookbook collection of my own.....perhaps even to rival that of the library!"

Ruth Hanrahan

Sweet Potato Soup with a Kick

"My son Michael is a chef in Vail, and this is one of his favorite recipes. He once served it to Gerald and Betty Ford, and has a picture of himself standing at their table."

- 1/4 **cup bacon fat**
- 1 **pound red onions, chopped**
- 1 **leek, trimmed and chopped**
- 2 **cloves garlic**
- 1 **jalapeño chile pepper, seeds removed, and finely chopped**
- 1½ **pounds sweet potatoes, peeled and cut into ½" chunks**
- 2 **quarts chicken broth**
- 1/4 **teaspoon dried thyme**
- 1/4 **teaspoon ground nutmeg**
- **salt and pepper** *(to taste)*
- 1 **cup heavy cream**
- 1/2 **cup sour cream** *(or as needed)*

- In a large skillet place the bacon fat and heat it on medium until it is melted and hot. Add the onions, leeks, garlic and jalapeño chile pepper. Sauté them for 5 minutes, or until the onions are tender.
- Add the sweet potatoes, chicken broth, thyme and nutmeg. Bring the ingredients to a boil over high heat.
- Reduce the heat to low and simmer the ingredients for 15 minutes, or until the potatoes are tender.
- Place the mixture in a food processor and purée it for 1 minute, or until it is smooth.
- Add the salt, pepper and cream, and blend them in well.
- Garnish each serving with a dollop of sour cream.

serves 8

Red Violet Black Beans

"This is a simple recipe that is very versatile. The beans can be used on tostadas or in tacos, mixed with salsa for a bean dip, or made into a soup by adding some broth. I keep a big batch in my freezer to use as I need them over a period of time."

- 1 **pound black beans, cleaned and rinsed**
- 6 **cups water** *(or as needed)*
- 2 **cloves garlic, finely chopped**
- 2 **tablespoons lard** *(or to taste)*
- **salt** *(to taste)*

- In a large stockpot place the beans, water and garlic, and bring them to a boil over medium heat. Cover the pot with a lid, reduce the heat to low, and simmer the beans for 3 hours, or until they are tender *(add more water if needed)*.
- In a food processor place the cooked beans. Purée them so that a chunky paste is formed.
- Add the lard and salt, and blend them in.

serves 4 to 6

Veggie Eggs Benedict

"This is a popular vegetarian dish that we serve for breakfast. Other vegetables such as tomatoes or mushrooms may be substituted for the green peppers."

- **2 tablespoons olive oil**
- **1 red bell pepper, seeded and thinly sliced**
- **1 green bell pepper, seeded and thinly sliced**
- **2 tablespoons butter**
- **2 tablespoons flour**
- **½ teaspoon salt**
- **¼ teaspoon white pepper**
- **1 cup milk**
- **2 large egg yolks**
- **⅓ cup Swiss cheese, grated**
- **2 teaspoons lemon juice, freshly squeezed**
- **1 teaspoon Dijon mustard**
- **3 English muffins, halved and toasted**
- **6 large eggs, poached**
- **1 teaspoon paprika** *(or to taste)*
- **½ cup Parmesan cheese, freshly grated**

- In a medium sauté pan place the olive oil and heat it on medium high until it is hot. Add the bell peppers, and sauté them until they are crisp and tender. Set them aside and keep them warm.
- In a medium saucepan place the butter and heat it on medium until it is melted and hot. Add the flour, salt and white pepper. Whisk and cook the mixture for 1 minute.
- Add the milk and whisk the sauce until it is smooth.
- While stirring constantly, bring the sauce to a boil and let it thicken. Remove the pan from the heat.
- In a small bowl place the egg yolks and lightly beat them. Add a small amount of the hot white sauce and blend it in.
- Add the egg mixture to the sauce in the pan.
- Add the cheese and heat it until it is melted.
- Remove the pan from the heat.
- Add the lemon juice and mustard, and stir them in.
- On each of 6 individual serving plates place a muffin half. Spoon on the bell peppers. Place a poached egg on top. Ladle on the sauce. Sprinkle on the paprika and Parmesan cheese.

serves 6

Chorizo Eggplant Parmesan

"If you are fond of Eggplant Parmesan, you definitely will love this recipe. It calls for the addition of chorizo sausage, which adds a wonderful New Mexican spicy flavor."

- 2 **medium eggplants, peeled, sliced into ¼" rounds, sprinkled with salt, allowed to sit for 1 hour, then rinsed and patted dry**
- 3 **eggs, well beaten**
- 2 **cups dried bread crumbs, ground**
- ½ **cup vegetable oil** *(or as needed)*
- 3 **cups spaghetti sauce** *(your favorite)*
- 1 **pound chorizo sausage, cooked and drained of grease**
- 2 **cups mozzarella cheese, grated**
- ⅓ **cup Parmesan cheese, freshly grated**

- Preheat the oven to 350°.
- Dip each slice of eggplant first into the eggs and then into the bread crumbs so that it is well coated.
- In a large skillet place the oil and heat it on medium until it is hot. Add the eggplant slices and fry them for 3 minutes on each side, or until they are browned.
- In a square greased baking dish place some of the spaghetti sauce and spread it out evenly.
- In this order, make layers of the eggplant, chorizo, mozzarella cheese and sauce, ending with a layer of the sauce. Sprinkle the Parmesan cheese on top.
- Bake the casserole for ½ hour, or until everything is hot.
- Remove the dish from the oven and let it cool for 15 minutes.

serves 8

"Raton is a small, friendly town with lots of outdoor activities and beautiful clear skies. It's the kind of place where, if you go to the store and forget your wallet, you can take the groceries home and pay for them the next day."

John Hanrahan

Chile Rellenos

"Twenty-five years ago we moved into an old house in Colorado. I found this recipe written on a piece of paper stuck inside an old Mexican cookbook that the previous owners had left in the cupboard. It's so good that I've been making it ever since."

- 1 **16-ounce can tomatoes** *(with juice)*
- ¼ **cup yellow onions, finely chopped**
- 1 **beef bouillon cube**
- ⅛ **teaspoon pepper**
- ⅛ **teaspoon ground cinnamon**
- 2 **cups Monterey Jack cheese, grated**
- 2 **cups Swiss cheese, grated**
- 8 **large poblano chile peppers, roasted, peeled, seeds and stems removed**
- 8 **egg yolks, lightly beaten**
- 2 **tablespoons water**
- ¼ **cup flour**
- ½ **teaspoon salt**
- 8 **egg whites, beaten stiff**
- ½ **cup shortening** *(or as needed)*
- 1 **tablespoon fresh cilantro, chopped**

- In a blender place the tomatoes, onions, bouillon, pepper and cinnamon. Blend them together so that they are smooth.
- Place the mixture in a medium saucepan. Bring it to a boil over medium heat. Reduce the heat to low and simmer the sauce for 5 minutes. Keep it warm.
- In a medium bowl place the two cheeses and combine them together.
- Stuff each of the 8 peppers with ½ cup of the cheese mixture. Set them aside.
- In another medium bowl place the egg yolks and water, and stir them together. Add the flour and salt, and beat them with an electric mixer for 5 minutes, or until the mixture is thick.
- Add the egg whites and fold them in.
- In a large heavy skillet place the shortening and heat it on medium until it is melted and hot *(the shortening should be ½" deep)*.
- For each pepper, pour ⅓ cup of the batter into the skillet so that it is in the shape of the pepper. Let the batter fry for 30 to 40 seconds, or until it begins to set. Place the pepper on top of the batter. Pour another ⅓ cup of batter on top of the pepper. Fry the relleno for 2 minutes, or until the bottom is brown. Turn the relleno over and fry it for another 2 minutes, or until the bottom is brown. Remove it from the skillet and drain it on paper towels.
- On each of 8 individual plates place one of the peppers. Pour the tomato sauce on top. Sprinkle on the cilantro.

serves 8

Pork Medallions with Mushroom Wine

"I make this dish when I am serving an elegant five-course meal. The breading of saltine crackers gives the pork a very nice texture and flavor."

- **½ pound bacon, cut into 1" pieces**
- **1 cup yellow onions, chopped medium**
- **½ pound fresh mushrooms, sliced**
- **2 pounds pork tenderloin, cut into ½" thick rounds**
- **2 eggs, beaten**
- **2 cups saltine cracker crumbs, finely ground**
- **2 teaspoons salt**
- **¼ teaspoon pepper**
- **1 cup dry white wine**

- Preheat the oven to 300°.
- In a medium skillet place the bacon and fry it so that it is lightly browned. Remove it from the pan, drain it on paper towels and set it aside.
- To the skillet with the bacon grease add the onions and mushrooms. Sauté them for 4 minutes, or until the onions are tender. Remove the vegetables from the pan *(reserve the grease)*, drain them on paper towels and set them aside.
- Dip each piece of pork first into the eggs and then into the cracker crumbs so that both sides are well coated.
- Place the medallions in the bacon grease and fry them for 2 minutes on each side, or until they are lightly browned *(do not let them burn)*.
- Sprinkle them with the salt and pepper.
- In a medium casserole dish, in this order, make layers of the pork, mushrooms and bacon.
- Pour the wine on top.
- Cover the dish with a lid.
- Bake the pork for 1 hour, or until it is done.

serves 8

Stuffed Chicken with Gorgonzola Cheese Sauce

"This is one of the richest and most delicious chicken dishes I have ever eaten. When I serve it to my guests, they become both very quiet and noisy at the same time.....not talking, but making small sounds of pleasure as they eat it."

Stuffed Chicken

1 tablespoon olive oil
½ cup pepperoni, chopped
2 tablespoons shallots, finely chopped
1½ cups sweet basil pesto
1½ cups Fontina cheese, grated
salt and pepper *(to taste)*
6 6-ounce boneless chicken breasts, skins removed, and pounded to ¼" thick
2 eggs, beaten
1½ cups dried bread crumbs, ground
6 tablespoons unsalted butter
Gorgonzola Cheese Sauce *(recipe on next page)*

- In a medium skillet place the oil and heat it on medium until it is hot. Add the pepperoni and shallots, and sauté them for 5 minutes, or until the shallots are tender. Remove the skillet from the heat.
- Add the pesto, cheese, salt and pepper, and stir them in.
- Let the ingredients cool for 10 minutes.
- In the center of each of the chicken breasts, place some of the filling. Tuck in the ends and roll the chicken up so that the filling is secure *(use toothpicks to secure them if necessary)*.
- Dip each roll first into the eggs and then into the bread crumbs so that it is well coated.
- Place the chicken in a medium baking dish. Cover the dish with foil and chill the chicken in the refrigerator for 1 hour.
- Preheat the oven to 350°.
- In a large heavy skillet place the butter and heat it on medium until it is melted and hot. Place the chicken rolls in the skillet with the seam side down. Sauté them for 5 minutes on each side, or until they are lightly browned all over.
- In a lightly greased baking dish place the chicken with the seam side down.
- Bake the chicken for 15 minutes.
- Slice each roll into ½" thick rounds.
- In the center of each of 6 individual serving plates spoon on some of the Gorgonzola Cheese Sauce. Fan out the rounds on top.

serves 6

Gorgonzola Cheese Sauce

1½ cups half & half
1½ teaspoons shallots, finely chopped
½ cup Gorgonzola cheese, crumbled
½ cup Parmesan cheese, freshly grated
salt and pepper *(to taste)*

- In a medium saucepan place the half & half and shallots, and simmer them for 5 minutes.
- Add the Gorgonzola cheese and stir it in so that it is melted.
- Add the Parmesan cheese, salt and pepper, and stir them in.
- Cook the sauce on very low heat for 5 to 7 minutes, or until it thickens.

makes approximately 2½ cups

"When I create new dishes I first start with a recipe from a cookbook or food magazine. From there I will add and delete different ingredients until I finally come up with a variation that is uniquely my own."

Ruth Hanrahan

Secret Carrot Cake with Cream Cheese Frosting

"I was given this recipe by my son's girlfriend. It originally called for grated carrots, but I could never get them to cook right at our high altitude, and the cake always came out raw in the middle. So finally I decided to try baby food carrots, and that did the trick. Now it comes out perfect every time, no matter what the altitude. People tell me it's the best carrot cake in the world."

Secret Carrot Cake

2 cups flour
1⅔ cups sugar
4 eggs, lightly beaten
1¼ cups vegetable oil
2 small jars baby food carrots
2 teaspoons baking soda
1½ teaspoons ground cinnamon
1 teaspoon salt
½ cup walnuts, chopped
½ cup pecans, chopped
Cream Cheese Frosting *(recipe follows)*

- Preheat the oven to 350°.
- In a large bowl place all of the ingredients *(except for the nuts and frosting)* and blend them together with an electric mixer so that they are smooth.
- Add the nuts and mix them in.
- Place the batter in a greased and floured medium cake pan.
- Bake the cake for 45 minutes, or until a wooden toothpick inserted in the center comes out clean.
- Frost the cake with the Cream Cheese Frosting.

serves 10 to 12

Cream Cheese Frosting

1 8-ounce package cream cheese
4 tablespoons butter, softened
1 teaspoon vanilla extract
4 cups powdered sugar

- In a medium bowl place the cream cheese, butter and vanilla. Beat them together with an electric mixer so that they are smooth and creamy.
- While constantly blending, slowly add the powdered sugar.

frosts 1 cake

Poppy Seed & Strawberry Cake

"This cake tastes as beautiful as it looks. Be sure that you display it to your guests before you slice it up."

- 1 **box yellow cake mix** *(with pudding)*
- 4 **eggs**
- 1 **cup sour cream**
- ½ **cup butter, melted**
- ½ **cup champagne** *(or cream sherry)*
- ½ **cup poppy seeds**
- 4 **cups strawberries, sliced**
- 1 **cup heavy cream, whipped and sweetened**

- Preheat the oven to 350°.
- In a large bowl place all of the ingredients *(except for the strawberries and cream)*, and blend them together with an electric mixer for 5 minutes.
- Place the batter in a greased and floured bundt pan.
- Bake the cake for 45 minutes, or until a wooden toothpick inserted in the center comes out clean.
- Invert the cake onto a serving plate and let it cool completely.
- Slice the cake in half horizontally. Remove the top half and set it aside. Place ½ of the strawberries and whipped cream on top of the bottom half. Place the other cake half back on top.
- Spread on the rest of the whipped cream.
- Place the remaining strawberries on top.

serves 10 to 12

"Ruth and I love to listen to our guests tell us about their travels. We dream of the time when we can repeat some of their adventures."

John Hanrahan

Salsa del Salto

Post Office Box 1468
El Prado, New Mexico 87529
(505) 776-2422
Mary Hockett & Dadou Mayer, Innkeepers

Although this elegant inn, designed by architect Antoine Predock, is on the road to Taos Ski Valley, close to Taos Pueblo, and just north of the beguiling attractions of Taos, guests may not want to leave even to ski or river-raft. A private tennis court, heated pool and hot tub are on the premises, and paintings by Taos artists adorn the guest rooms, all of which feature king-size beds and mountain and mesa views. Add to this breakfasts created by a French chef, and it's small wonder no one wants to depart.

Recipes

Basil Pesto Soup

"Rich with a basil pesto and garlic background, this is a marvelous French vegetable soup. Each ingredient can be tasted by itself, while at the same time blending with everything else to produce a brand-new taste."

- **1 tablespoon olive oil**
- **1½ cups tomatoes, peeled and finely chopped**
- **⅓ cup carrots, finely chopped**
- **1 leek, finely chopped**
- **1 shallot, finely chopped**
- **3 cloves garlic, finely chopped**
- **5 cups chicken broth**
- **½ cup potatoes, sliced into thin rounds**
- **1 stalk celery, finely chopped**
- **½ cup fresh green beans, snapped into small pieces**
- **1 bay leaf**
- **1 teaspoon salt**
- **½ teaspoon pepper**
- **1 cup fresh noodles** *(your favorite)*
- **⅓ cup Gruyere cheese**
- **4 teaspoons fresh basil, finely chopped**
- **1 clove garlic, finely chopped**
- **1 tablespoon olive oil**

- In a medium stockpot place the first tablespoon of olive oil and heat it on medium until it is hot. Add the tomatoes, carrots, leeks, shallots and the 3 cloves of chopped garlic. Sauté them for 4 minutes, or until the carrots are just tender.
- Add the chicken broth, potatoes, celery, beans, bay leaf, salt and pepper. Stir everything together well.
- Reduce the heat to low and simmer the soup for 40 minutes. Remove the bay leaf.
- Add the noodles and cheese, and stir them in. Simmer the soup for 5 minutes.
- In a small mortar place the basil, the 1 clove of garlic and the second tablespoon of olive oil. Crush the ingredients together so that a paste is formed.
- Add the paste to the soup and stir it in.

serves 4

"I was born and raised in France, but have lived in the United States for over 30 years. New Mexico is my favorite place in the world, and Taos is my favorite place in New Mexico. I love the big sky, clear air, beautiful mountains, and all of the wonderful outdoor activities that are available. Here I feel very close to nature."

Dadou Mayer

Ratatouille

"Ratatouille is a classic French vegetable dish, and every family has its own recipe. The secret to its success is that you must sauté each vegetable separately, because each one takes a different amount of time to cook."

2½ cups eggplant, peeled and cubed
salt *(as necessary)*
¼ cup olive oil
1 cup yellow onions, thinly sliced
2 cloves garlic, minced
3 cups zucchini, sliced into ¼" rounds
4 green bell peppers, seeded and sliced
2 cups tomatoes, peeled, seeds removed, and quartered
½ cup pitted black olives
2 teaspoons dried basil
½ teaspoon dried oregano
¼ cup olive oil
salt and pepper *(to taste)*

- Into the bottom of a colander place a layer of the eggplant. Sprinkle ½ teaspoon of the salt evenly on top. Repeat this process for the rest of the eggplant. On top of the last layer of eggplant place a heavy plate so that the excess moisture will be squeezed out. Let the eggplant drain for 40 minutes. Rinse it well, pat it dry and set it aside.
- In a large saucepan place the first ¼ cup of oil and heat it on medium until it is hot. Add the onions and garlic, and sauté them for 3 minutes, or until they are lightly browned.
- One vegetable at a time, sauté the eggplant, zucchini and green bell peppers so that they are slightly crisp. Remove each vegetable from the pan and set it aside.
- Add the tomatoes and deglaze the pan.
- Return all of the sautéed vegetables to the pan. Add the olives, basil, oregano, the second ¼ cup of oil, the salt and pepper.
- Reduce the heat to low and simmer the ingredients for 30 minutes, or until the liquid is mostly absorbed.

serves 8

"I design my menu according to what looks fresh and good in the market. Never do I plan a menu in advance because there is always the chance that an ingredient won't be available.....and then I'm in trouble!"

Dadou Mayer

Squash Blossom Omelette with Sauce Aurore

"Incredibly savory and delicate, this omelette and sauce must be prepared deftly, and with speed. The recipe comes from the south of France, where you can buy beautiful yellow squash blossom bouquets at the outdoor markets."

Squash Blossom Omelette

- 2 **tablespoons butter**
- 7 **eggs, beaten**
- 1½ **ounces squash blossoms, washed, dried and shredded**
- 3 **teaspoons fresh parsley, finely chopped**
- ¼ **teaspoon garlic powder**
- ¼ **teaspoon ground nutmeg**
- **salt and white pepper** *(to taste)*
- **Sauce Aurore** *(recipe follows)*

- In a large omelette pan place the butter and heat it on medium until it is melted and hot. Add the eggs. Briskly shake the pan to distribute them evenly. Sprinkle the squash blossoms, parsley, garlic, nutmeg, salt and white pepper on top.
- Cook the omelette for 3 minutes, or until the edges are set. Tilt the pan and fold the upper third of the omelette to the center. Tilt the pan the other way and fold over another third of the omelette.
- Slide the omelette onto a plate. Turn it over so that the folded edges are on the bottom. Place the Sauce Aurore on top.

serves 4

Sauce Aurore

- 1½ **tablespoons clarified butter**
- 1½ **tablespoons flour**
- 1 **cup warm milk**
- ⅛ **teaspoon garlic powder**
- ⅛ **teaspoon ground nutmeg**
- **salt and white pepper** *(to taste)*
- 1 **tablespoon tomato purée**
- ½ **cup heavy cream** *(or as needed)*
- 1 **teaspoon butter, softened**

- In a medium skillet place the clarified butter and heat it on medium until it is hot. Sprinkle the flour into the butter and stir it in. While stirring constantly, cook the mixture until it foams and bubbles. Remove the pan from the heat.
- Add the milk and whisk it in well.
- Return the pan to the heat and bring it to a low boil. While whisking constantly, cook the mixture for 2 minutes. Add the garlic, nutmeg, salt and white pepper. Stir them in well. Add the tomato purée and whisk it in.
- Slowly add and stir in the cream so that the sauce is of pouring consistency.
- Add the butter and gently stir the sauce just twice.

makes approximately 1½ cups

Sautéed Rabbit à la Claude

"Claude is the chef at the St. Bernard restaurant in Taos, and this recipe comes from his hometown region in France. If you are not fond of rabbit, then chicken, turkey or other wild game may be substituted."

- ½ **cup olive oil**
- 1 **whole rabbit, cut into quarters**
- ½ **cup flour**
- 1 **cup chicken broth**
- 1 **cup dry white wine**
- 1 **cup yellow onions, coarsely chopped**
- 2 **carrots, halved and sliced lengthwise**
- 2 **cloves garlic**
- 1 **Bouquet Garni** *(herbs of your choice tied in a cheesecloth)*
- 6 **slices bacon, cut into pieces**
- ⅓ **cup yellow onions, chopped medium**
- 1 **cup beef stock**
- 2 **drops Tabasco sauce**
- **salt and pepper** *(to taste)*

- Preheat the oven to 350°.
- In a heavy large skillet place the oil and heat it on medium until it is hot. Dredge the rabbit in the flour and then place it in the skillet. Sprinkle on any remaining flour. Sauté the rabbit pieces on all sides so that they are lightly browned.
- In a large casserole dish place the rabbit, chicken broth, wine, the 1 cup of onions, the carrots, garlic and Bouquet Garni. Cover the casserole with a lid.
- Poach the rabbit in the oven for 1 hour, or until it is done.
- In the same large skillet place the bacon and cook it on medium so that it is lightly browned. Add the ⅓ cup of onions and sauté them until they are lightly browned.
- Remove the rabbit from the casserole and place it in the skillet.
- Remove the vegetables from the stock and discard them.
- To the skillet add the beef stock, Tabasco, salt and pepper. Gently stir them in.
- While stirring occasionally, bring the liquid to a boil. Simmer it for 5 minutes.

serves 4

Ham Morandelle

"This is a classic dish from the south of France. The sauce is really delicious.....subtle and light, with a slight tang from the mustard."

4 tablespoons butter
2 tablespoons vegetable oil
2½ pounds cooked ham, sliced into ¼" thick pieces
3 tablespoons shallots, finely chopped
8 tablespoons Madeira wine
5 tablespoons cognac
4 tablespoons heavy cream
4 tablespoons Dijon mustard
1 tablespoon tomato paste
freshly ground pepper *(to taste)*

- In a medium skillet place the butter and oil. Heat them on medium until the butter is melted and they are hot. Add the ham slices and sauté them for 1 minute, or until they are lightly browned. Remove the ham from the skillet and drain off all but 2 tablespoons of the drippings.
- Add the shallots and sauté them for 2 minutes, or until they are just tender.
- While stirring constantly, add the Madeira and cognac. Scrape off the bits from the bottom of the skillet. Let the liquid mixture bubble until the juice is slightly thickened.
- In a small saucepan place the cream, mustard and tomato paste. Cook and stir the ingredients on high so that the mixture comes to a boil. Reduce the heat to low and simmer the sauce for 1 minute.
- Add the sauce and the pepper to the skillet, and whisk them in well.
- Return the ham slices to the skillet. Cook the ingredients so that everything is hot.

serves 6

"Although I am quite competent in the kitchen, I leave most of the cooking to my husband Dadou, because he can do it twice as fast and twice as well as I can."

Mary Hockett

Onion Tart

"Savory and delicate, this is a wonderful tart recipe that always pleases our guests."

2 slices bacon, cut into ½" pieces
1½ cups yellow onions, thinly sliced
⅛ teaspoon ground nutmeg
2 cups milk
2 tablespoons flour
¼ cup heavy cream
3 eggs, beaten
¼ cup fresh parsley, chopped
¼ cup fresh chives, chopped
½ teaspoon fresh thyme
salt and pepper *(to taste)*
1 9-inch Tart Shell *(recipe on next page)*

- Preheat the oven to 350°.
- In a medium skillet place the bacon and heat it on low. Sauté it for 5 minutes, or until it begins to brown. Add the onions and sauté them until they are translucent.
- Add the nutmeg and gently stir it in.
- In a small bowl place the milk and flour, and whisk them together so that the flour dissolves.
- Add the milk-flour mixture to the skillet and whisk it in.
- Add the remaining ingredients *(except for the tart shell)* and whisk them in well. Cook and stir the mixture for 3 minutes *(do not let it boil).*
- Pour the mixture into the prepared tart shell.
- Bake the tart for 40 minutes, or until it is set and lightly browned.

serves 8

"I find running a Bed & Breakfast to be quite enjoyable. Our guests are gracious and their positive feedback makes all of our hard work worthwhile. It is always a pleasure to see people enjoy themselves."

Mary Hockett

Tart Shell

"This is a basic, easy, foolproof tart shell recipe that can be used with any dessert or entrée filling."

1½ cups flour
¼ teaspoon sugar
⅛ teaspoon salt
2 tablespoons shortening
1 egg, beaten
3 tablespoons water *(or as needed)*

- On a flat surface place the flour. Make a well in the center. Sprinkle the sugar and salt around the edges of the flour.
- Into the well place the shortening and egg. Combine the ingredients together with a fork.
- Add the water as necessary so that a dough is formed.
- Knead the dough 20 times, or until it is smooth.
- Form the dough into a ball.
- Cover it with a cloth and let it sit for 2 hours.
- On a lightly floured surface, roll out the dough to fit a 9" pie plate or tart pan.
- Place the dough in the pan.
- Form a decorative border around the top edge.

makes one 9" tart shell

"Although I am a classically trained French chef, I have become addicted to New Mexico green chile. I use it in many of my dishes, and enjoy the challenge of successfully combining the flavors of French cuisine with those of the Southwest."

Dadou Mayer

Sierra Mesa Lodge

Fort Stanton Road • Post Office Box 463
Alto, New Mexico 88312
(505) 336-4515
Larry & Lila Goodman, Innkeepers

Mountain views, pine forests and skies that go on forever are the setting for this lovely residence near Ruidoso, about 180 miles southeast of Albuquerque. Horse racing, hiking, horseback riding, golfing, fishing and winter sports are nearby attractions, along with shops and restaurants. An indoor spa bath, charming guest rooms with period furnishings, and afternoon refreshments will relax the most weary traveler. And the breakfasts are elegant as well as lavish.

Recipes

Goodman's Minestrone

"Loaded with fresh vegetables, minestrone is a nutritious, filling soup that is almost a complete meal in itself. This recipe is one of the best I've ever tasted."

- **1/3 cup olive oil**
- **1/4 cup butter**
- **1 cup yellow onions, finely chopped**
- **1 1/2 cups potatoes, peeled and diced into 1/2" cubes**
- **1 cup carrots, chopped**
- **1/2 cup celery, chopped**
- **1/2 pound green beans, snapped into 1" pieces**
- **6 cups water**
- **1 1/3 cups green cabbage, shredded**
- **1 16-ounce can whole tomatoes** *(with liquid)*
- **1 cup fresh spinach, washed, deveined and coarsely chopped**
- **1 1/3 cups zucchini, chopped**
- **6 beef bouillon cubes**
- **1 teaspoon salt**
- **1 16-ounce can white beans, drained**
- **1 16-ounce can red kidney beans, drained**
- **1/2 cup Parmesan cheese, freshly grated**

- In a large stockpot place the oil and butter, and heat them on medium until the butter is melted and hot. Add the onions, potatoes, carrots, celery and green beans. Sauté them for 10 minutes, or until they are lightly browned.
- Add the water, cabbage, tomatoes, spinach, zucchini, bouillon and salt. While stirring occasionally, bring the ingredients to a boil over high heat.
- Reduce the heat to low and simmer the soup for 45 minutes, or until the vegetables are tender.
- Add the canned beans and stir them in.
- Simmer the soup for 15 minutes, or until it is slightly thickened.
- Sprinkle the Parmesan cheese on top of each serving.

serves 4 to 6

"At our inn we strive to provide our guests with thoughtful service, quiet charm, and warm hospitality.

Larry Goodman

Lila's Chinese Chicken Salad

"I studied Chinese cooking for two years, and this is one of my favorite dishes that I learned how to make. The preparation takes some time, but once everything is ready, it takes only minutes to put together."

2 tablespoons light soy sauce
2 tablespoons regular soy sauce
2 cloves garlic, crushed
4 teaspoons rice vinegar
2 teaspoons sugar
2 teaspoons sesame oil
½ teaspoon Tabasco sauce
½ teaspoon dry Chinese mustard
1 cup boneless chicken, boiled, shredded and fried in sesame oil
1 cup celery, chopped small
1 cup cucumbers, peeled, seeded and chopped small
½ cup red cabbage, shredded
⅓ cup carrots, grated
3 tablespoons scallions *(white part only),* **finely chopped**
¼ cup water chestnuts, sliced
1 cup bean sprouts
¼ cup slivered almonds
1 small head iceberg lettuce, shredded
¼ pound vermicelli pasta, fried in hot oil until puffed, and drained on paper towels

- In a small bowl place the two soy sauces, garlic, vinegar, sugar, sesame oil, Tabasco and dry mustard. Whisk them together well.
- Place 2 tablespoons of the dressing in a large bowl and reserve it.
- Cover the original small bowl with plastic wrap and chill it in the refrigerator.
- Add the chicken to the 2 tablespoons of dressing and toss it in well. Let it sit for 15 minutes.
- Add the celery, cucumbers, cabbage, carrots, scallions, water chestnuts, bean sprouts and almonds. Mix everything together.
- Add the lettuce and the chilled dressing, and toss them in well.
- Sprinkle the fried vermicelli on top of each serving.

serves 4

Mom's Beef Brisket

"Fork tender and full of spicy flavors, this dish is the perfect thing to serve for your family Sunday dinner."

1	**7-pound beef brisket**
	salt *(to taste)*
	water *(as necessary)*
1	**cup yellow onions, thinly sliced**
1	**clove garlic, chopped**
1	**teaspoon paprika**
¼	**teaspoon garlic salt**
1	**bay leaf**
½	**teaspoon dried oregano**
3	**cups potatoes, peeled and sliced**

- Preheat the oven to 400°.
- In a large roasting pan place the beef brisket with the fat side down. Sprinkle it with the salt. Add enough water so that it comes up halfway in the pan. Add the onions and garlic.
- Place the pan on the stove and bring the water to a boil on medium high heat. Reduce the heat to low and simmer the ingredients for 10 minutes.
- Add the paprika, garlic salt, bay leaf and oregano.
- Cover the pan tightly with foil and place it in the oven.
- Reduce the heat to 350°.
- Bake the brisket for 2 hours.
- Add the potatoes and bake the brisket for 1 hour more, or until the potatoes are done.
- Remove the meat from the pan and thinly slice it against the grain.
- Return the slices to the pan. Roast the brisket and potatoes *(uncovered)* for ½ hour.

serves 6 to 8

"To be a successful innkeeper you must be very friendly and enjoy being around people. Many of our guests have never been to a Bed & Breakfast before, but once they have the experience, they are hooked!"

Lila Goodman

Sierra Mesa Lodge

Linguini & Eggs Frittata

"I developed this recipe when we were raising our kids, as a way to use up leftover spaghetti. The parsley and basil really make it come to life."

- **4 eggs, lightly beaten**
- **½ cup milk**
- **1⅓ cups yellow onions, chopped and sautéed in olive oil**
- **⅓ cup Parmesan cheese, freshly grated**
- **2 tablespoons fresh parsley, chopped**
- **1 tablespoon dried basil**
- **1 teaspoon salt**
- **½ teaspoon pepper**
- **½ pound linguini, cooked al dente and drained**

- In a large bowl place all of the ingredients *(except for the linguini)* and combine them together well.
- Add the linguini and gently toss it in.
- Spray two large skillets *(the same size)* with no-stick cooking spray. Heat them on medium until they are hot.
- Place the mixture in one of the skillets and spread it out evenly in the pan. Cook it *(without stirring)* for 6 minutes, or until the bottom is browned.
- Invert the other skillet over the frittata. Carefully turn the skillets over so that the frittata falls into the empty skillet. Fry the frittata for 5 minutes more, or until it is browned on both sides.

serves 4

"My husband and I have traveled in many foreign countries and, as a consequence, have sampled a variety of different ethnic cuisines. One of our great joys is trying to incorporate the different tastes into dishes that the typical American palate will enjoy."

Lila Goodman

Aunt Irene's Stuffed Cabbage

"Aunt Irene is from Hungary, and this is one of the recipes that she brought from the old country. The cabbage flavor is quite mild, and tastes slightly sweet and sour, along with a strong paprika and onion flavor."

- **1 head green cabbage, boiled until tender and cored**
- **1½ pounds ground beef, cooked and drained**
- **1⅓ cups yellow onions, finely chopped**
- **2 eggs, beaten**
- **½ cup dried bread crumbs, crushed**
- **2 tablespoons Hungarian paprika**
- **salt and pepper** *(to taste)*
- **1 28-ounce can sauerkraut**
- **2 cups yellow onions, thinly sliced**
- **1 28-ounce can stewed tomatoes** *(with juice)*
- **salt** *(to taste)*
- **water** *(as needed)*

- Remove 12 leaves from the cabbage head. Shred the remaining cabbage.
- In a medium bowl place the beef, chopped onions, eggs, bread crumbs, paprika, salt and pepper. Combine the ingredients together well.
- In the middle of each of the 12 cabbage leaves place some of the meat mixture.
- Roll the leaves up into small logs, tucking the ends in as you roll so that they are secure.
- In a large stockpot, in this order make layers of the shredded cabbage, sauerkraut, onion slices and cabbage rolls. Place the stewed tomatoes on top. Sprinkle on the salt. Add enough water to cover the ingredients.
- Simmer the cabbage rolls on low heat for 2 hours.

serves 6 to 8

"We spent most of our lives in southern California, where our neighbors hardly even waved or said hello. But here in Ruidoso, if we run into someone we just saw two days ago, we are greeted with big warm hugs and kisses. We will never leave this place.....it is perfect."

Lila Goodman

Mostaccioli Chicken Casserole

"This is an excellent, flavorful low-fat recipe. The great thing is that people love it, and never realize that they are eating something that is so healthy."

1 tablespoon vegetable oil
1 cup yellow onions, chopped medium
4 cloves garlic, finely chopped
1 pound boneless chicken, skin removed, and cut into 1" pieces
1 28-ounce can whole tomatoes *(with liquid),* **coarsely chopped**
3 tablespoons tomato paste
1¼ teaspoons dried basil
¾ teaspoon dried oregano
¼ teaspoon dried thyme
1 10-ounce package mostaccioli, cooked al dente and drained
1 10-ounce package frozen spinach, thawed, chopped and drained
½ cup Parmesan cheese, freshly grated

- In a large skillet place the oil and heat it on medium until it is hot. Add the onions and garlic, and sauté them for 3 minutes, or until they start to brown.
- Add the chicken and sauté it for 4 to 6 minutes, or until it is done.
- Add the tomatoes, tomato paste, basil, oregano and thyme. Bring the ingredients to a boil. Reduce the heat to low and simmer the mixture for 5 minutes.
- Preheat the oven to 350°.
- In a large bowl place the chicken mixture, pasta, spinach and ¼ cup of the Parmesan cheese. Combine the ingredients well.
- Place the mixture in a greased baking dish. Sprinkle the remaining cheese on top.
- Bake the casserole for 20 minutes, or until the cheese is browned and everything is hot.

serves 4 to 6

"Owning a Bed & Breakfast is perfect for a person like me, someone who is retired. It keeps me busy, but I don't have to really work all that hard. If we have guests I'm happy, and if we don't have guests I'm still happy!"

Larry Goodman

Hungarian Cholent

"My Hungarian grandmother used to make this recipe, which is wonderful on a cold winter day. The longer you bake it, the better it tastes. If you have any left over, add a little water and bake it some more the next day."

1	**5-pound beef brisket**		**water** *(as necessary)*
1	**marrow bone** *(optional)*	1	**teaspoon paprika**
1	**pound navy beans, cleaned and washed**		**salt and pepper** *(to taste)*
1	**cup yellow onions, thinly sliced**	½	**pound barley**

- In a large oven-proof stockpot place the beef brisket, bone, beans and onions. Add enough water to cover the ingredients.
- Add the paprika, salt and pepper.
- Cover the pot with a lid and simmer the brisket on low heat for 1 hour.
- Add the barley and stir it in. Cook the ingredients *(uncovered)* for 15 minutes.
- Replace the lid and cook the ingredients for 1 hour.
- Preheat the oven to 350°.
- Place the ingredients in a large casserole dish and cover it with a lid.
- Bake the beef for 3½ hours *(occasionally check the dish to see if more water is needed)*.
- Remove the lid and bake the casserole for 1 hour more.

serves 4 to 6

"I don't like bland food.....I like things to have a strong flavor that is easily recognizable. This preference is reflected in the dishes that I make, which usually elicit definite responses (mostly positive!) from our guests."

Larry Goodman

Goodman's Chocolate Chip Streusel Cake

"Our repeat guests are always asking us to make this cake, which is the most popular dessert we serve. It's rich and chocolatey, with a light, sponge-like texture."

1 6-ounce package chocolate chips
1 cup walnuts, chopped
1 teaspoon ground cinnamon
⅓ cup brown sugar
½ cup sugar
1 stick butter, softened
1 cup sugar
2 eggs
1 cup sour cream
1 teaspoon baking soda
1 teaspoon baking powder
1 teaspoon salt
2 teaspoons vanilla extract
2 cups flour, sifted

- Preheat the oven to 350°.
- In a medium bowl place the chocolate chips, walnuts, cinnamon, brown sugar and the ½ cup of sugar. Mix the ingredients together and set the bowl aside.
- In a large bowl place the butter and the 1 cup of sugar. Beat them together with an electric mixer so that they are creamy.
- Add the eggs, sour cream, baking soda, baking powder, salt and vanilla. Blend them together so that the mixture is smooth.
- Add the flour and mix it in.
- In the bottom of a greased tube pan place ⅓ of the chocolate chip mixture. Place ½ of the batter on top. Repeat the process, ending with the streusel on top.
- Bake the cake for 45 minutes, or until a wooden toothpick inserted in the center comes out clean.

serves 10

"When I was twelve years old I joined the Boy Scouts and was made the chief cook at our summer camp. Ever since then I have loved to work with food and create new recipes."

Larry Goodman

Aunt Margaret's Hungarian Pastries

"These pastries are so buttery that they literally melt in your mouth. In this recipe we stuff them with apricot preserves, but any sweet fruit or berries will do. I especially like them stuffed with a mixture of cinnamon, sugar and nuts."

2 sticks butter, softened
2 cups flour
1 8-ounce package cream cheese, softened
apricot preserves *(as needed)*

- In a medium bowl place all of the ingredients *(except for the apricot preserves)* and blend them together with an electric mixer. Cover the bowl with plastic wrap and chill it in the refrigerator for 1 hour.
- Preheat the oven to 350°.
- On a lightly floured surface place the dough. Knead it 10 times, or until it is smooth. Roll the dough out so that it is ½" thick. Cut it into 12 triangles. In the center of each triangle place a teaspoon of the apricot preserves. Fold the 3 points to the center.
- Place the pastries on an ungreased cookie sheet. Bake them for 12 to 15 minutes, or until they are lightly browned.

makes 12 pastries

Russian Tea Cakes

"These are sweet, hard little cakes that are the perfect thing to eat with a cup of hot tea in the afternoon."

¼ cup butter, softened
1 cup sugar
2 egg yolks
¼ cup vegetable oil
¼ cup sour cream
1 teaspoon vanilla extract
2 cups flour
1 dash salt
1 cup nuts, chopped
1 cup golden raisins
½ cup powdered sugar *(or as needed)*

- Preheat the oven to 350°.
- In a large bowl place the butter and sugar, and mix them together so that they are creamy. Add the egg yolks and beat them in. Add the oil, sour cream and vanilla, and beat them in well. Add the flour, salt, nuts and raisins, and mix them in.
- Divide the dough into 3 portions. On a lightly floured surface roll each portion into a log that is 1½" in diameter. Place the logs on a greased cookie sheet. Bake them for 35 to 45 minutes, or until they are browned.
- Remove the logs from the oven. Sprinkle them liberally with the powdered sugar. Let the logs cool. Cut the cookies into 1" slices.

makes approximately 12 cookies

Territorial Inn

215 Washington Avenue
Santa Fe, New Mexico 87501
(505) 989-7737
Lela McFerrin, Innkeeper

Imagine what it was like at the turn of the century to live in splendor on Washington Avenue, a block from the Santa Fe Plaza.....that's what you'll discover at the Territorial Inn. Here, where Santa Fe society set the standards for the Territory, you too may enjoy the rose garden and shady trees, crackling open fires, elegant antique furnishings and the luxury of breakfast in bed, featuring fresh pastries, fruit and coffee. Among the modern touches appreciated by today's guests are cable TV, a gazebo-enclosed hot tub and off-street parking.

Recipes

Territorial Inn Bread Pudding

"This is a rich, delicious German recipe that can be served either as a special breakfast entrée, or as a dessert. Good toppings to accompany it are maple sauce, hard sauce or crème anglaise."

4 cups white bread, crusts removed, and cubed
1½ cups apples, peeled, cored and chopped
2 ripe bananas, peeled and mashed
⅓ cup brown sugar
1½ cups half & half
2 eggs, lightly beaten
1 teaspoon ground cinnamon
1 teaspoon ground nutmeg
1 teaspoon vanilla extract
¼ cup white sugar

- Preheat the oven to 350°.
- In a large bowl place the bread cubes and set them aside.
- In a medium bowl place the apples, bananas, brown sugar, half & half, eggs, cinnamon, nutmeg and vanilla. Mix the ingredients together so that they are well blended.
- Pour the wet mixture over the bread cubes and mix them together well so that the bread is soaked.
- Place the mixture in a medium greased baking pan. Sprinkle the white sugar on top.
- Bake the pudding for 40 minutes, or until it is firm.

serves 8

"On sunny days we serve breakfast on the patio.....maybe strawberries and cream with granola and homemade muffins, fresh juices, and coffee or tea. It's a very pleasant experience."

Lela McFerrin

Lela's Blueberry Sauce

"I needed a sauce to put on simple fruit dishes and thought that blueberries would work well with almost everything.....including pancakes, waffles or even ice cream. An option is to add several tablespoons of vodka to the sauce, which makes it thicker."

2 cups fresh blueberries, washed and drained

½ cup sugar

2 tablespoons lemon juice, freshly squeezed

¼ teaspoon ground cinnamon

- In a medium saucepan place all of the ingredients and mix them together. While stirring occasionally, cook the mixture on low heat for 30 minutes.
- Remove the sauce from the heat and let it cool.
- Store it in the refrigerator.

makes approximately 2 cups

"When my husband and I decided to turn our home into a Bed & Breakfast, we did our research in a really enjoyable way. We spent ten months traveling around the country and stayed in different inns, noting everything in detail."

Lela McFerrin

Territorial Peach Crisp

"You can make this recipe more nutritious by adding some wheat germ and wheat bran to the topping. I love to serve it in the spring or summer, when the peaches are fresh and delicious."

6 **cups peaches, peeled, seeded and sliced**
¼ **cup brandy** *(or apple juice)*
1 **lemon, juiced and zested** *(outer yellow part grated off)*
¾ **cup flour**
½ **cup rolled oats**
½ **cup unsalted butter, softened**
¾ **cup brown sugar**
1 **teaspoon ground cinnamon**
½ **teaspoon ground ginger**
¼ **teaspoon ground nutmeg**

- Preheat the oven to 350°.
- In a large bowl place the peaches, brandy, lemon juice and lemon zest. Mix the ingredients together.
- Place the peach mixture in a medium-size buttered baking pan and set it aside.
- In a medium bowl place the flour, oats, butter, brown sugar, cinnamon, ginger and nutmeg. Mix the ingredients together so that they are well blended and crumbly.
- Sprinkle the topping on top of the peaches.
- Bake the crisp for 30 minutes, or until it is golden brown and bubbly.

serves 6 to 8

"Although Santa Fe is becoming touristy, its main character remains unspoiled. Many visitors leave here murmuring, 'This is the way to live'."

Lela McFerrin

Territorial Stuffed Pears

"The basis of this recipe comes from an old River Road cookbook that I got in Louisiana. Apples can be substituted for pears. It's very simple to make and has a delicious, homey flavor."

4 pears, peeled and cored
¼ cup pineapple juice
2 tablespoons water
¼ cup raisins
2 tablespoons walnuts, finely chopped
2 tablespoons sugar
1 tablespoon lemon juice, freshly squeezed
½ cup light corn syrup

- Preheat the oven to 350°.
- In a small baking pan place the pears. Add the pineapple juice and water to the pan.
- In a small bowl place the raisins, walnuts, sugar and lemon juice. Mix the ingredients together.
- Stuff the center of each pear with the filling. Drizzle the corn syrup on top.
- Cover the pan tightly with foil.
- Bake the pears for 1 hour, or until they are tender.

serves 4

"One time we had a guest who wanted to propose to his girlfriend in one of our rooms, with dinner brought in from a local restaurant. As a special touch, we put rose petals on the bed. The next morning the couple came down with big smiles on their faces, so we knew she had accepted!"

Lela McFerrin

Apple Cranberry Crisp

"Here is an easy, delicious recipe that everyone loves. The cranberry sauce combined with the apples is what makes the taste so good."

- **3 medium baking apples, peeled, cored and thinly sliced**
- **¾ teaspoon ground cinnamon**
- **1½ cups cranberry sauce** *(with whole cranberries)*
- **¾ cup rolled oats**
- **⅓ cup flour**
- **¾ cup brown sugar, packed**
- **½ cup butter, softened**

- Preheat the oven to 350°.
- In a small baking pan place the apples. Sprinkle the cinnamon on top. Pour the cranberry sauce over the apples so that they are thoroughly covered.
- In a small bowl place the oats, flour and brown sugar. Mix the ingredients together.
- Add the butter and cut it in with a pastry blender so that the mixture is crumbly.
- Sprinkle the topping over the cranberry sauce.
- Bake the crisp for 35 minutes, or until the top is lightly browned and the apples are tender.

serves 6

"People who stay at Bed & Breakfast inns are a unique breed. They often become fast friends with both the innkeeper and many of the other guests."

Lela McFerrin

Vogt Ranch House

Post Office Box 716
Ramah, New Mexico 87321
(505) 783-4362
Anita Davis, Innkeeper

Off the beaten track in west-central New Mexico at the foot of the Zuni Mountains is the former home of Evon Z. Vogt, who was a sheep rancher, newspaper publisher and the first custodian of El Morro National Monument. The ranch house, built in 1915 of Anasazi Indian ruin rocks, was a center for many noted scholars, artists and writers, and is still owned by the family. The frontier flavor is accented with Navajo rugs, a Kalamazoo cookstove, a bear pelt on the wall and traditional hospitality.....including a hearty ranch breakfast.

Recipes

Avocado Mousse

"This is a rich and delicious way to use avocados. For a beautiful presentation, serve it in a ring over a bed of lettuce. Then fill the center with chicken or seafood mixed with French dressing, and garnish it with carrot shavings and fresh parsley sprigs."

2 cups ripe avocados, peeled, pitted and mashed
½ cup mayonnaise
⅓ cup scallions, finely chopped
¼ cup fresh cilantro, chopped
1 lemon, freshly squeezed
1 teaspoon Crystal Louisiana Hot Sauce
½ teaspoon salt
1 small package lime Jello, well mixed with 1 cup boiling water and cooled until just syrupy
¾ cup heavy cream, whipped stiff
8 red leaf lettuce leaves, washed, dried and tough ends removed

- In a large bowl place the avocados, mayonnaise, scallions, cilantro, lemon juice, hot sauce and salt. Beat them together well so that the mixture is smooth.
- Add the Jello mixture and stir it in.
- Add the whipped cream and gently fold it in.
- Place the avocado mixture in a medium-size ring mold.
- Chill it in the refrigerator for at least 4 hours.
- On a serving plate place the lettuce leaves with the curly ends toward the edge.
- Place the mousse in a shallow pan of warm water for 1 minute to loosen it.
- Unmold it onto the serving plate.

serves 4 to 6

"Sometimes our guests tell us that if only it were possible, they would love to stay here and live for the rest of their lives."

Anita Davis

Winter Squash Medley

"Here is another 'what to do with all the winter squash from the garden' recipe.....and it's a really good one. The honey and sunflower seeds are the secret."

- **¼ stick butter**
- **2 cups winter squash, peeled and diced medium**
- **⅓ cup yellow onions, diced medium**
- **¾ cup celery, chopped**
- **1 clove garlic, crushed**
- **1 teaspoon whole wheat flour**
- **¼ teaspoon salt**
- **¼ teaspoon pepper**
- **1 tablespoon honey**
- **¼ cup salted sunflower seeds**
- **¼ cup fresh parsley, chopped**

- In a large skillet place the butter and heat it on medium until it is melted and hot. Add the squash, onions, celery and garlic. Sauté them for 2 minutes.
- Add the flour, salt and pepper, and stir them in.
- Add the honey and sunflower seeds, and stir them in.
- Cook the mixture for 5 minutes, or until the squash is al dente *(do not overcook)*.
- Sprinkle on the parsley.

serves 4

"I feel that Vogt Ranch lies in one of the last undiscovered parts of America. The views are forever, and there are beautiful mesas and an abundance of wildlife."

Anita Davis

Cilantro Beets

"This dish is a good way to get people to eat beets because the cilantro and lime juice mellow the beet flavor. If the beets you use are not naturally sweet, then add a little sugar."

3 tablespoons butter
2 cups beets, peeled and grated
1 clove garlic, crushed
1 tablespoon lime juice, freshly squeezed
2 tablespoons fresh cilantro, chopped
salt and pepper *(to taste)*

- In a medium skillet place the butter and heat it on medium until it is melted and hot. Add the beets and garlic, and sauté them for 3 minutes, or until they are tender but still crisp *(do not overcook)*.
- Remove the skillet from the heat.
- Add the lime juice, cilantro, salt and pepper. Gently stir them in.

serves 4 to 6

Jicama Salad

"One day I spontaneously concocted this dish for a salad. My mother took a taste and said, 'Yum, this is really good! I want the recipe!' so I wrote it down as best as I could, and we both have enjoyed it ever since."

3 cups jicama, peeled and cut into thin matchsticks
½ cup walnuts, chopped
¼ cup plain yogurt
¼ cup mayonnaise
3 tablespoons lemon juice, freshly squeezed
1 tablespoon Dijon mustard

- In a large bowl place all of the ingredients and toss them together well.
- Cover the bowl with plastic wrap and chill it in the refrigerator for 30 minutes.

serves 4 to 6

Grandma Shirley's Corn Bake

"My grandma gave me this recipe and I've been making it for over twenty years. But I think that the recipe must somehow be getting around, because recently several people have given it to me, raving about how great it is."

1 15-ounce can corn, drained
1 15-ounce can cream style corn
1 cup green chile peppers, roasted, peeled and chopped
2 cups cheddar cheese, grated
2 eggs, slightly beaten
1 cup cornmeal
6 tablespoons vegetable oil
1 teaspoon garlic salt

- Preheat the oven to 350°.
- In a large bowl place all of the ingredients and stir them together well.
- Place the mixture in a greased 9" x 12" glass cake pan.
- Bake it for 30 minutes, or until it is firm.

serves 8 to 10

"Because our location is so remote, the guests are my contact with the outside world. They bring us current news, different points of view, ideas and stories.....I feel like a traveler without really traveling!"

Anita Davis

Vogt Tamale Pie

"This is my mom's recipe, which she made when I was growing up. It's a wonderful old standard that will always be popular."

2	**tablespoons vegetable oil**
1	**clove garlic, crushed**
¾	**cup yellow onions, chopped**
1½	**pounds lean ground beef**
1	**teaspoon red chile powder** *(or to taste)*
	salt and pepper *(to taste)*
1	**15-ounce can stewed tomatoes**
1	**tablespoon brown sugar**
2	**teaspoons Worcestershire sauce**
1	**teaspoon lemon juice, freshly squeezed**
2	**cups cooked cornmeal mush**
½	**cup pitted black olives, sliced**

- Preheat the oven to 350°.
- In a large skillet place the oil and heat it on medium until it is hot. Add the garlic and onions, and sauté them for 3 minutes, or until they are translucent.
- Add the beef, red chile powder, salt and pepper. Cook and stir the mixture for 10 minutes, or until the beef is browned.
- Add the tomatoes, brown sugar, Worcestershire sauce and lemon juice. Stir them in well.
- Place the mixture in a 2-quart casserole dish.
- Spread the cornmeal mush on top.
- Sprinkle on the olives.
- Bake the pie for ½ hour, or until the pie is set and everything is hot.

serves 4

"My grandfather Vogt used to have 10,000 head of sheep on the ranch, and so he had lots of sheepherders working for him. They would make coffee on the trail by pouring boiling water over coffee grounds, and then adding a pinch of salt and an eggshell. I've tasted coffee made this way and it's delicious!"

Anita Davis

Bengali Chicken Curry

"A Bengali friend of mine used to make this dish, which is a complete meal in one pan. Somehow when I make it, it doesn't taste quite as good as when he made it."

2 tablespoons vegetable oil
1 medium yellow onion, chopped
3 cloves garlic, crushed
3 cardamom seeds
1 stick cinnamon
4 whole cloves
8 peppercorns
2 bay leaves
½ inch fresh ginger root, peeled and grated
4 chicken breast halves, skin and bones removed, and cut into thirds
2 cups water
1 teaspoon ground cumin
1 teaspoon ground turmeric
1½ teaspoons ground coriander
1 teaspoon red chile powder
½ teaspoon sugar
1 teaspoon salt *(or to taste)*
2 medium potatoes, peeled, cubed and steamed
1½ cups cauliflower florets, steamed
2 cups raw white rice, cooked

- In a medium large skillet place the oil and heat it on medium high until it is hot. Add the onions, garlic, cardamom seeds, cinnamon stick, cloves, peppercorns, bay leaves and ginger. Sauté the ingredients for 3 minutes.
- Add the chicken and sauté it for 5 minutes.
- Transfer everything from the skillet to a large stockpot.
- Add the water and stir it in.
- Add the cumin, turmeric, coriander, red chile powder, sugar and salt. Stir everything together well.
- Simmer the ingredients for 45 minutes, or until the chicken is done.
- Add the potatoes and cauliflower, and stir them in. Cook the ingredients for 3 minutes.
- Let the curry cool. Remove the cinnamon stick and bay leaves.
- Refrigerate the curry overnight.
- Gently heat the curry before serving *(do not overcook or the vegetables will be soggy)*.
- Serve it on top of the rice.

serves 6 to 8

Ranch Style French Toast with Peaches

"When I make a basic dish like french toast, I like to think of something different and interesting to do with it. That's how I came up with this popular recipe. The orange flavor of the Tang in the batter is the secret."

4	**eggs, beaten**
1	**cup buttermilk**
1	**teaspoon Tang**
1/4	**teaspoon ground cinnamon**
1/2	**teaspoon vanilla extract**
8	**slices sourdough bread**
1	**tablespoon margarine** *(or as needed)*
1/4	**cup sugar**
1	**teaspoon cornstarch**
1/2	**teaspoon ground cinnamon**
1	**19-ounce can sliced peaches** *(with juice)*

- In a medium bowl place the eggs, buttermilk, Tang, the 1/4 teaspoon of cinnamon and the vanilla. Whisk them together well.
- Place the bread slices in the bowl and dip them on both sides.
- In a large skillet place the margerine and heat it on medium low until it is melted and hot. Add the bread slices and cook them for 2 to 3 minutes on each side, or until they are browned.
- In a small bowl place the sugar, cornstarch and the 1/2 teaspoon of cinnamon. Mix them together well.
- In a medium saucepan drain off the juice from the peaches. Add the sugar mixture. Mix and stir the sauce on medium heat until it thickens.
- Add the peaches and cook them until they are heated through.
- Serve the French Toast with the hot peaches on top.

serves 4

"When I was growing up on the ranch we always had a vegetable garden, egg-laying chickens and milk cows. My dad made us do everything by hand and my mother hated to go to the grocery store. This self-sufficient attitude has stayed with me all my life."

Anita Davis

Pecan Ice Box Cookies

"The title for this recipe comes from the fact that you can store the dough in the freezer or refrigerator for a long time, and then slice off portions as you need them. This way the cookies are always freshly baked."

1 cup butter, softened to room temperature
½ cup brown sugar
½ cup white sugar
1 egg, slightly beaten
1 teaspoon vanilla extract
½ cup pecans, finely chopped
2 cups flour
½ teaspoon baking soda
¼ teaspoon salt

- In a large bowl place the butter, brown sugar and white sugar. Beat them together with an electric mixer so that they are creamy.
- Add the egg and blend it in well.
- Add the vanilla and pecans, and mix them in.
- In a medium bowl sift together the flour, baking soda and salt.
- Add the egg mixture to the flour mixture, and blend it in well.
- Place the dough on a lightly floured surface. Form it into a log that is 2" in diameter.
- Wrap the dough with plastic wrap and place it in the refrigerator for 2 hours, or until it is well chilled.
- Preheat the oven to 350°.
- Slice ¼" thick cookies from the roll.
- Place them on an ungreased cookie sheet so that they are 1" apart.
- Bake them for 10 minutes, or until they are lightly golden.

makes approximately 4 dozen cookies

Orange Bowknots with Icing

"This is grandma's old recipe that she would make for our family every Christmas morning. We kids would decorate the bowknots with green and red dried cherries."

- **1¼ cups milk, scalded**
- **½ cup shortening**
- **⅓ cup sugar**
- **1 teaspoon salt**
- **2 eggs, slightly beaten**
- **¼ cup orange juice, freshly squeezed**
- **2 tablespoons orange peel, zested** *(outer orange part grated off)*
- **1 package dry yeast**
- **5 cups flour**
- **1 cup powdered sugar**
- **¼ cup butter, softened**
- **2 tablespoons orange juice, freshly squeezed**
- **1 teaspoon orange zest**

- In a large bowl place the scalded milk, shortening, sugar and salt. Mix the ingredients together well. Let the mixture sit for 15 minutes, or until it is lukewarm.
- Add the eggs, the ¼ cup of orange juice, the 2 tablespoons of orange zest and the yeast. Blend the ingredients together well.
- Add the flour and stir it in.
- Let the mixture sit for 10 minutes.
- On a floured surface place the dough and knead it 20 times, or until it is fairly smooth. Cover the dough with a light cloth and let it rise for 2 hours.
- Roll out the dough into a long rectangle that is 10" wide and ½" thick. Cut the dough, widthwise, into strips that are 10" long and ½" wide.
- Tie each strip into a knot. Place the strips on a cookie sheet and let them rise for 40 minutes.
- Preheat the oven to 350°.
- Bake the bowknots for 15 minutes, or until they are brown. Remove them from the cookie sheet and let them cool for 15 minutes.
- In a small bowl place the powdered sugar, butter, the 2 tablespoons of orange juice and the 1 teaspoon of orange zest. Beat them together with an electric mixer so that they are creamy and spreadable.
- Spread the icing on each bowknot.

makes approximately 48 bowknots

Water Street Inn

427 West Water Street
Santa Fe, New Mexico 87501
(505) 984-1193
Dolores & Al Dietz, Innkeepers

Guests don't even have to get out of their cozy beds for breakfast in this historic restored adobe inn.....their choice arrives in their rooms on a tray. A private patio or balcony may make a perfect breakfast spot. But, though it may be difficult to leave the guest rooms, with their brick floors, fireplaces, oriental rugs, and antique furniture, the Santa Fe Plaza is just four blocks away, a temptation to get moving.

Recipes

Water Street Sangria

"Simple, light and delicious, this is a perfect beverage to serve in the summertime."

- **1** **6-ounce can frozen orange juice**
- **1** **6-ounce can frozen lemonade**
- **2** **fifths burgundy wine**
- **2** **quarts club soda**
- **sugar** *(to taste)*
- **orange and lemon slices** *(to garnish)*

- In a large punch bowl place the orange juice, lemonade and wine. Stir them together so that the concentrates are dissolved.
- Add the club soda and sugar, and stir them in. Float the orange and lemon slices on top. Serve the Sangria over ice.

serves 20 to 30

B's Shrimp Dip

"When I serve this dip to guests, it can be totally gone in ten minutes. People simply devour it!"

- **1** **pound shrimp, peeled, deveined, boiled in seasoned water and drained**
- **1½** **pounds cream cheese, softened**
- **8** **scallions, chopped**
- **1** **can water chestnuts, drained**
- **½** **cup mayonnaise**
- **1½** **tablespoons Dijon mustard**
- **2** **teaspoons Worcestershire sauce**
- **1** **teaspoon dried basil**
- **1½** **lemons, juiced**
- **3** **splashes Tabasco sauce**
- **salt and pepper** *(to taste)*

- In a food processor place the shrimp and pulse it. Place the shrimp in a medium bowl and set it aside.
- To the food processor add the remaining ingredients and purée them so that they are smooth.
- Add the mixture to the shrimp and stir them together.

makes approximately 1 quart

Hot Crab Dip

"As long as I can remember I have been making this dip. It has a spicy, Cajun flavor, and is always a big success when I serve it as an appetizer."

4 tablespoons butter
4 tablespoons flour
1 teaspoon salt
¼ teaspoon pepper
2 cups milk
4 ounces cream cheese, softened
2 tablespoons butter
2 tablespoons olive oil
1 cup yellow onions, finely chopped
¾ cup green bell peppers, seeded and finely chopped
7 stalks celery, chopped small
3 cloves garlic, minced
2 6-ounce cans white lump crab meat
1½ tablespoons lemon juice, freshly squeezed
¼ teaspoon Worcestershire sauce
¼ teaspoon Tabasco sauce
¼ teaspoon cayenne pepper
1 teaspoon dried parsley
salt and pepper *(to taste)*

- In a small saucepan place the 4 tablespoons of butter and heat it on medium until it is melted and hot. Add the flour, the 1 teaspoon of salt and the ¼ teaspoon of pepper. Whisk them in well.
- While whisking constantly, slowly add the milk. Continue to whisk the mixture so that it is smooth and thick.
- Add the cream cheese and stir it in for 1 minute, or until it is melted. Remove the sauce from the heat and set it aside.
- In a large skillet place the 2 tablespoons of butter and the olive oil, and heat them on medium until the butter is melted and they are hot. Add the onions, bell peppers and celery. Sauté the vegetables for 10 minutes, or until they are tender.
- Add the garlic and sauté it for 2 minutes.
- Add the vegetables and crab to the white sauce, and stir them in.
- Add the remaining ingredients. Cook and stir the mixture for 5 minutes on medium heat, or until the dip bubbles.
- Place the dip in a chafing dish and keep it heated.

makes approximately 5 cups

Southwestern Pesto Roll

"This is a marvelous appetizer dish that always receives rave reviews. Serve it with melba rounds and then get ready to rake in the compliments from your guests."

- 8 **ounces light cream cheese, softened**
- 8 **ounces skim milk ricotta cheese**
- 1 **14" x 16" piece cheesecloth, soaked with water and then wrung out**
- 3 **cloves garlic**
- 5 **bunches fresh basil**
- ½ **cup Romano cheese, freshly grated**
- ½ **cup olive oil** *(or as needed)*
- 3 **jalapeño chile peppers, chopped**
- ½ **cup pecans, toasted**
- **pepper** *(to taste)*

- In a medium bowl place the cream cheese and ricotta cheese, and beat them together with an electric mixer so that they are combined.
- Place the cheesecloth flat on a cookie sheet. Spread the cheese mixture on top of the cheesecloth so that it forms a 5" x 11" rectangle.
- Place the cookie sheet in the freezer
- In a food processor place the garlic, basil, Romano cheese, olive oil and jalapeño chile peppers. Purée them together so that they are smooth *(add more olive oil if necessary)*.
- Add the pecans and pepper. Pulse the ingredients for 5 seconds, or until the nuts are in tiny pieces *(not ground)*.
- Remove the cookie sheet from the freezer. Spread the pesto evenly on top of the cheese. Let the cheese sit for 10 minutes, or until it is slightly thawed.
- Using the cheesecloth to lift the cheese, roll it up into a log so that the cheese and pesto make a spiral in the center.
- Place the pesto roll on a serving plate. Chill it in the refrigerator for 30 minutes.

serves 6 to 8

"I come from southern Louisiana, in the heart of the Creole country, and I grew up loving hot, spicy foods. So it was not hard for me to adapt to the cuisine of northern New Mexico, with all of its wonderful green and red chiles."

Dolores Dietz

Anne's Corn Pudding

"We make a number of different corn puddings, and this particular recipe comes from my daughter-in-law. It is one of our favorites because of its rich, delicious taste."

- 1 **tablespoon unsalted butter**
- 1 **white onion, finely chopped**
- ½ **cup white wine**
- ½ **teaspoon salt**
- ¼ **teaspoon pepper**
- 6 **ears corn, kernels cut off**
- 2 **cans evaporated skim milk**
- 3 **eggs**
- 1 **egg yolk**
- 2 **tablespoons flour** *(Wondra Flour, if possible)*
- ¾ **cup Parmesan cheese, freshly grated**
- 1 **bunch fresh basil, chopped**
- ¼ **cup Parmesan cheese, freshly grated**

- Preheat the oven to 350°.
- In a large skillet place the butter and heat it on medium until it is melted and hot. Add the onions and sauté them for 5 minutes.
- Add the wine and cook it until the liquid is evaporated.
- Add the salt, pepper and corn, and sauté them for 3 minutes.
- In a medium bowl place the milk, eggs, egg yolk and flour. Whisk them together well.
- Add the ¾ cup of Parmesan cheese and the basil, and whisk them in.
- Spray a large casserole dish with Pam.
- Place the corn mixture in the dish. Pour the egg mixture on top and lightly stir it in. Sprinkle on the ¼ cup of Parmesan cheese.
- Bake the casserole for 20 minutes.
- Lower the oven temperature to 325°.
- Bake it for 30 to 45 minutes more, or until it is well set.

serves 8

Shrimp Etoufée

"The word 'etoufée' means 'smothered'. This recipe is a favorite southern Louisiana dish, that often is served in place of a gumbo. Other kinds of shellfish may be substituted for the shrimp."

- **½ stick butter**
- **¾ cup yellow onions, chopped medium**
- **½ cup green bell peppers, seeded and chopped medium**
- **1½ cups water**
- **1½ teaspoons tomato paste**
- **1½ teaspoons cornstarch**
- **3 cloves garlic, finely chopped**
- **1 teaspoon salt**
- **½ teaspoon black pepper**
- **½ teaspoon ground red pepper**
- **½ teaspoon Worcestershire sauce**
- **1 teaspoon lemon juice, freshly squeezed**
- **1 cup scallions, finely chopped**
- **1 pound fresh shrimp, cleaned and deveined**
- **2 cups white rice, cooked**

- In a large saucepan place the butter and heat it on very low until it is melted. Add the onions and bell peppers. While stirring occasionally, simmer them for 30 to 45 minutes, or until they are extremely soft *(smothered)*.
- Add the water, tomato paste and cornstarch. Stir them in well.
- Add the garlic, salt, black pepper, red pepper and Worcestershire sauce. Stir them in well.
- Cover the pan with a lid, reduce the heat to low and simmer the ingredients for 30 minutes.
- Remove the lid. Add the lemon juice, scallions and shrimp.
- Cook the mixture for 6 to 8 minutes. Adjust the seasonings if necessary.
- Remove the pan from the heat and let it sit for 10 minutes.
- Serve the etoufée over the rice.

serves 4 to 6

"I love Santa Fe, because not only is it physically beautiful and intellectually stimulating, it also is a town that allows people to do their own thing. There is a marvelous 'live and let live' attitude, which is one of its main attractions."

Al Dietz

Fennel Breakfast Pudding

"Rich, creamy, and slightly spicy, this is an adaptation of an old Louisiana recipe. The Egg Beaters are yolk-free eggs that can be found in the frozen foods section of your grocery."

1 tablespoon vegetable oil
1 pound turkey sausage
1 teaspoon fennel seeds
½ loaf French bread, broken into 1" pieces
1 can evaporated skim milk
2 cartons Egg Beaters, thawed
¾ cup Swiss cheese, grated
4 scallions, chopped
1 teaspoon dry mustard
½ teaspoon cayenne pepper
¼ teaspoon salt

- In a large skillet place the oil and heat it on medium until it is hot. Add the sausage and fennel, and sauté them for 5 minutes, or until the sausage is lightly browned.
- Remove the skillet from the heat and let it cool.
- Add the remaining ingredients and stir them in well.
- Place the mixture in a lightly greased baking pan. Cover the pan with foil and chill it in the refrigerator for 8 hours *(or overnight)*.
- Preheat the oven to 350°.
- Remove the foil from the pan.
- Bake the pudding for 45 minutes, or until it is set.

serves 6 to 8

"When I create a new dish in the kitchen I have one main desire.....to make it taste really good. The health food aspect is important, but the flavor takes definite priority."

Dolores Dietz

Our Buttermilk Biscuits

"You can keep this dough refrigerated in a tight container, then cut off a small portion each morning. This way you can have fresh biscuits daily, without having to make them from scratch."

5 cups flour
3 tablespoons sugar
2 tablespoons baking powder
1 teaspoon baking soda
1 teaspoon salt
1 cup Crisco butter-flavored shortening
2 cups buttermilk
1 package dry yeast, dissolved in 2 tablespoons warm water

- In a large bowl place the flour, sugar, baking powder, baking soda and salt. Mix them together well.
- Add the Crisco and cut it in with a pastry blender so that pea-size crumbs are formed.
- In a small bowl place the buttermilk and the dissolved yeast, and stir them together. Add the liquids to the flour mixture, and combine the ingredients so that a dough is formed.
- Preheat the oven to 400°.
- On a lightly floured surface place the dough and roll it out so that it is ½" thick. Cut out the biscuits with a floured biscuit cutter. Place them on a greased cookie sheet.
- Bake the biscuits for 10 minutes, or until they are lightly browned and a wooden toothpick inserted in the center comes out clean.

makes approximately 24 biscuits

Whole Wheat Buttermilk Pancakes

"These light and thin pancakes are a cross between a crêpe and a regular pancake. They are delicious with a fruit-flavored syrup or berry preserves."

3 egg whites, lightly beaten
1 cup buttermilk
½ cup white flour
½ cup whole wheat flour
2 tablespoons vegetable oil
1 tablespoon sugar
1 teaspoon baking powder
½ teaspoon baking soda
½ teaspoon salt

- In a large bowl place all of the ingredients. Beat them together with an electric mixer so that the batter is smooth.
- Heat a large, lightly oiled skillet *(or griddle)* to medium high. Using a ⅓ measuring cup, pour the pancakes into the skillet. Cook them for 3 minutes on each side, or until they are lightly browned.

serves 4

Tiny Pecan Tarts

"This is a fun, delicious dessert that is very easy to make. You can take the idea of the tiny tart shells and fill them with apples, berries, or any favorite pie filling."

1 3-ounce package cream cheese, softened
½ cup butter, softened
1 cup flour
¾ cup brown sugar
1 egg
1 tablespoon butter, softened
1 teaspoon vanilla extract
½ teaspoon salt
1 cup pecan pieces, chopped small

- Preheat the oven to 350°.
- In a medium bowl place the cream cheese and the ½ cup of butter. Beat them together with an electric mixer so that they are creamy.
- Add the flour and blend it in well.
- Cover the bowl with plastic wrap and chill it in the refrigerator for 1 hour.
- Shape the dough into 1" balls.
- Form each ball into the shape of a cup with your thumbs, and then press it into a tiny ungreased muffin tin.
- In another medium bowl place the brown sugar, egg, the 1 tablespoon of butter, vanilla and salt. Beat the ingredients together.
- In the bottom of the pastry cups place ½ of the pecans.
- Pour the egg mixture on top.
- Sprinkle on the rest of the pecans.
- Bake the tarts for 20 to 25 minutes, or until they are lightly golden.
- Remove them from the oven and let them cool.

makes approximately 24 tiny tarts

Prune Spice Cake with Buttermilk Sauce

"Moist and flavorful, this is one of the most popular cakes that we serve for breakfast. People always want the recipe, and then are shocked to see that it contains prunes."

Prune Spice Cake

- **2 cups sifted flour**
- **1 teaspoon baking soda**
- **½ teaspoon baking powder**
- **1½ teaspoons ground cinnamon**
- **1 teaspoon ground nutmeg**
- **1 teaspoon allspice**
- **½ teaspoon salt**
- **3 eggs**
- **1¼ cups sugar**
- **½ cup vegetable oil**
- **1 cup prunes, cooked, pitted and chopped**
- **1 cup buttermilk**
- **1 cup pecans, toasted and chopped**
- **Buttermilk Sauce** *(recipe follows)*

- Preheat the oven to 350°.
- In a medium bowl place the flour, baking soda, baking powder, cinnamon, nutmeg, allspice and salt. Mix them together well.
- In a large bowl place the eggs, sugar and oil. Blend them together with an electric mixer.
- Add the prunes and stir them in.
- While stirring constantly, alternately add the buttermilk and the flour mixture to the egg mixture.
- Add the pecans and stir them in well.
- Place the batter in 2 greased and lightly floured tube pans.
- Bake the cakes for 30 minutes, or until a wooden toothpick inserted in the center comes out clean.
- Remove the cakes from the pans.
- Pour the Buttermilk Sauce on top of each serving.

makes 2 cakes

Buttermilk Sauce

- **1 cup sugar**
- **½ cup buttermilk**
- **1 stick butter**
- **1 teaspoon light corn syrup**
- **½ teaspoon baking soda**

- In a medium saucepan place all of the ingredients and heat them on medium until the butter is melted, the sugar is dissolved and the sauce is hot.

makes approximately 2 cups

W.E. Mauger Estate

701 Roma Avenue N.W.
Albuquerque, New Mexico 87102
(505) 242-8755
Chuck Silver & Brian Miller, Innkeepers • Lorraine Tripp, Manager

A brick Victorian mansion rescued from oblivion in downtown Albuquerque surprises guests to this lovely old inn, who expect New Mexico to always mean adobe. The well-to-do at the turn of the century, however, wanted tall Queen Anne-style residences, and that's what Maude Talbott had built in 1897, and later sold to the Mauger family in 1907. The completely restored home was opened in 1987 as an inn. After a full breakfast, guests may walk to the convention center, Old Town, local museums and downtown.

Recipes

Very Mellow Yams

"This is an excellent sweet potato dish to serve on Thanksgiving or Easter. The oats and cranberries give it a delicate, subtle flavor."

- ½ **cup flour**
- ½ **cup brown sugar**
- ½ **cup rolled oats**
- ½ **teaspoon ground cinnamon**
- ⅓ **cup butter**
- 2 **cups fresh cranberries**
- 2 **tablespoons white sugar**
- 1 **24-ounce can sweet potatoes, drained** *(reserve the liquid)*

- Preheat the oven to 350°.
- In a large bowl place all of the ingredients *(except for the sweet potatoes and reserved liquid)* and mix them together well.
- In a medium casserole dish place alternate layers of the cranberry mixture and the sweet potatoes. Pour the reserved liquid on top.
- Cover the dish.
- Bake it for 35 minutes, or until everything is hot.

serves 6 to 8

Spinach Surprise

"We don't waste much in our kitchen, and this recipe was developed as a way to use our leftover bread crusts. It's very easy and very good. To make it richer, add small cubes of cream cheese."

- 8 **eggs, lightly beaten**
- ½ **cup milk**
- 2 **cups bread crusts, cubed**
- 1 **1-pound package frozen spinach**
- 1 **8-ounce carton cottage cheese**
- 1½ **cups Swiss cheese, grated**
- 1 **package onion soup mix**
- ½ **cup pitted black olives, chopped**
- 1 **tablespoon fresh garlic, chopped**

- Preheat the oven to 350°.
- In a large bowl place all of the ingredients *(except for ½ cup of the cheese)* and combine them together well.
- Place the mixture in a greased medium baking pan and spread it out evenly. Sprinkle the remaining cheese on top.
- Bake the casserole for 45 minutes, or until it is set.

serves 4 to 6

Turkey Sausage Egg Bake

"All of our dishes are prepared the night before, chilled overnight, and then baked before serving the next day. According to our guests, this particular recipe is one of our most delicious. They love the way it's a complete meal in itself."

½ pound Italian spicy turkey sausage
1 green bell pepper, seeded and chopped
1 red chile pepper, roasted, peeled and chopped
½ cup yellow onions, chopped
1 medium tomato, chopped
1 pound package frozen hash browns, thawed
1 teaspoon seasoned salt *(or to taste)*
1½ cups cheddar cheese, grated
8 eggs

- Preheat the oven to 350°.
- In a large skillet place the sausage and cook it on medium heat so that it is brown. *(Do not drain the grease.)* Add the bell peppers, red chile peppers, onions and tomatoes. Sauté them for 5 minutes, or until the onions are tender.
- Add the hash browns and sauté them for 5 minutes. Add the seasoned salt and stir it in.
- Add the cheese and heat it for 2 minutes, or until it just begins to melt.
- Place the mixture in a lightly greased medium baking pan. Make 8 divots in the mixture with a spoon. Place one egg in each divot.
- Bake the casserole for 30 minutes, or until the eggs are done.

serves 8

"I used to be an architectural designer in Los Angeles. I bought and renovated magnificent old mansions, and then sold them. Many of the homes belonged to old movie stars like Charlie Chaplin, Rudolph Valentino and Claudette Colbert. Then, the bottom fell out of the real estate market.....so here I am in Albuquerque, living a much slower, healthier and happier life."

Chuck Silver

Downtown Breakfast Burritos

"Vegetarians, as well as meat eaters, love these burritos. They have a lot of different, tasty ingredients, and make for a very satisfying and filling meal."

8 eggs, lightly beaten
¼ cup milk
1 cup potatoes, cooked and chopped
½ cup whole kernel corn
½ cup green chile peppers, roasted, peeled and chopped
1 green bell pepper, seeded and chopped
1 medium tomato, chopped
½ cup pitted black olives, chopped
½ stick butter
1 dozen flour tortillas, warmed
1 cup red enchilada sauce, heated
2 cups sharp cheddar cheese, grated

- Preheat the oven to 400°.
- In a large bowl place the eggs and milk, and whisk them together well.
- Add the potatoes, corn, green chile peppers, bell peppers, tomatoes and olives. Combine the ingredients together well
- In a large skillet place the butter and heat it on medium until it is melted and hot. Add the egg and vegetable mixture, and sauté it for 5 minutes, or until the eggs are softly cooked.
- Place some of the mixture in the center of each tortilla. Fold the tortilla up into the shape of a pillow. Wrap each burrito with foil.
- Place the burritos on a baking sheet and heat them in the oven for 15 minutes. Remove them from the oven and take off the foil. Spoon on the sauce and sprinkle on the cheese.
- Preheat the oven to broil.
- Broil the burritos for 1 minute, or until the cheese is melted.

serves 12

"The day-to-day operations of running a Bed & Breakfast are fairly mundane.....bookkeeping, cleaning, repairing and cooking. What makes it all worthwhile are the incredible people that we meet."

Lorraine Tripp

Grandma Elaine's Tuna Rice Casserole

"This is my foster mother's famous tuna casserole. It is the only casserole I would ever eat as a kid, and it is really, really good. She always claimed that no soup other than Campbell's would work."

1 **tablespoon butter**	1 **can tuna**
¾ **cup yellow onions, chopped medium**	1 **can Campbell's cream of mushroom soup**
3 **celery stalks, chopped medium**	1 **can Campbell's cream of chicken soup**
½ **cup uncooked rice**	1 **can dry onion rings**

- Preheat the oven to 350°.
- In a large bowl place all of the ingredients *(except for the onion rings),* and mix them together well.
- Place the mixture in a greased medium casserole dish.
- Bake the casserole *(covered)* for 1 hour.
- Sprinkle the onion rings on top.
- Bake the casserole *(uncovered)* for 5 minutes, or until the onion rings are browned.

serves 4 to 6

"I used to write out recipes for our guests, but now I don't do that. Instead, I hand them a notebook and pencil, and say, 'I'll dictate and you take notes.' So, having this cookbook with our recipes will be wonderful!"

Chuck Silver

Old Town Strata

"There are many fillings (instead of green chile and bacon) that will work with this strata. Some examples that I've tried are crab and corn, tomatoes and green peppers and onions, and turkey and broccoli."

- **8 eggs**
- **½ cup milk**
- **½ package taco mix**
- **8 slices bread, crusts removed**
- **2 cups cheddar cheese, grated**
- **½ cup green chile peppers, roasted, peeled and chopped**
- **8 ounces bacon, cooked, drained and crumbled**
- **2 teaspoons fresh parsley, chopped**
- **½ teaspoon paprika**

- In a large bowl place the eggs, milk and taco mix. Whisk them together well.
- Dip each bread slice into the mixture so that it is well soaked *(reserve the remaining liquid)*.
- In the bottom of a lightly greased medium baking pan place the bread slices so they make 1 layer. Sprinkle ½ cup of the cheese on top.
- To the remaining egg mixture add the green chile peppers and bacon, and stir them in.
- Pour the mixture on top of the cheese in the baking pan and spread it out evenly.
- Sprinkle the remaining cheese on top.
- Sprinkle on the parsley and paprika.
- Cover the pan with foil and chill it in the refrigerator for at least 6 hours *(or overnight)*.
- Preheat the oven to 350°.
- Remove the foil and bake the casserole for 45 minutes, or until it is set.

serves 8

W.E. Mauger Estate

Chuck's Chicken Reuben

"This chicken casserole is one of my favorite dishes for many reasons....the flavor is unique, it freezes beautifully, it's even better the next day, it's easy to make, and people love it. The interesting thing is that you cannot taste the sauerkraut and the Thousand Island dressing seems to disappear, but both are necessary for the unique taste."

2 pounds chicken, skin and bones removed, and cut into bite-size pieces
salt and pepper *(to taste)*
1 cup mushrooms, sliced
½ cup pitted black olives, sliced
1 cup sauerkraut, rinsed and drained
8 ounces mozzarella cheese, grated
1 cup Kraft's Thousand Island salad dressing

- Preheat the oven to 350°.
- In the bottom of a 9" x 13" casserole dish, evenly place the chicken. Sprinkle on the salt and pepper. Layer on the mushrooms, olives, sauerkraut and cheese.
- Pour the salad dressing on top.
- Cover the dish with a lid.
- Bake the chicken for 45 minutes, or until it is done.

serves 6

"People who stay at Bed & Breakfasts are a caliber above your average tourist. They are honest, respectful, grateful, intelligent.....and they all love to talk! Friendships are formed here that last forever."

Brian Miller

Frances's Noodle Pudding

"We serve this for breakfast with sour cream and applesauce. Many of our guests are surprised by the taste and texture, and don't really know that it contains noodles. I've given out the recipe a hundred times."

1 pound egg noodles, cooked al dente and drained
6 eggs, lightly beaten
1 cup cottage cheese
1 cup sour cream
½ cup milk
½ cup sugar
1 8-ounce package cream cheese, cut into 1" pieces
½ cup pineapple chunks
½ cup dates, chopped
½ cup raisins
½ cup walnuts, chopped
2 tablespoons ground cinnamon
1 cup corn flakes

- Preheat the oven to 350°.
- In a large bowl place all of the ingredients *(except for the corn flakes)* and mix them together well.
- Place the mixture in a greased medium baking pan.
- Sprinkle the corn flakes on top.
- Bake the casserole for 45 minutes, or until it is set.

serves 8

"Cooking is very relaxing to me. I love to putter around in the kitchen, cutting, chopping and creating new recipes. For practicality, I like dishes that you can prepare the night before and that freeze well. Also, I try to avoid red meat."

Chuck Silver

Chile Pepper Guide

About Chile Peppers

Americans have discovered the excitement of hot and spicy foods, and as a result, the use of chile peppers (genus *Capsicum*) has exploded in popularity. There are up to 200 identified varieties of chiles, each one with a unique taste and quality of heat. Chiles can be purchased fresh, dried, frozen, canned, crushed, and powdered. When working with any form of chile peppers, remember to be careful about touching your eyes with your hands because the heat will burn them. Many people use rubber gloves when handling chiles. If you eat a bite of food that is too hot, the best antidote for the heat is a dairy product such as milk, yogurt, ice cream, or a starch, such as rice or bread. Contrary to popular opinion, cold beer and water do not work.

For those of you who do not have access to the different chile peppers and Southwestern ingredients called for in these recipes, some mail order sources are listed on page 8. For more information on chile peppers, two excellent books that you can purchase are **The Whole Chile Pepper Book** by Dave DeWitt and Nancy Gerlach, and **The Great Chile Book** by Mark Miller.

How to Roast Chile Peppers

Place the peppers on a rack over a gas flame, on a grill, or under a broiler. The skin should blacken and blister all over. Do this quickly, so the flesh won't burn. Then place the peppers in a bowl, cover it with plastic wrap, and let the peppers "sweat" for about 10 minutes so that the skin loosens. Pull the skin off with your fingers. If the skin sticks, gently scrape it off with the back of a knife blade. Don't wash the peppers. Remove the seeds with a spoon or the tip of a knife.

Types of Chile Peppers

Anaheim: Long, green chile, similar to the New Mexico green chile, only milder and not as sharply defined in flavor. Excellent roasted. Good stuffed, in stews, and sauces. Widely available. Mild heat.

Ancho: A dried red-ripe poblano chile, 3 to 5 inches long and 2 to 4 inches wide. Reddish brown in color and very wrinkled. The most commonly used dried chile in Mexico. Sweet, with a fruity flavor of cherries and dried plums. Medium hot.

Arbol: Small dried red chiles, usually serrano, but sometimes cayenne or Thai chiles. Good toasted. Widely available. Extremely hot.

Bell, green: Bright green, sweet, and mild. Good stuffed and baked, grilled, or roasted. Available everywhere. No heat.

Bell, red: Very sweet and crisp. Good raw, grilled, and roasted. Almost always available. No heat.

Bell, yellow: Sweet, crisp, and fruity. Usually available. No heat.

Cascabel: Dried version of a Mexican chile, which, when ripe, looks like an Italian cherry pepper. Nutty-sweet flavor. Good toasted whole in oil. Medium hot.

Cayenne: Bright red dried pepper, 2 to 4 inches long and ½ inch across. Pungent heat. Can be used whole in soups, stews, and sauces, but usually are sold ground as a seasoning powder. Very hot.

Chile Caribe: Crushed dried New Mexican red chile peppers. Comes packed in supermarkets as "crushed red chile flakes". Varies in flavor and heat.

Chile Molido: Ground dried New Mexican red chile peppers. Varies in flavor and heat.

Chimayó Red Chile Powder: Ground dried red chiles from Chimayó, New Mexico. Highly prized for its excellent flavor. Hot, smoky, sweet, and nutty. Mild to hot.

Chipotle, dried: A smoked jalapeño, 2 to 4 inches long, light dusty brown in color. Good toasted. Used in soups and salsas. Very hot.

Chipotle, in adobo sauce: Canned, dried, smoked jalapeños that are simmered in a tomato-vinegar sauce. Widely available. Very hot.

Green (New Mexico): Fresh, related to the Anaheim, but with a much fuller flavor. Wonderful roasted. Used in sauces, stews, soups, or just eaten plain. Comes frozen or canned in most markets, but fresh is far superior. Frozen is preferred to canned. Also known as "Hatch". Mild to hot heat.

Guajillo: Dried red chile, about 4 inches long and reddish brown in color. Nutty-rich flavor. Good in salsas and moles. Mildly hot.

Habanero: Fresh, dark green to orange to red. About 2 inches long and 1½ inches wide. One of the hottest chiles in the world. Distinct flavor. Goes well with tropical fruits and tomatoes. Fierce heat!

Jalapeño: Fresh, dark green chile, about 2 top 3 inches long. The most popular chile in the United States. Readily available. Excellent raw or roasted. Comes in red and yellow as well. Medium to high heat.

Japone: Small, thin dried red chiles with a unique, sharp heat. Thai or arbol chiles may be substituted. Very hot.

Morita: A type of dried smoked jalapeño with a sweet, smoky flavor. Used in soups and salsas. Medium high heat.

Mulato: A type of dried poblano. Dark brown with a slight licorice and tobacco flavor. Used in moles, sauces, stews, and soups. Low to medium low heat.

Pasado: A New Mexico or Anaheim chile that has been roasted, peeled, and dried. About 4 inches long and 1 inch wide. Sweet, toasty, dusty flavor. Good for flavoring stews and soups. Medium hot.

Pasilla: Dried chile, also known as "chile negro". About 5 to 7 inches long and 1 inch wide, with dark and wrinkled skin. Sometimes the fresh poblano or the dried ancho and mulato are mistakenly called "pasillas". Deep, rich, almost cocoa-flavor. Used in moles and salsas. Low to medium heat.

Pequin: Tiny dried red chiles. Fiery, sharp, sweet and nutty flavor. Easy to find. Very hot.

Poblano: Fresh, dark green and purple-black chile, 4 to 5 inches long and 3 inches wide. Always roasted or cooked. Good for rellenos or made into sauces and moles. Rich and meaty. Low heat.

Red Chile Powder: Ground dried red chiles. Varies in quality of flavor and heat.

Sambal Chile: Asian chile. Comes in paste form. Can be found in Asian stores and larger markets. Extremely hot.

Serrano: Fresh green small chile with a clean, sharp heat. Extremely easy to find. Very hot.

Tabasco: Fresh or dried chiles from Louisiana. Used to make tabasco sauce. Very, very hot.

Thai: Thin, fresh green or dried red chiles, about 1½ inches long and ¼ inch wide. Used in Southeast Asian cooking. Found in specialty stores. Very hot.

Index

Cookbook Order Form

Quantity	Book Title	Price	Total
____	***Chile, Corn & Croissants*** *(softbound)* .... *Delicious recipes from New Mexico Inns • 374 recipes • 368 pages*	*$17.95*	________
____	***Santa Fe Lite & Spicy Recipe*** *(softbound)* .... *Lighter, healthier recipes from Santa Fe chefs • 350 recipes • 336 pages*	*$16.95*	________
____	***Santa Fe Hot & Spicy Recipe*** *(softbound)* .... *Hot new recipes from Santa Fe chefs • 392 recipes • 352 pages*	*$16.95*	________
____	***Santa Fe Recipe*** *(softbound)* .... *Recipes from favorite local restaurants • 300 recipes • 305 pages*	*$14.95*	________
____	***Taos Recipe*** *(softbound)* .... *Restaurant recipes from Taos, New Mexico • 170 recipes • 177 pages*	*$12.95*	________
____	***Southern California Beach Recipe*** *(hardbound)* .... *Recipes from favorite coastal restaurants • 335 recipes • 352 pages*	*$17.95*	________
____	***Grant Corner Inn Breakfast & Brunch Cookbook*** *(spiral bound)* . . *Recipes from Santa Fe's famous Grant Corner Inn • 263 recipes • 192 pages*	*$13.95*	________

BOOK TOTAL: __________

For shipping charges, please enclose $3.00 for the first book and $1.50 for each additional book.

SHIPPING TOTAL: __________

TOTAL AMOUNT ENCLOSED: __________

Ship to: ______________________________

Address: ______________________________

City: ______________________________

State: ______________ Zip: __________

Make check or money order payable to **Tierra Publications**. Send it to:

Tierra Publications
2801 Rodeo Road, Suite B-612
Santa Fe, New Mexico 87505
(505) 983-6300

(MasterCard and Visa phone orders accepted)

Notes